COLIN H.H. MCNAIRN, formerly a professor in the Faculty of Law at the University of Toronto, is a practising barrister and solicitor in Toronto.

As the state comes to play a larger role in the community the question of the extent to which government is subject to the general law of the land assumes increasing importance. This book examines the limits of two related forms of state immunity: crown or governmental immunity from statute and intergovernmental immunity. The first results from the rule of statutory construction that the crown, representing the executive government, is not bound by legislation except by express words or necessary implication. The second is of a constitutional order and provides a degree of freedom to each level of authority in a federal system from the laws of the other level of authority.

The author considers, in separate chapters, the effect which statutes can have upon a government when it confronts the legal system in tort proceedings, in criminal actions, as a party to a contract, as a creditor, and as a potential taxpayer. Some of the particular questions that are canvassed are as follows: Can the crown recover damages against a subject beyond the limit of liability prescribed by statute? Is a servant of the crown, such as a member of the armed forces, liable to conviction for a traffic offence committed while in the course of his duty? Is the Commonwealth of Australia as a landlord limited in what it may charge its tenants by state rent control legislation? Can a provincial liquor board import supplies for resale free of Canadian customs duties?

The author's examination of judicial decisions on intergovernmental immunity, one of the most difficult areas of constitutional law, exposes the confusion that exists as to the precise scope of the immunity. One of the principal purposes of this book is to impose some order on this jurisprudential chaos and to suggest directions of approach for the future.

This incisive analysis of a crucial area of the law will be of interest to all who are concerned with governmental accountability as well as to jurists, judges, and lawyers.

COLIN H.H. MCNAIRN

Governmental and Intergovernmental Immunity in Australia and Canada

UNIVERSITY OF TORONTO PRESS
Toronto and Buffalo

032863

© University of Toronto Press 1977
Toronto and Buffalo
Printed in Canada

Canadian Cataloguing in Publication Data

McNairn, Colin H.H., 1939–
Governmental and intergovernmental immunity in Australia and Canada

Includes index.
ISBN 0-8020-2241-3

1. Privileges and immunities – Canada. 2. Privileges and immunities –
Australia. 3. Executive power – Canada. 4. Executive power – Australia.
I. Title.

KE4715.M32   342′.71′06   C77-001383-X

This book has been published during the
Sesquicentennial year of the University of Toronto

To Marian and to my Parents

Preface

The research for this book was begun during the 1973-4 academic session while I was on sabbatical leave from the Faculty of Law at the University of Toronto. During that period I enjoyed the hospitality and facilities of the University of Melbourne Law School. The project was supported during the sabbatical year by a Leave Fellowship award from the Canada Council.

Publication has been assisted by a grant from the Law Foundation of Ontario and a grant from the Social Science Research Council of Canada, using funds provided by the Canada Council. I am grateful to the University of Toronto Press for undertaking to publish the book and, in particular, to Prudence Tracy who as supervising editor has piloted the manuscript through to publication.

I would like to acknowledge the assistance of Nancy Douglas, Patricia Ward, and Deborah Ward, who typed various drafts of the manuscript. And, finally, I wish to express appreciation to my wife Marian for her assistance in the tedious task of proofreading.

C.H.H.M.
Toronto
March 1977

Contents

032863

4
Statutes affecting the criminal and contractual liability of the crown

5
The effect of statutes upon the crown as creditor

6
The crown as taxpayer

xi Contents

Introduction

The political systems of Australia and Canada have a number of important features in common. Both are federal jurisdictions with constitutions originally given force, except in their conventional aspects, by imperial legislation. Each of the enacted constitutions contemplates a parliamentary system of government on the Westminster model with those modifications necessary to accommodate the federal principle. And in their federal elements the two constitutions have many close but little explored parallels.

The head of state in both Australia and Canada is Her Majesty the Queen, the reigning monarch of the United Kingdom. The two countries inherited from the UK a single set of principles, which form part of the common law, concerning the accountability of the sovereign as the representative of executive authority. The basic theory is that the sovereign in the latter capacity is a legal entity which can incur liabilities in the same way as other persons. In its legal relationships the sovereign is often referred to, however, in an abstract sense as the 'crown,' though technically that term describes a 'chattel now lying in the Tower [of London].'[1]

It is a well-established principle of the common law then that the crown is subject to the law of the land. However, that law as it applies to the crown is not always the same as would apply to subjects. This is because the crown enjoys certain special and peculiar privileges, when not displaced by statute, which are part of the royal prerogative. Thus, for example, it has been given priority for its debts ahead of those of any other person. These characteristics of executive authority, based as they are in the common law, pertain in both Australia and Canada.

This book is about the potential confrontations between the exercise of executive and legislative powers and how they are to be resolved. In particular it concerns the extent to which Her Majesty, as the head of an executive government,

1 Maitland *Selected Essays* (1936), at 116

is subject to statute law. That question has two distinct aspects, requiring consideration of a prerogative or constructional rule, on the one hand, and of a rule of federal constitutional law, on the other.

In the first place the crown enjoys a form of immunity from statutory control as a result of the rule that it is not bound by legislation except by express words or a necessary implication. Since the crown or Her Majesty personifies the executive government, it is common practice to use 'government' in a loose sense as synonymous with the former expressions. While the government is not itself a legal entity the word carries the notion that it is the state and not Her Majesty simply in a personal role that enjoys those rights and is subject to those liabilities which belong to the crown. Hence the immunity which results from the interpretation of statutes so as not to affect the crown may be described as 'governmental immunity.' In considering that immunity the judicial decisions of a number of countries within the community of nations that make up the Commonwealth have been taken into account in this book. An attempt has been made, however, to be fairly exhaustive in relation to the Australian and Canadian jurisprudence within that larger framework.

The second kind of immunity which will be examined is intergovernmental immunity. That expression describes the constitutional freedom which is enjoyed by either level of authority in a federal system from the laws of the other level of authority. It is a function of the federal division of responsibility and is largely implicit in the basic constitutional instrument.

The immunity is, once again, one that is enjoyed technically by Her Majesty. The sovereign, however, presides nominally over a number of governments within the Australian and Canadian federations. The latter circumstance is the result of the distribution of executive power between the central and constituent political units of each of those nations. In order to distinguish between the different capacities in which the crown manifests itself it is appropriate to refer to Her Majesty or the crown 'in right of' a state or province or 'in right of' a particular nation. Accordingly, we may speak variously of the crown in right of Australia, Canada, the state of Victoria, the province of Ontario, etc. Or we may speak simply of Australia or the Commonwealth (of Australia), Canada, the state of Victoria, the province of Ontario, etc. as shorthand expressions for the crown in those rights. Generic reference is sometimes made to the state or provincial crown to distinguish from what is described simply as the federal crown. Put in these terms, intergovernmental immunity as it arises in Australia and Canada involves a consideration of the freedom of the federal crown from state or provincial legislation and of the freedom of the state or provincial crown from federal legislation.

Judicial decisions from both Australia and Canada present a very confused picture of intergovernmental immunity. A major purpose of this comparative-review is to offer a rational and orderly approach to the subject and to suggest judicial and legislative directions for the future. Wherever possible, insights that may be gained from the experience in Australia are drawn upon in examining the position in Canada and vice versa.

Some of the particular issues that have arisen in the cases involving a claim to either or both forms of immunity are illustrative of the matters that are canvassed in the following chapters. Can the crown recover damages against a subject beyond the limit of liability prescribed by statute? Is a servant of the crown, such as a member of the armed forces, liable to conviction for a traffic offence committed while in the course of his duty? Is the Commonwealth of Australia as a landlord limited in what it may charge its tenants by state rent control legislation? Can a provincial liquor board import supplies for resale free of Canadian customs duties?

The first two chapters of this book explore the general principles of governmental and intergovernmental immunity. The chapters which follow examine the extent of the immunity, of either variety, which the crown enjoys when it is a party to tort proceedings, when its contractual or criminal liability is in question, when it is a creditor, and when it is a potential taxpayer.

GOVERNMENTAL AND INTERGOVERNMENTAL IMMUNITY
IN AUSTRALIA AND CANADA

1

Governmental Immunity from Statute

GENERAL DESCRIPTION OF IMMUNITY

Statute law does not govern the crown in the same way as it does other legal entities. The special position of the sovereign in this respect has been stated as follows: the crown is not bound by a statute unless expressly named or included by necessary implication. In the absence of such particular extension to the crown it is sometimes said, more specifically, that an enactment shall not affect such matters as the property, rights, title, prerogatives, or interests of the crown.[1] The general rule may also be put positively in terms of an immunity of the crown from statute if it is not specially included therein.

The rule has been described both as a feature of the royal prerogative and as a canon of construction for legislation creating a presumption in favour of the crown.[2] These characterizations carry a different emphasis but are not inherently inconsistent. Though the rule may be attributed to the prerogative it is important to keep in mind that, unlike most other forms of the prerogative, this particular privilege does not have to be positively asserted by the crown.[3] The crown will be regarded as outside the reach of a statute absent its special inclusion whether or not it insists upon such treatment. This is implicit in the constructional nature of the rule.

1 See, for example, *A.G.* v *Hancock*, [1940] 1 K.B. 427, at 439, appl'd in *A.G.* v *Randall*, [1944] K.B. 709, at 712 (C.A.); *Minister for Works (W.A.)* v *Gulson* (1944), 69 C.L.R. 338, at 363 & 366–7 *per* Williams J.
2 See *Madras Electric Supply Corp.* v *Boarland*, [1955] A.C. 667 (H.L.). In Australia a preference has sometimes been expressed for the view that the rule is one of construction; see *Roberts* v *Ahern* (1904), 1 C.L.R. 406, at 417–18, and *Downs* v *Williams* (1971), 126 C.L.R. 61, at 85–6 *per* Windeyer J, dissenting.
3 *Madras Electric Supply Corp.* v *Boarland*, [1955] A.C. 667, at 689 *per* Lord Reid, but cf at 694 *per* Lord Keith (H.L.); *Inland Revenue Comm'rs* v *Whitworth Park Coal Co.*, [1958] Ch. 792, at 824 (C.A.), decision aff'd at [1961] A.C. 31 (H.L.).

At one time the opinion prevailed that certain kinds of statutes could be taken, by their very nature, to bind the crown. It was said that the King is impliedly bound by statutes providing for the 'public good,' under which may be subsumed other similar categories of statutes[4] that were often described separately.[5] The king was also thought to be subject to statutes affecting 'inferior rights as belong indifferently to the King or to a subject.'[6] He could not, however, be deprived by statute 'of any part of his ancient prerogative or of those rights which are incommunicable and are appropriated to him as essential to his regal capacity,' without being included expressly or by necessary implication.[7] In *Bombay* v *Municipal Corporation of Bombay*[8] the Privy Council expressly rejected the former limitation upon crown immunity as too open-ended, since 'every statute must be supposed to be "for the public good," at least in intention,'[9] and as inconsistent with authority.[10] The second limitation upon crown immunity has also been discredited.[11] The conclusion is therefore apt that the rule for determining the effect of statutes upon the crown should no longer be stated 'in terms or with limitations which on occasion may have appeared appropriate in earlier times.'[12]

The important aspects of governmental immunity in its contemporary form are considered in the sections which follow.

THE RIGHTS OF THE CROWN WHICH ARE SECURED

In Canada there is a discernible judicial tendency, which is reminiscent of the

4 Viz. statutes for the relief of the poor, for the advancement of learning, religion, and justice, to give a remedy against a wrong, to prevent fraud, injury, or wrong, see *Bacon's Abridgement of the Law* (7th ed 1832), vol. 6, at 462, and *Chitty's Prerogatives of the Crown* (1820), at 382.

5 See the *Magdalen College* case (1615), 77 E.R. 1235; *Bacon's Abridgement*, at 462; *Chitty's Prerogatives*, at 382; *A.G.* v *Goldsbrough* (1889), 15 V.L.R. 638, at 654, aff'd on other grounds, ibid, at 660 (F.C.), *Sydney Harbour Trust Comm'rs* v *Ryan* (1911), 13 C.L.R. 358, at 365–6 & 370; *R* v *Hay*, [1924] V.L.R. 97, at 99; *R* v *McLeod*, [1930] 4 D.L.R. 226, at 228 & 229 (N.S.S.C. in banco).

6 *Hardcastle on Statutes* (1st ed 1879), at 180–1

7 Ibid, at 180–1. And see the following cases which take this distinction, *Campbell* v *Judah* (1884), 7 L.N. 147 (Que. Sup. Ct); *Sydney Harbour Trust Comm'rs* v *Ryan* (1911), 13 C.L.R. 358, at 365 per Griffith CJ; *Lowden* v *Sydney Harbour Trust Comm'rs* (1920), 21 S.R. (N.S.W.) 59, at 64 (F.C.), *R* v *Hay*, [1924] V.L.R. 97, at 99.

8 [1947] A.C. 58 (P.C.)

9 Ibid, at 63

10 Ibid. See, in addition to the cases referred to there, *R* v *Pouliot* (1888), 2 Ex. C.R. 49, at 60–1; *R* v *Le Blanc* (1930), 1 M.P.R. 1 (N.B.S.C., App. Div.).

11 Consider *Bombay* v *Municipal Corp. of Bombay*, [1947] A.C. 58, esp. at 64 (P.C.), *Minister for Works (W.A.)* v *Gulson* (1944), 69 C.L.R. 338, at 363–4 per Williams J.

12 Per Barwick CJ in *Commonwealth* v *Rhind* (1966), 119 C.L.R. 584, at 598

earlier era, to limit the kinds of crown rights which are entitled to the security afforded by governmental immunity in the statutory form which the rule now takes in that country. The Ontario Interpretation Act contains a provision, essentially paralleling that in several other jurisdictions, in these terms:

No Act affects the rights of Her Majesty, Her Heirs or successors, unless it is expressly stated therein that Her Majesty is bound thereby.[13]

In *Dominion Building Corporation* v *The King*,[14] which involved a contract claim against the crown, the Privy Council said that the 'rights of Her Majesty' in this provision meant 'the accrued rights of [Her] Majesty.'[15] It did not cover 'mere possibilities such as rights which, but for the alteration made in the general law by the enactment under consideration, might have thereafter accrued to [Her] Majesty, under some future contract.'[16] On this basis a provincial enactment, to the effect that time was of the essence of a contract only when the parties to it had so provided, was applied against the crown even though it did not purport to bind the sovereign expressly. Consequently the corporate claimant was able to succeed notwithstanding its earlier delays, the contract in question being silent as to whether the time fixed for its performance constituted a material condition.

The statement of the Judicial Committee, recited above, might be taken to suggest that governmental immunity only insulates the crown from any retroactive application of legislation since it refers simply to the 'accrued rights' of Her Majesty as protected against general statutory incursions. But, as will be suggested in a subsequent chapter, the case may properly be viewed as standing for the proposition that a general statutory provision may not alter the effect of the express terms of a contract to the prejudice of the crown though it may, as in this case, govern the implications that may be drawn from such terms.[17] In other words, the right of Her Majesty which is secured when the contractual commitments of the crown are in issue is limited to the right to contract on such terms as the crown may choose including, for example, a term that time is of the essence of the contract.

In *Gartland Steamship Co.* v *The Queen*[18] a section of the federal Interpretation Act,[19] similar to that of the Ontario Act, was also invoked unsuccessfully by

13 R.S.O. 1970, c 255, s 11
14 [1933] A.C. 533 (P.C.)
15 Ibid, at 548, appl'd in *R* v *Board of Transport Comm'rs* (1967), 65 D.L.R. (2d) 425 (S.C.C.)
16 [1933] A.C. 533, at 548 (P.C.)
17 See at 98–105, infra.
18 (1960), 22 D.L.R. (2d) 385 (S.C.C.)
19 R.S.C. 1952, c 158, s 16. This section was changed in significant respects by S.C. 1967–8, c 7, s 16.

the crown. The federal authority attempted through this proceeding to recover damages against a shipowner in an amount over and above the statutory limit of liability, arguing that it was not bound by the latter restriction. The Supreme Court of Canada refused, however, to grant recovery in excess of the prescribed maximum. Locke J, giving the judgment of the court on this point, said;

[i]t cannot be said that the Royal prerogative ever extended to imposing liability upon a subject to a greater extent than that declared by law by legislation lawfully enacted. The fact that liability may not be imposed upon the Crown, except by legislation in which the Sovereign is named or that any other prerogative rights are not to be taken as extinguished unless the intention to do so is made manifest by naming the Crown, does not mean that the extent of liability of a subject may be extended in a case of a claim by the Crown beyond the limit of liability effectively declared by law.[20]

This statement seems to assume that the only rights of the crown which are beyond the reach of general legislative alteration are those of a prerogative nature, at least when governmental immunity takes the particular statutory form which it did in that case. Indeed, Locke J had said earlier that the purpose of the relevant Interpretation Act provision was 'to prevent the infringement of prerogative rights of the Crown other than by express enactment in which the Sovereign is named.'[21] But to so confine governmental immunity is not consistent with other authority,[22] except on a very broad view of the rights that are included within the royal prerogative that is probably excessive in light of the current conservative view of the scope of the crown's special privilege.

Though the larger pronouncements in these two cases require qualification, the outcome of both is symptomatic of a judicial preference for restricting governmental immunity. The specification of 'the rights of Her Majesty' as secured by the statutory version of the rule has provided the interpretive opportunity for achieving that end. Many of the Interpretation Acts, however, are not as amenable to this particular approach. They indicate that a statute, not expressly binding upon the crown, is not to affect either the rights or the prerogatives of Her

20 (1960), 22 D.L.R. (2d) 385, at 400 (S.C.C.), appl'd in *R* v *Murray* (1967), 60 D.L.R. (2d) 647 (S.C.C.), and *B.C. Telephone Co.* v *Marpole Towing Ltd* (1970), 17 D.L.R. (3d) 545 (S.C.C.)
21 (1960), 22 D.L.R. (2d) 385, at 400 (S.C.C.)
22 Consider, for example, *R* v *Pouliot* (1888), 2 Ex. C.R. 49, see esp. at 62; *Re Silver Brothers Ltd*, [1932] A.C. 514 (P.C.)(considered in detail infra, at 119–24); *R* v *Rhodes*, [1934] 1 D.L.R. 251 (Ont. S.C.), *Re Sask. Gov't Ins. Office & City of Saskatoon*, [1948] 2 D.L.R. 30 (Sask. C.A.), *Pounder* v *Carl Shaum Constr. Ltd* (1972), 26 D.L.R. (3d) 284 (Ont. S.C.).

Majesty and that such a statute shall not be treated as 'binding on Her Majesty.'[23] These various forms of expression limiting the impact of statutes upon the crown may be assumed to have some independent content. Thus it is more difficult to dismiss a crown claim to immunity in that it may be appropriately put in terms of one or other formulation.

If the incidence of a statute upon prerogative rights is in question it may be important to determine the precise character of the particular prerogative which is the basis of the argument for immunity. The availability of various prerogative claims depends on the presence of certain underlying circumstances. For example, the crown is entitled to the undistributed personal property of a corporation as *bona vacantia* if the corporation has been effectively dissolved. It also succeeds to the personalty of an individual who dies intestate if the deceased is without lawful successors. A general statute, not dealing specially with this particular prerogative, may determine when a specific conditioning element is satisfied. A general corporations act may provide for revival of a corporation after its dissolution, with retroactive effect, so that a corporation is not effectively terminated for all purposes when it is formally dissolved. And a legitimation act may give an intestate next of kin which he would not otherwise have. The effect, in each case, is to confine the situations in which the crown is entitled to property under the prerogative. But such legislation need not bind the crown expressly or by necessary implication.[24] The reason is that the prerogative gives no rights to the crown

23 The Interpretation Acts or Ordinances of the following jurisdictions follow this formula: Alberta (R.S.A. 1970, c 189, s 13), Canada (R.S.C. 1970, c I-23, s 16), Manitoba (R.S.M. 1970, c 180, s 15), Newfoundland (R.S. Nfld. 1970, c 182, s 13), Northwest Territories (R.O.N.W.T. 1974, c I-3, s 13), Nova Scotia (R.S.N.S. 1967, c 151, s 13), Yukon Territory (R.O.Y.T. 1971, c I-3, s 12(1)). And see, for a partial adoption of this formula, the Quebec Civil Code, art. 9, the Acts Interpretation Act, 1954–71 (Qd), s 13, and the Acts Interpretation Act 1931 (Tas.), s 6(6). The Interpretation Acts of the following jurisdictions are, in the relevant respect, on the Ontario pattern: New Brunswick (R.S.N.B. 1973, c I-13, s 32), New Zealand (Acts Interpretation Act 1924 (N.Z.), s 5(k)), Prince Edward Island (R.S.P.E.I. 1974, c I-6, s 10), Quebec (R.S.Q. 1964, c 1, s 42), Saskatchewan (R.S.S. 1965, c 1, s 7). See also the Interpretation Act, 1897 (N.S.W.), s 14, and the Acts Interpretation Act, 1954–71 (Qd), s 30, which are confined in their operation, however, to private acts affecting the property of individuals.

24 As to the first kind of statute, see *A. G. of B.C.* v *Royal Bank & Island Amusement Co.*, [1937] 3 D.L.R. 393 (S.C.C.), disting'd in *R* v *Lincoln Mining Syndicate Ltd* (1959), 19 D.L.R. (2d) 273 (S.C.C.). As to the second kind of statute, there is authority to the contrary, viz. *Re W*, [1925] 2 D.L.R. 1177 (Ont. S.C.), which in fact concerned *bona vacantia* rather than escheat as the judgment would indicate, see 'Annotation,' 1 D.L.A. 903. But that decision was given without reference to *Re Stone*, [1925] 1 D.L.R. 60 (S.C.C.), which, though not precisely on point, suggests that *Re W* was wrongly decided, see 'Annotation,' 1 D.L.A. 903. Moreover *Re W* was seriously doubted in *Re Cummings*, [1938] O.R. 486 (H.C.), aff'd ibid, at 654 (C.A.). See also *Rumrell* v *Henderson* (1872), 22 U.C.C.P. 180.

at all whenever a statute indicates that a factor, that is a prerequisite to the very existence of the crown's special privilege, is not present. Such a statute cannot be said to affect the rights of the crown in any pertinent sense under the rule of governmental immunity.

The federal constitutional arrangement imposes some limits upon the operation of governmental immunity. In Australia and Canada it is accepted that the courts have the inherent right to review legislation to determine whether it comes within the limits of legislative authority under the constitution. The courts act in a sense as referees of the federal system. It is fundamental to this role that judicial review not be significantly inhibited by statute. That proposition is well established in Canada.[25] It follows from this supervening principle that governmental immunity cannot put the rights of the crown beyond the reach of a statute which would assist in securing the effective judicial review of legislation. Thus, for example, a general statutory provision must be available for use against the crown to freeze its property pending a decision on the validity of legislation conferring the property interest on the crown.[26] The crown cannot be afforded immunity from the general statutory provision in this situation. If it were, crown property could be dissipated before the court was able to determine whether the legislation creating it was valid. A judicial determination that the statute was invalid would then be a somewhat futile gesture. The review role of the court would have been significantly impaired in these circumstances which, as a constitutional matter, cannot be permitted.

IMMUNITY ONLY FROM PREJUDICIAL STATUTES

Statutes, or indeed a single statute, may have differing impacts upon the crown. But governmental immunity is only enjoyed from statutory provisions as they operate to the prejudice of the crown. If the effect of a statute is neutral or beneficial, in terms of the position of the crown, it will include the crown without express reference or a necessary implication to this effect in accordance with its general tenor.

Madras Electric Supply Corporation v *Boarland*[27] is illustrative. The Madras Electric company contested the imposition upon it of a particular tax. The levy was rightfully demanded only if it could be said that the company had sold its

25 See Strayer *Judicial Review of Legislation* (1968), c 3. And cf *Motor Transport Comm'r* v *Antill Ranger & Co.*, [1956] A.C. 527 (P.C.), and *Amax Potash Ltd* v *Government of Sask.*, (1976), 71 D.L.R. (3d) 1.
26 Cf *B.C. Power Corp.* v *B.C. Electric Co.* (1962), 34 D.L.R. (2d) 274 (S.C.C.), foll'd by McLean J A in *Canex Placer Ltd* v *A.G. of B.C.* (1975), 58 D.L.R. (2d) 241 (B.C.C.A.), but disting'd in *Calder* v *A.G. of B.C.* (1973), 34 D.L.R. (3d) 145, at 226 (S.C.C.).
27 [1955] A.C. 667 (H.L.).

business to 'another person' within the meaning of a section of the UK Income Tax Act. Since the purchaser of the company's business was in fact the crown, it was argued that the general language of the act was not competent to embrace the circumstances of the transaction of sale that had taken place in this case. Hence it was maintained that the company was free of the tax. The House of Lords rejected this argument. Had the section in question been a charging provision, admittedly it would not have brought in the crown as a taxpayer if expressed with a similar level of generality. But, as their lordships observed, the function of this section was to prescribe a method of computing the tax payable by a vendor, which in this instance was not the crown, in the event of the sale of a business. And the context did not indicate that the word 'person' in this provision should necessarily bear the same meaning as it had in the charging section of the act. There was no call, therefore, for resorting to the presumption that the crown was not bound by the statute since it was not actually or potentially burdened as a consequence of giving the word 'person' in the relevant section its natural meaning as inclusive of the crown.

In *Broken Hill Associated Smelters Pty* v *Collector of Imposts (Victoria)*[28] the same general term was held not to include the crown though the contrary conclusion would not have prejudiced the crown in any application of the section in question. That section, which was part of the Victorian Stamps Act, required a licence and a fee of companies which effected insurance with any 'person' outside the state of Victoria. The High Court decided that the appellant company, which had taken out insurance with Her Majesty's imperial government, was not obliged to secure a licence under this provision, 'person' being interpreted so as not to encompass the crown. It was evident that the statutory requirement was designed simply to guard against evasions of the general insurance licensing scheme which the statute established. That scheme involved an obligation upon any 'person' writing insurance in Victoria to take out a licence which must, in its generality, exclude the crown as the subject of direct regulation. Thus the word 'person' in the section at issue was treated, in the interests of logical consistency, to exclude the crown given the interrelationship between that section and the primary licensing provision. This result was reached notwithstanding that to include the crown in the former section would not directly prejudice it. The decision demonstrates the importance to be attached to the general purpose of a statute and the interdependency between sections in determining whether the crown should be included within a general expression in a provision which could not, of itself, place any burden upon the crown.

The crown has often been treated as entitled to the advantage of legisla-

28 (1918), 25 C.L.R. 61

tion.[29] In this respect it need not be specially included within the range of beneficiaries of an enactment. But the crown cannot secure the benefit of a statute which specifically excludes the crown from its reach,[30] which is clearly intended to apply only to subjects of the crown,[31] or which affords a remedy which is inconsistent with the nature and character of the crown.[32]

The question of prejudice or otherwise may be complicated by the fact that a given statutory provision operates with one effect upon the crown as representing one government but with another effect upon the crown as representing another government. For example, a federal statute creating a priority in bankruptcy for a debt owed to the federal authority operates positively as far as the crown in the federal right is concerned. But if that provision were to be interpreted so as to postpone any competing claim of a state or provincial government, the crown in that right would be clearly disadvantaged. In this situation it has been held that a distinction should be made between the crown in its different aspects. And, in so far as it would be prejudicial to a provincial government, such a provision ought not to be interpreted as affecting its claim, in the absence of an express statement that the crown is bound.[33]

AVOIDANCE OF THE RULE: ASSUMPTION OF STATUTORY BURDENS WITH STATUTORY BENEFITS

By taking advantage of legislation the crown will be treated as having assumed the attendant burdens, though the legislation has not been made to bind the crown expressly or by necessary implication. The force of the rule of immunity is avoided by the particular conduct of the crown and the integrity of the relevant statutory provisions, beneficial and prejudicial.

The principle is evident in the British Columbia Court of Appeal judgment in *Attorney General of British Columbia* v *Royal Bank and Island Amusement Company*.[34] The Amusement Company had been stricken from the companies' regis-

---

29 See, for example, *R* v *Fraser* (1877), 11 N.S.R. 431 (C.A.); *R* v *Powell* (1885), 2 W.N. (N.S.W.) 9, and *R* v *Canadian Accident & Fire Assurance Co.*, [1948] 4 D.L.R. 660 (N.B.S.C.).

30 *Nisbet Shipping Co.* v *The Queen*, [1955] 4 D.L.R. 1 (P.C.)

31 *Hamilton* v *The King* (1917), 35 D.L.R. 226 (S.C.C.)

32 See *Commonwealth* v *Anderson* (1960), 105 C.L.R. 303, at 311–13 *per* Dixon CJ, McTiernan J concurring, and see also at 314 *per* Kitto J, at 318 *per* Menzies J, & at 318–25 *per* Windeyer J.

33 *Re Silver Brothers Ltd* [1932] A.C. 514 (P.C.)

34 [1937] 1 W.W.R. 273 (B.C.C.A.), decision aff'd on other grounds at [1937] S.C.R. 459. This decision is in accord with early English authority, viz. *Crooke's* case (1691), 89 E.R. 540, and *R* v *Cruise* (1852), 2 Ir. Ch. R. (N.S.) 65, see Gordon, 'How Far Privative or Restrictive Enactment Binds the Crown' (1940), 18 *Can. Bar Rev.* 751.

ter pursuant to the provincial Companies Act, and hence dissolved, at a time when it had money on deposit with the Royal Bank. It was subsequently restored to the register, the effect of which, under the terms of the same statute, was that it was deemed to have continued in existence as if it had never been struck off. In the meantime, however, the crown had advanced a claim to the bank deposit on the ground that it became part of its traditional entitlement as *bona vacantia*. The crown maintained that the section of the Companies Act providing for restoration to the register and prescribing its consequences did not bind the crown and thus could not subsequently reduce its claim. This contention was rejected by the court, for the crown had to invoke the act to establish its claim. In so doing it could not 'rely on that part of the Act by which the right is acquired and ignore that part which (if its true construction warrants it) puts an end to the right temporarily enjoyed.'[35] Similarly if the crown takes advantage of a statute which creates or extends a right and the statute introduces a limitation period for the assertion of that new or extended right, then the crown is obliged to comply with the time limitation.[36]

It is not essential, however, that the benefit and the restriction upon it occur in one and the same statute for the notion of crown submission to operate.[37] Rather, the crucial question is whether the two elements are sufficiently related so that the benefit must have been intended to be conditional upon compliance with the restriction.[38] That, of course, may be a more likely conclusion the narrower the statutory focus. But it is nonetheless a possible conclusion even though the range of consideration must be extended to distinctive statutes or statutory provisions.

Reliance upon a statute may, however, be for such a limited purpose that the crown ought not, as a result, to be taken to have assumed the attendant burdens. Such is the case when a statute is resorted to for a purely defensive reason, for example to give notice under a registration scheme of the existence of a crown

35 [1937] 1 W.W.R. 273, at 294 *per* Macdonald J A
36 *Re Excelsior Elec. Dairy Mach. Ltd*, [1923] 3 D.L.R. 1176, at 1179 (Ont. S.C.); *A.G. of Can.* v *Tombs*, [1946] 4 D.L.R. 516 (Ont. Co'y Ct), decision rev'd on other grounds, ibid, at 519 (Ont. C.A.); *Minister of Works* v *Pinchbeck*, [1969] S.A.S.R. 240 (F.C.). But cf *R* v *Rutherford*, [1927] 4 D.L.R. 434 (Ont. S.C., App. Div.).
37 Consider *Housing Comm'n of N.S.W.* v *Panayides* (1963), 63 S.R. (N.S.W.) 1 (F.C.) (doubted in its holding, on the particular facts of the case, in *Commonwealth* v *Rhind* (1966), 119 C.L.R. 584, at 599–600), and *Reid* v *Canadian Farm Loan Bd*, [1937] 4 D.L.R. 248 (Man. K.B.), which is considered at length infra, at 110–11.
38 A sufficient nexus between the benefits of one provincial statute and the burdens of another could not be discerned in *Re Rowe & Man.*, [1942] 4 D.L.R. 754 (Man. K.B.), and *Deeks McBride Ltd* v *Vancouver Associated Contractors Ltd*, [1954] 4 D.L.R. 844 (B.C.C.A.).

claim.[39] The use of a statute in this way may be distinguished from active reliance to secure positive rights, the assumption of the burdens of a statute being a possible consequence only of the latter circumstance.[40]

The invocation by the crown of a statutory provision will not normally constitute the abandonment of a prerogative which is exercisable independently of statute.[41] The special privileges which are peculiar to the crown are not compromised quite so readily. Therefore, the crown remains free of the burdens of the statute in the sense that it can fall back on a persisting prerogative to achieve those ends which otherwise could only be realized through and subject to the statute. But there are some situations in which the crown's resort to statute may indicate an effective waiver of the relevant prerogative. This would be the case, for instance, when the statute relied on provides a remedy which, when pursued by the crown, is a complete substitute for a prerogative remedy.[42] In these circumstances, reliance upon the statute will be inconsistent with the preservation of the right to resort to the prerogative. Only then, the prerogative having been waived, is it possible to treat the crown as necessarily subject to the burdens of a statute which it has invoked in circumstances in which it enjoys a special privilege.

There are two other notions, which may be referred to conveniently at this point, that are related to the principle that the assumption of the benefit of a statute carries with it the attendant burdens. The first is that by entering, or having to enter, regularly into transactions of a kind that are statutorily regulated, the crown should be taken as subjected to the burdens of that system of regulation. This has been offered as a reason for treating the provisions of a bills of exchange statute as binding upon the crown or one of its agencies.[43] But general reliance, rather than particular reliance in the matter at issue, has never been a

---

39 As in *Re Buckingham*, [1922] N.Z.L.R. 771, see 774, and *Emerson v Simpson* (1962), 32 D.L.R. (2d) 603, see 607 (B.C.S.C.).

40 *Deeks McBride Ltd v Vancouver Associated Contractors Ltd*, [1954] 4 D.L.R. 844, at 847 (B.C.C.A.).

41 See, for example, *R v Bank of N.S.* (1885), 11 S.C.R. 1, at 22 *per* Strong J; *N.S.W. Taxation Comm'rs v Palmer*, [1907] A.C. 179, at 185 (P.C.); *Crowther v A.G. of Can.* (1959), 17 D.L.R. (2d) 437, at 441 & 445-6 (N.S.S.C. in banco); *Emerson v Simpson* (1962), 32 D.L.R. (2d) 603 (B.C.S.C.); *R v Hamilton* (1962), 37 D.L.R. (2d) 545 (Man. Q.B.).

42 *Chitty's Prerogatives of the Crown* (1820), at 245; *Commonwealth v Anderson* (1960), 105 C.L.R. 303, at 311-12 *per* Dixon CJ & at 318 *per* Windeyer J; *Housing Comm'n of N.S.W. v Panayides* (1963), 63 S.R. (N.S.W.) 1, at 4 & 9 (F.C.). And cf *McCleery v The Queen* (1974), 48 D.L.R. (3d) 129 (F.C.A.).

43 See *Dalgety & Co. v The Crown* (1942), 49 W.A.L.R. 49, at 63, rev'd on other grounds at (1944), 69 C.L.R. 18, and *Bank of Montreal v Bay Bus Terminal (North Bay) Ltd* (1971), 24 D.L.R. (3d) 13, at 20 (Ont. H.C.), aff'd at (1972), 30 D.L.R. (3d) 24, see esp. at 25 (Ont. C.A.).

ground for submission to legislation and in other commercial activities the crown has been entitled to rely upon its immunity though those activities are extensively regulated by statute.[44]

The second notion is that by commencing legal action the crown submits itself to all the ordinary rules of practice and procedure of the chosen court.[45] While this is unobjectionable as a general proposition, it must be subject to an important qualification. The crown does enjoy certain prerogatives in procedural matters which it will not be deemed to have surrendered by the act of bringing suit.[46] The most important of these is the crown's prerogative right to refuse discovery.[47] This right is not lost when the crown initiates or joins proceedings. Consequently the crown cannot become subject to a requirement to give discovery under the rules of practice that normally pertain in the court in which proceedings have been taken.[48] Of course, this prerogative may be particularly overborne by the express terms or a necessary implication of a statute.[49] Or it may be excluded by a provision assimilating the rights of the parties in crown proceedings generally with those in proceedings between subjects.[50] Finally, in actions involving an agency of the crown, the capacity to sue and be sued, conferred on the agency by its constitutive statute, may be construed as enabling suit only in accordance with the ordinary procedure pertaining between subjects, thus precluding the crown from relying upon its immunity from discovery.[51] But other-

44 See, for example, *Re Buckingham*, [1922] N.Z.L.R. 771; *R v Sanford*, [1939] 1 D.L.R. 374 (N.S.S.C. in banco); *Re Mar-Lise Industries Ltd* (1968), 5 D.L.R. (3d) 487, at 493–5 *per* Ferguson J, dissenting (Ont. C.A.).

45 *R v Fawcett* (1900), 13 Man. R. 205, at 211 (K.B.); *Bartlett v Osterhout*, [1931] 3 D.L.R. 609, at 609 (Ont. S.C.). And cf *R v The Ship 'City of Windsor'* (1896), 5 Ex. C.R. 223. Limitation bars are not included within the rules to which the crown may submit itself, see *A.G. of Can. v Rhode* (1957), 8 D.L.R. (2d) 89, at 91 (Sask. Dist. Ct).

46 See *A.G. of Ont. v Toronto Junction Recreation Club* (1904), 8 O.L.R. 440, at 442 (H.C.).

47 See *Thomas v The Queen* (1874), L.R. 10 Q.B. 31; *Crombie v The King*, [1923] 2 D.L.R. 542 (Ont. S.C., App. Div.).

48 See *A.G. of B.C. v Kandahar Consol. Gold Mines Ltd*, [1939] 1 W.W.R. 303 (B.C.S.C.); *Central Can. Potash Co. v A.G. of Sask.* (1974), 50 D.L.R. (3d) 560 (Sask. C.A.).

49 As, for example, in the Proceedings against the Crown Act, R.S.O. 1970, c 365, s 12, and the Crown Proceedings Act, 1972 (S.A.), s 7.

50 See *Jamieson v Downie*, [1923] A.C. 691 (P.C.); *Commonwealth v Miller* (1910), 10 C.L.R. 742; *Heimann v Commonwealth* (1935), 54 C.L.R. 126. And see infra, at 71.

51 See *A. Goninan & Co. v South Australian Harbours Bd*, [1931] S.A.S.R. 128 (F.C.); *Skinner v Commissioner for Rys* (1937), 37 S.R. (N.S.W.) 261 (F.C.). And cf *Ex p. The Milk Board; Re Farmers' Fertilizers Corp.* (1935), 35 S.R. (N.S.W.) 583 (F.C.); *Housing Comm'n of N.S.W. v Imperial Paint Mfrs Pty* (1956), S.R. (N.S.W.) 312 (F.C.); *Langlois v Canadian Commercial Corp.* (1956), 5 D.L.R. (2d) 410 (S.C.C.). But a

wise the crown's special privilege in this matter persists and is not waived by the commencement or joinder of proceedings by the crown.

In principle it would seem that the crown, in initiating an action, ought to be subject not only to the court's rules of practice and procedure which do not conflict with its prerogatives but to its jurisdictional limitations. This is especially so if the authority of the court is statutorily defined. But the matter is complicated once again by the prerogative, for the crown has the peculiar privilege of suing in the forum of its own choosing.[52] It may be doubted, however, that that privilege would now be viewed as entitling the crown to judicial relief beyond the limits of the statutory competence of the chosen tribunal.[53]

THE BENEFICIARIES OF IMMUNITY

The benefit of governmental immunity accrues not only to the crown but to agents and servants acting on its behalf.[54] While a crown agency may be created to engage in functions which are thought to be non-governmental in character this does not have the effect of denying immunity from statutory regulation to such an entity.[55] The immunity is enjoyed indifferently by those that perform traditional government roles and those that do not. What is crucial is the test considered earlier, that is whether the crown would be prejudiced, in this instance by the inclusion of its servant or agent within the general terms of the legislation.[56]

crown agency will not be subjected, as a result of such a construction, to a statute of limitations; *Chief Secretary of N.S.W.* v *Oliver Food Prods Pty* (1960), S.R. (N.S.W.) 435 (F.C.).

52 *Bradlaugh* v *Clarke* (1883), 8 App. Cas. 354, at 375 (H.L.); *R* v *Grant* (1896), 17 P.R. 165 (C.A.); *R* v *McCarthy* (1919), 46 D.L.R. 456 (Exch.), aff'd by the Supreme Court, see Morse Ex. Ct Dig., at 15.

53 *Housing Comm'n of N.S.W.* v *Panayides* (1963), 63 S.R. (N.S.W.) 1, at 4–5 *per* Sugerman J, Manning J concurring (F.C.); *Commonwealth* v *Rhind* (1966), 119 C.L.R. 584, at 598 *per* Barwick CJ, McTiernan J concurring, but see also at 607 *per* Menzies J.

54 There is a third category of 'Crown instrumentality' comprising persons who are *in consimili casu* with servants of the crown, the members of which have been accorded immunity from taxing legislation, see infra, at 128–9.

55 *North Sydney Municipal Council* v *Housing Comm'n of N.S.W.* (1948), 48 S.R. (N.S.W) 281, at 287 (F.C.). This circumstance has sometimes been taken, however;
   (a) to indicate that such an entity is not a crown agent at all but a body quite independent of the crown (see Hogg *Liability of the Crown* (1971), at 209–10, and McNairn, 'The Ontario Crown Agency Act' (1973), 6 *Ottawa L. Rev.* 1, at 2), and
   (b) to support a conclusion that such an entity ought to be treated as bound by necessary implication by a statute which does not mention the crown specifically as bound by its terms (see *Downs* v *Williams* (1971), 126 C.L.R. 61, at 89–90 *per* Windeyer J, dissenting).

56 See also infra, at 921–5.

The construction of a statute so as to exclude the crown from a general expression may redound to the benefit of a subject who is not a servant or agent of the crown.[57] Take the case of rent control legislation which, in accordance with the rule of governmental immunity, would not affect crown lands without their special inclusion. That being so, a tenant of the crown would also be free of the burden of such legislation in the event that he entered into a sub-lease of such lands.[58] A statute of this kind operates *in rem*[59] and the rule of immunity saves all crown lands from its burdens even in respect of transactions to which the crown is not a party. There have been a few other cases in which a subject appears to receive the advantage of immunity when he can show that the application to him of an enactment would prejudice the crown in a fairly immediate and significant way.[60] For one, a contractor engaged to do work for the government on crown lands has been held free of the statutory obligation to obtain a permit under a licensing scheme involving approval and inspection of the work.[61] Otherwise the rights of the crown to the use and enjoyment of its property would be affected.[62] But in every case in which governmental immunity has been accorded it is in reality on behalf of and for the ultimate benefit of the crown though others may receive incidental advantages.

EXPRESS WORDS OR A NECESSARY IMPLICATION
THAT THE CROWN IS BOUND

The classic description of governmental immunity makes it very clear that the crown can be affected by certain statutes, namely those which bind it expressly or by necessary implication.[63] The meaning of the latter phrase was considered

---

57 Consider *Broken Hill Associated Smelters Pty* v *Collector of Imposts (Vict.)* (1918), 25 C.L.R. 61, discussed supra, at 9.

58 *Clark* v *Downes* (1931), 145 L.T. 20; *Rudler* v *Franks*, [1947] K.B. 530 (C.A.).

59 For the significance of this factor see further, *R* v *Gay* (1959), 20 D.L.R. (2d) 170 (Ont. C.A.).

60 See *Re Automatic Telephone & Electric Co's Application*, [1963] 2 All E.R. 302 (C.A.).

61 *Lower Hutt City* v *A.G.*, [1965] N.Z.L.R. 65 (C.A.), foll'd in *Wellington City Corp.* v *Victoria University*, [1975] 2 N.Z.L.R. 301. And cf *Ottawa* v *Shore & Horwitz Constr. Co.* (1960), 22 D.L.R. (2d) 247 (Ont. H.C.), which reached a similar result but on the basis of federal constitutional considerations. But see *Engineered Homes Ltd* v *Popil*, [1974] 4 W.W.R. 357 (Alta. Dist. Ct).

62 Consider *Bank voor Handel en Scheepvaart* v *Administrator of Hungarian Property*, [1954] A.C. 584, at 607 & 615 (H.L.); *Wynyard Investments Pty* v *Commissioner for Rys (N.S.W.)* (1955), 93 C.L.R. 376, at 395.

63 For subordinate legislation to bind the crown it has been assumed that this criterion must be satisfied by the regulation or other statutory instrument sought to be applied against the crown, as well as by the enabling legislation under which it has been adopted, see *Minister for Works (W.A.)* v *Gulson* (1944), 69 C.L.R. 338, esp. at 364 *per* Williams J.

by the Privy Council in *Bombay* v *Municipal Corporation of Bombay*.[64] There is a necessary implication that the crown is bound, the Judicial Committee said, '[i] f it can be affirmed that, at the time when the statute was passed and received the royal sanction it was apparent from its terms that its beneficent purpose must be wholly frustrated unless the Crown were bound.'[65] At the same time the test applied by the High Court of Bombay, from which the appeal had been taken, was rejected as too restrictive of the scope of governmental immunity. That court had decided that the crown was bound by necessary implication simply if the statute could not otherwise operate in a reasonably smooth and efficient manner. On that view crown land, having regard to its prevalence in the city of Bombay, was held to be subject to the statutory power of the municipality to carry its drains across any property within its territorial limits. The criterion substituted by the Privy Council dictated a reversal of that disposition.

The escape from immunity afforded by the qualification contained in the rule itself is, on this approach, quite restricted. The crown must be included expressly or, if not, the statute must be seen to be virtually meaningless were the crown not bound. This position has been adhered to in a number of subsequent cases in Australia.[66]

Latterly, the notion of total frustration of the beneficent purpose of a statute has come under strain, given the circumstances in which some courts have been willing to find that that result would ensue were the crown not bound.[67] And a more limited immunity than that indicated by the quotation recited above is suggested by another passage in the *Bombay* opinion, which must of course be read against the facts of the case. In particular the Judicial Committee said at an earlier point in the judgment that a necessary implication that the crown is bound will be found, '[i] f ... it is manifest from the very terms of the statute that it was the intention of the legislature that the Crown should be bound.'[68] In fact this statement, which happens also to accord with earlier authority,[69] has been preferred

64 [1947] A.C. 58 (P.C.)
65 Ibid, at 63
66 *North Sydney Municipal Council* v *Housing Comm'n of N.S.W.* (1948), 48 S.R. (N.S.W.) 281 (F.C.); *Public Curator of Qd* v *Morris* (1951), 51 S.R. (N.S.W.) 402, at 416 *per* Herron J, dissenting (F.C.); *Randwick Municipal Council* v *Commissioner for Gov't Transport* (1966), 85 W.N. (Pt 1) (N.S.W.) 351; *Downs* v *Williams* (1971), 126 C.L.R. 61, at 87–8 *per* Windeyer J, dissenting, & at 94 *per* Gibbs J, dissenting.
67 See *Alexander* v *Munia* (1969), 14 W.I.R. 58 (Guyana C.A.); *Kent* v *Minister for Works* (1973), 2 A.C.T.R. 1, app. dismissed without reference to this point, *sub. nom. Johnson* v *Kent*, at (1975), 132 C.L.R. 164; *Re Pacific Western Airlines Ltd*, (1976), 66 D.L.R. (3d) 507 (F.C.A.), rev'd at (1977), 14 N.R. 21 (S.C.C.).
68 [1947] A.C. 58, at 61 (P.C.)
69 See, for example, *Roberts* v *Ahern* (1904), 1 C.L.R. 406, at 418, and *Minister for Works (W.A.)* v *Gulson* (1944), 69 C.L.R. 338, at 347 *per* Latham CJ, at 357 *per* Rich J & at 363–5 *per* Williams J.

in a number of post-*Bombay* Australian cases.[70] These developments indicate a general retreat from the more rigorous application of the *Bombay* decision.

A necessary implication that the crown is bound by a particular statutory provision will not be drawn from the fact that the crown is expressly exempted from the operation of other provisions in the same statute. The latter specification will be assumed to have been included *ex abundante cautela* and not as demonstrating that the crown is otherwise bound by the legislation.[71] On the other hand the presence of a section declaring expressly that some portions of an act are to bind the crown has been used to support the conclusion that other portions of the statute ought not to be taken as binding the crown by necessary implication.[72]

In Canada, at the federal and provincial levels,[73] and in two Australian states,[74] the rule of governmental immunity has been given statutory form in a section of the Interpretation Act.[75] It is generally the case that the special position enjoyed by the sovereign in relation to statutes pertains 'unless it is expressly stated that

70 Viz. *Public Curator of Qd* v *Morris* (1951), 51 S.R. (N.S.W.) 402 (F.C.); *Wynyard Investments Pty* v *Commissioner for Rys (N.S.W.)* (1955), 93 C.L.R. 376, at 389; *Kaye* v *A.G. of Tas.* (1956), 94 C.L.R. 193, at 204 *per* Williams J; *Downs* v *Williams* (1971), 126 C.L.R. 61, at 87–8 *per* Windeyer J, dissenting. And cf *Commonwealth* v *Rhind* (1966), 119 C.L.R. 584, at 598 *per* Barwick CJ, McTiernan J concurring. See also *Premchand Nathu & Co.* v *Land Officer*, [1963] A.C. 177 (P.C.).

71 *Gorton Local Health Bd* v *Prison Comm'rs*, [1904] 2 K.B. 165n, at 169n; *Hornsey U.D.C.* v *Hennell*, [1902] 2 K.B. 73, at 80–1; *Repatriation Comm'n* v *Kirkland* (1923), 32 C.L.R. 1, at 17 *per* Higgins J, and see also at 8–9 & 22; *Bombay* v *Municipal Corp. of Bombay*, [1947] A.C. 58, at 64–5 (P.C.); *North Sydney Municipal Council* v *Housing Comm'n of N.S.W.* (1948), 48 S.R. (N.S.W.) 281, at 285 (F.C.); *C.B.C.* v *A.G. of Ont.* (1959), 16 D.L.R. (2d) 609, at 618 (S.C.C.); *Re Pacific Western Airlines Ltd,* (1977), 14 N.R. 21 (S.C.C.).

72 *Re Bonham* (1879), 10 Ch. D. 595, at 601–3 (C.A.); *Broken Hill Associated Smelters Pty* v *Collector of Imposts (Vict.)* (1918), 25 C.L.R. 61, at 66 *per* Isaacs & Rich JJ; *R* v *Sanford*, [1939] 1 D.L.R. 374, at 381 (N.S.S.C. in banco); *Minister of Works* v *Pinchbeck*, [1969] S.A.S.R. 240, at 244 *per* Bray CJ (F.C.). And cf *Public Curator of Qd* v *Morris* (1951), 51 S.R. (N.S.W.) 402 (F.C.).

73 British Columbia is the exception since its Interpretation Act imports the presumption that the crown is bound by statute unless it is specifically provided otherwise, see S.B.C. 1974, c 42, s 13.

74 Namely Queensland and Tasmania

75 The provisions of the Canadian Interpretation Acts or Ordinances are as follows; R.S.A. 1970, c 189, s 13, R.S.M. 1970, c 180, s 15, R.S.N.B. 1973, c I-13, s 32, R.S.Nfld 1970, c 182, s 13, R.O.N.W.T. 1974, c I-3, s 13, R.S.N.S. 1967, c 151, s 13, R.S.P.E.I. 1974, c I-6, s 10, R.S.Q. 1964, c 1, s 42, R.S.S. 1965, c 1, s 7, R.O.Y.T. 1971, c I-3, s 12(1). See also the Quebec Civil Code, art. 9. The Australian provisions are as follows; Acts Interpretation Act, 1954–71 (Qd), s 13, and the Acts Interpretation Act, 1931 (Tas.) s 6(6).

Her Majesty is bound' by the legislation in question, or words to that effect.[76] Thus, there is an omission to state, independently at least, the second limiting factor of immunity. No reference is made to the fact that the immunity does not extend to the crown when there is a necessary implication to the effect that the crown is bound by the legislation in question. This may be explained on the basis of a legislative assumption that a necessary implication is subsumed under, or adds nothing to the mention of, an express statement. Alternatively, it may be a deliberate attempt to limit the opportunities for arguing against immunity more narrowly than at common law. If the former view is correct, governmental immunity in its statutory form is, in this particular respect, simply a restatement of the common law. But it represents an enlargement beyond its traditional scope on the latter view. There is judicial support for each of these conclusions.[77]

The narrower version of the statutory immunity, reflecting the conventional rule, is to be preferred. In the first place the common law rule has itself been frequently put in similar terms. It has been said simply that the crown is not bound by statute except expressly, no mention being made of the effect of a necessary implication.[78] And, secondly, the adverb 'expressly' is in fact capable of embracing a necessary implication as is evident from the meaning given to it in other contexts.[79] Perhaps the most closely analogous circumstance in which the larger

76 There are two exceptions viz. the Interpretation Act, R.S.C. 1970, c I-23, s 16 (see *Re Pacific Western Airlines Ltd* (1977), 14 N.R. 21 (S.C.C.), and the English version of s 42 of the Interpretation Act, R.S.Q. 1964, c 1. However, as to the latter section the Official Languages Act, S.Q. 1974, c 6, s 2, now requires that any discrepancy between the English and French text of a Quebec statutory provision be resolved in favour of the French version if the discrepancy is not effectively eliminated by the application of the ordinary rules of construction.

77 As to the first possible conclusion, see *Cushing* v *Dupuy* (1880), 5 App. Cas. 409, at 419–20 (P.C.); *Crombie* v *The King*, [1923] 2 D.L.R. 542, at 547 (Ont. S.C., App. Div.); *Re Sask. Gov't Ins. Office & City of Saskatoon*, [1948] 2 D.L.R. 30, at 33 (Sask. C.A.); *Kaye* v *A.G. of Tas.* (1956), 94 C.L.R. 193, at 204 *per* Williams J. See also the New Zealand case of *Harcourt* v *A.G.*, [1923] N.Z.L.R. 686, at 689–91. As to the second possible conclusion, see *Re W*, [1925] 2 D.L.R. 1177, at 1179 (Ont. S.C.); *Re Silver Brothers Ltd*, [1932] A.C. 514, at 523 (P.C.); *R* v *Rhodes*, [1934] 1 D.L.R. 251, at 255 (Ont. S.C.); *M.N.R.* v *Roxy Frocks Mfg Co.* (1937), 62 B.R. 113, esp. at 124 *per* Barclay J (C.A.); *McArthur* v *The King*, [1943] 3 D.L.R. 225, at 257 (Exch.); *Murray* v *Cold Road Pty*, [1969] Q.W.N. no. 15, at 31 (F.C.).

78 See, for example, *Bacon's Abridgment of the Law* (7th ed 1832), vol. 6, at 462; *Théberge* v *Laudry* (1876), 2 App. Cas. 102, at 106 (P.C.), appr'd in *Re Wi Matua's Will*, [1908] A.C. 448, at 449 (P.C.).

79 See *Chorlton* v *Lings* (1868), L.R. 4 C.P. 374; *Metropolitan Dist. Ry* v *Sharpe* (1880), 5 App. Cas. 425 (H.L.); *Rose* v *Hvric* (1963), 108 C.L.R. 353. And cf *Shanmugam* v *Commissioner for Registration of Indian and Pakistani Residents*, [1962] A.C. 515 (P.C.), appl'd in *R* v *Young*, [1969] Qd R. 417 (C.C.A.). But see *Walton* v *Bank of N.S.*

meaning of 'expressly' has been adopted is in the interpretation of legislation denying power to courts to order costs against or in favour of the crown except where expressly authorized. That too is a restatement of a special privilege enjoyed by the sovereign at common law.[80] Legislation which carries a necessary implication that costs may be awarded to or against the crown has been treated as an express authorization enabling such an award.[81] So also legislation on other subjects ought to be capable of extension to the crown by necessary implication even though the statutory form of governmental immunity likewise envisages legislation affecting the crown only where it is so provided expressly.

STATUTES CONCERNING THE SUBJECT MATTER OF A PREROGATIVE

If a statute deals particularly with the subject matter of a prerogative, providing a privilege or immunity which reflects the special position of the crown at common law, then that statute doubtless binds the crown. There must be a necessary implication to this effect because the very subject matter of the statute is rights which pertain to the crown. Thus, when the statute governs, the crown is limited by its terms if it happens to restrict the crown in either a substantive or a procedural way.[82] But this leaves untouched the question of when the statute is in fact controlling. If the crown relies upon it it may be subject to its burdens. But that is not a likely conclusion, as we have seen, if the crown is possessed of a prerogative which it can resort to independently of the statute to achieve its ends. We would normally have to determine, therefore, whether the prerogative is still extant or is effectively abrogated by the creation of a statutory régime of rights or immunities. If the prerogative is displaced, then the statute will govern exclusively and the crown will be bound by it whether by relying upon it or by necessary implication. If the prerogative is not displaced the statute will not necessarily govern. The crown will usually be able to have recourse in this event to its

(1964), 43 D.L.R. (2d) 611, at 620–1 (Ont. C.A.), decision aff'd on other grounds at (1965), 52 D.L.R. (2d) 506 (S.C.C.).

80 See *Lord Advocate* v *Dunglas* (1842), 8 E.R. 381 (H.L.); *Johnson* v *The King*, [1904] A.C. 817 (P.C.).

81 See *Watson* v *Howard*, [1924] 4 D.L.R. 564 (B.C.C.A.), appr'd in *R* v *McLane*, [1927] 1 W.W.R. 701 (B.C.C.A.); *R* v *Hassell*, [1937] 1 W.W.R. 726 (B.C.S.C.); *Re Browne*, [1944] 1 D.L.R. 365 (B.C.S.C.). The British Columbia Crown Costs Act which was under consideration in these cases was repealed by the Crown Proceedings Act, S.B.C. 1974, c 24, s 16(3).

82 Cf *N.S.W.* v *Bardolph* (1934), 52 C.L.R. 455, at 496 *per* Rich J, appr'd in *Cudgen Rutile (No. 2) Pty* v *Chalk*, [1975] A.C. 520, at 533 (P.C.).

traditional privileges even though these may be more extensive than those provided by statute.

The leading authority on the question of when the prerogative is circumscribed by statute is *Attorney General v De Keyser's Royal Hotel, Ltd.*[83] In that case the UK government had requisitioned hotel premises under the Defence of the Realm Acts. But there was a failure to agree on an appropriate sum by way of compensation. Proceedings were initiated by the hotel company to establish its right to compensation under the legislation. The crown, in response, maintained that its acquisition of the hotel was equally supportable under the royal prerogative. That being the case there was no legal obligation to provide any compensation at all. The House of Lords concluded, however, that since the statute empowered the crown to do the same thing as it could have done by virtue of the prerogative the latter was completely displaced. Otherwise the statutory imposition upon the crown of limitations, which did not inhere in the prerogative itself, would have been a futile gesture. Lord Dunedin put the general principle rather more narrowly in this way: 'if the whole ground of something which could be done by the prerogative is covered by the statute it is the statute that rules.'[84]

Legislation has been held to replace, generally or in particular contexts, the doctrine of *bona vacantia*,[85] the power to grant a petition of right to enable proceedings against the crown,[86] the priority of the crown as creditor,[87] and some of the functions of the crown as *parens patriae*.[88] But the common law right of the crown to dismiss its servants at its pleasure, which may only be a prerogative, strictly speaking, in the case of military servants,[89] is often found to persist notwithstanding fairly detailed statutory regulation of government employment relationships.[90] And, most recently, in *Barton v Commonwealth*,[91] the prerogative

---

83 [1920] A.C. 508 (H.L.)
84 Ibid, at 526
85 *Re Azoff-Don Commercial Bank*, [1954] Ch. 315; *Re Mitchell*, [1954] Ch. 525
86 *R v Dalgety & Co.* (1944), 69 C.L.R. 18. And see as to the prerogative power to refer a matter to the Judicial Committee, *Commonwealth v Qd* (1975), 7 A.L.R. 351, at 375 *per* Jacobs J, McTiernan J concurring.
87 *Food Controller v Cork*, [1923] A.C. 647 (H.L.); *Re Denton Sub-divisions Pty* (1968), 89 W.N. (Pt 1)(N.S.W.) 231
88 *Re A.B.*, [1954] 2 Q.B. 385; *Re B*, [1962] Ch. 201 (C.A.). See also *Laker Airways Ltd v Department of Trade*, [1976] 3 W.L.R. 537, aff'd at [1977] 2 All E.R. 182, [1977] 2 W.L.R. 234 (C.A.), as to the effect of legislation on the treaty-making prerogative.
89 Compare *Shenton v Smith*, [1895] A.C. 229, at 234–5 (P.C.), and *China Navigation Co. v A.G.*, [1932] 2 K.B. 197, at 214–15 (C.A.). But see *Kidd v The King*, [1924] Ex. C.R. 29.
90 See *Ryder v Foley* (1906), 4 C.L.R. 422; *Kaye v A.G. of Tas.* (1956), 94 C.L.R. 193; *Opoloto v A.G.*, [1969] E.A. 631 (C.A.). And cf *Rankin v The King*, [1941] 1 D.L.R. 14 (Exch.); *Deynzer v Campbell*, [1950] N.Z.L.R. 790, judgment of Finlay J (C.A.). But see *Gould v Stuart*, [1896] A.C. 575 (P.C.); *McCleery v The Queen* (1974), 48 D.L.R. (3d) 129 (F.C.A.).
91 (1974), 131 C.L.R. 477. For a good discussion of this case see Goldring, 'The Impact

power to seek the surrender of fugitives was held to survive the Australian Extradition Acts. Those enactments constitute the sole source of authority for extradition from and to countries with which Australia has pertinent treaty arrangements. The High Court considered the Commonwealth executive entitled, nonetheless, to ask Brazil to surrender two fugitives from Australian justice though there was no extradition treaty with that country. In invoking its prerogative in this situation[92] the Commonwealth was, notably, without limitation in the kinds of offences it might consider extraditable since it did not have to come within the confines of a treaty. Moreover it was quite incapable of promising reciprocal treatment of fugitives from Brazil, being a non-treaty state, in the face of the acts. These considerations led Barwick CJ to observe that the draftsman probably intended the acts to be exhaustive of extradition matters.[93] That did not deter him, however, from agreeing with Mason and Jacobs JJ that the prerogative remained available in the circumstances of this case.

The only conclusion that can be offered is that whether a special privilege of the crown is curtailed by statute may depend a good deal on the nature of the prerogative or other crown right which is at issue and the court's appreciation of its central importance to the state.[94]

A statute dealing with the subject matter of a prerogative may expressly preserve the special privileges of the crown, in which case, of course, there is no room for the *De Keyser* principle to operate.[95]

REFORM OF THE IMMUNITY RULE

In the province of British Columbia governmental immunity has been abolished by statute. This change was effected with the introduction of a new Interpretation Act,[96] in 1974, which substituted the following section for that which had provided for governmental immunity in the earlier versions of the statute;

13. Unless an enactment otherwise specifically provides, every Act, and every enactment made thereunder is binding upon Her Majesty.[97]

> of Statutes on the Royal Prerogative, Australian Attitudes as to the Rule in *Attorney-General* v *De Keyser's Royal Hotel Ltd* (1974), 48 *A.L.J.* 434.
>
> 92 McTiernan & Menzies JJ, however, proceeded on the assumption that as the Australian government had simply asked Brazil to detain the Bartons pending a request for extradition no prerogative, but simply general executive authority, was involved.
>
> 93 (1974), 131 C.L.R. 477, at 488
>
> 94 See also *Simpson* v *A.G.*, [1955] N.Z.L.R. 271 (C.A.).
>
> 95 *A.G. of N.S.W.* v *Butterworth & Co. (Australia)* (1938), 38 S.R. (N.S.W.) 195.
>
> 96 S.B.C. 1974, c 42
>
> 97 This provision was added pursuant to a recommendation of the Law Reform Commission of British Columbia, see *Report on Civil Rights (Project No. 3), Part I – Legal Position of the Crown* (1972), c VII.

In effect, then, the crown in right of British Columbia is now in no different position than any of its subjects in that it is embraced by the general words of provincial statutes even though that may be to its prejudice. If the crown is to be excluded from the reach of a statute the onus now rests with the legislature to so provide in specific terms.

This seems to be the more appropriate presumption, given the range of activities in which the crown and its agents are now engaged, the proliferation of regulation by statute and subordinate legislation, and the resultant increase in the opportunities for governmental immunity working to the prejudice of subjects.[98] It leaves open the possibility of the legislature giving special protection to the crown in particular circumstances as the situation might dictate. But the crown will have no privileged position, in the face of legislation, by default as it were. Indeed, we are probably quite justified in assuming that the merit of applying a given statute to the crown frequently receives little or no consideration. If that is so then the failure to mention the crown ought not to be attributed to any conscious decision that the crown should be free of the burdens of a statute.

The courts, especially in Canada, seem to have been less than happy with the present rule of governmental immunity. However, they have managed to do justice in many cases by taking a narrow view of the scope of protection which the rule affords. But of course there are limits to the flexibility of the courts in this matter which do not constrain the legislature.

98 See Williams *Crown Proceedings* (1948), at 54, and Hogg *Liability of the Crown* (1971), at 201-2.

2

Governmental and Intergovernmental Immunity in a Federal System

GOVERNMENTAL IMMUNITY

Interjurisdictional Operation

In a federation, such as that of the Australian states or the Canadian provinces, it is important to ascertain whether governmental immunity is capable of operating in an interjurisdictional context. A claim to governmental immunity across jurisdictional lines arises, typically, if the federal government argues that it is free of the burdens of local legislation on constructional grounds or if a state or provincial government presents a similar argument for standing outside federal legislation. Acceptance of either assertion involves the conclusion that governmental immunity is capable of benefiting not just the political division which has legislated but the other level of political authority in the federation. The competing position, which would result in a significantly narrower role for governmental immunity, is that immunity is only enjoyed by the crown in right of the legislating government. Thus, for example, federal legislation would bind the crown in right of a state or province according to its general tenor even though it was ineffective to bind the federal crown for failure to include the crown expressly or by necessary implication. This result presupposes that it is appropriate to make a distinction between the crown in the different capacities in which it is manifest in a federal setting for determining entitlement to governmental immunity.

It is sometimes said, however, that the crown is one and indivisible.[1] While that may be true in a limited sense the reality is that the crown is advised by different governments, which have separate 'purses'[2] and which are capable of con-

---

1 See, for example, *Amalgamated Soc'y of Eng'rs* v *Adelaide Steamship Co.* (1920), 28 C.L.R. 129, at 152.
2 See *Re Silver Brothers Ltd*, [1932] A.C. 514, at 524 (P.C.).

032863

tracting and suing in respect of their own particular interests. The fact that action is taken by various governments in the name of the one sovereign should not obscure the underlying differences in the real interests that are at stake. In practice, therefore, there are fundamental distinctions in the roles in which the crown may act.

In Canada it seems to be fairly well established that governmental immunity is capable of benefiting the federal government in relation to provincial statutes. There is a long line of authority holding provincial legislation inapplicable to the federal crown for failure to provide that Her Majesty is to be bound by it.[3] And the Privy Council decision in the Canadian appeal of Re Silver Brothers Ltd[4] demonstrates a like deference to the provincial crown in the event of federal legislation potentially restrictive of its interests.

In Silver Brothers the governments of the dominion and the province of Quebec had tax claims against the estate of a bankrupt company which were of a kind given priority by statutes of the respective jurisdictions. Quebec asserted that its claim should rank not only ahead of subjects but on a parity with the claim of the dominion. In accepting this contention the Privy Council read the federal statute giving priority to dominion tax claims 'over all other claims' as subject to the federal Interpretation Act's version of the rule of governmental immunity from statute. Thus the statutory priority of the federal authority was qualified so as not to prejudice the rights of the crown in its provincial aspect. The two government debts were, therefore, ranked pari passu. The province had

3 R v Berriman (1883), 4 O.R. 282 (H.C.J., Q.B.D.); R v L'Heureux (1913), 14 D.L.R. 604 (Exch.); G. Martinello & Co. v McCormick (1919), 50 D.L.R. 799 (S.C.C.); R v Rhodes, [1934] 1 D.L.R. 251 (Ont. S.C.); R v Sanford, [1939] 1 D.L.R. 374 (N.S.S.C. in banco); R v Star Kosher Sausage Mfg Co., [1940] 4 D.L.R. 365 (Man. K.B.); R v Verdun, [1945] 2 D.L.R. 429 (Exch.); A.G. of Can. v Rhode (1957), 8 D.L.R. (2d) 89 (Sask. Dist. Ct); Crowther v A.G. of Can. (1959), 17 D.L.R. (2d) 437, at 442 per MacDonald J, Parker J concurring (N.S.S.C. in banco); Ottawa v Shore & Horwitz Constr. Co. (1960), 22 D.L.R. (2d) 247, at 252 (Ont. H.C.); R v McInnes (1962), 7 C.L.Q. 234 (Ont. Mag. Ct); R v Hamilton (1962), 37 D.L.R. (2d) 545 (Man. Q.B.); R v City of Montreal (1972), 27 D.L.R. (3d) 349 (F.C.T.D.); R v Flintkote Co., [1976] 1 F.C. 249. And cf R v Richardson & Adams, [1948] 2 D.L.R. 305, at 324–5 per Estey J (S.C.C.); Palmer v The King, [1952] 1 D.L.R. 259, at 268 (Exch.); Engineered Homes Ltd v Popil, [1972] 4 W.W.R. 357 (Alta Dist. Ct). But see Reid v Canadian Farm Loan Bd, [1937] 4 D.L.R. 248, at 252 (Man. K.B.), appr'd in Majestic Mines Ltd v A.G. of Alta, [1941] 2 W.W.R. 353, at 356 (Alta S.C.), decision aff'd without reference to this point at [1942] 1 D.L.R. 474 (Alta C.A.) and [1942] 4 D.L.R. 593 (S.C.C.). And cf Independent Order of Foresters v The King, [1939] 2 D.L.R. 53, at 56 (Alta S.C.), appr'd on this point on appeal at [1940] A.C. 513, at 536 (P.C.).
4 [1932] A.C. 514 (P.C.). See also R v Le Blanc (1930), 1 M.P.R. 21 (N.B.S.C., App. Div.). And consider R v Board of Transport Comm'rs (1967), 65 D.L.R. (2d) 425

803280

asked for no more than that, having declined to press for an overriding priority over the federal government, to which it is doubtful that it would have been entitled.[5]

The assumption was made in this case, as it has been in a number of other decisions,[6] that the reference to Her Majesty in an interpretation act provision, to the effect that Her Majesty may only be bound by statute expressly, is not limited to the crown in the right of the legislating government. If it were, the Judicial Committee would not have been entitled to resort to the federal Interpretation Act in order to preserve the rights of the provincial crown. Put another way, the decision treats the benefits of immunity from statute as available to the crown in a right other than that of the legislating government.

The Australian case of *Federal Commissioner of Taxation* v *Official Liquidator of E.O. Farley Ltd*[7] also involved the reconciliation of claims to priority advanced by the central government and by the government of one of the constituent units of the federation in the administration of the assets of an insolvent company. The High Court decided that the two crown debts should be ranked equally. In so concluding, Evatt J applied the rule of construction that was invoked in the *Silver Brothers* case.[8] Rich J also relied on a presumption, based however on 'governmental comity and constitutional practice,' against interference with rights of the state, specifically those relating to the treasury.[9] No rule of interpretation, akin to either of these, was mentioned by the remaining four members of the court.[10] For them other circumstances favoured a narrow scope to the Commonwealth's priority. It had been argued that Commonwealth legisla-

(S.C.C.), which seems to assume that governmental immunity is enjoyed by the crown in right of a province from federal legislation.

5 See infra, at 121.
6 *R* v *Berriman* (1883), 4 O.R. 282 (H.C.J., Q.B.D.); *R* v *Star Kosher Sausage Mfg Co.*, [1940] 4 D.L.R. 365 (Man. K.B.); *Crowther* v *A.G. of Can.* (1959), 17 D.L.R. (2d) 437, judgment of MacDonald J, Parker J concurring (N.S.S.C. in banco); *R* v *Hamilton* (1962), 37 D.L.R. (2d) 545 (Man. K.B.); *R* v *McInnes* (1962), 7 C.L.Q. 234 (Ont. Mag. Ct); *R* v *Flintkote Co.*, [1976] 1 F.C. 249; *Re Pacific Western Airlines Ltd*, (1977), 14 N.R. 21 (S.C.C.). And see also *Dominion Building Corp.* v *The King*, [1933] A.C. 533 (P.C.), and *R* v *Board of Transport Comm'rs* (1967), 65 D.L.R. (2d) 425 (S.C.C.). But compare *Gauthier* v *The King* (1918), 40 D.L.R. 353, at 360 *per* Idington J (S.C.C.), and *Palmer* v *The King*, [1952] 1 D.L.R. 259, at 268 (Exch.). In *Ottawa* v *Shore & Horwitz Constr. Co.* (1960), 22 D.L.R. (2d) 247 (Ont. H.C.) the court relied, mistakenly, on the federal rather than the provincial Interpretation Act provision, see 252. And see *Bank of N.S.* v *The Queen* (1961), 27 D.L.R. (2d) 120, at 155 (Exch.), where a similar error was made.
7 (1940), 63 C.L.R. 278
8 Ibid, at 326
9 Ibid, at 292
10 Latham CJ, Starke, Dixon & McTiernan JJ

tion which required that a liquidator set aside sufficient funds to satisfy federal tax claims created a priority for such claims. It was in the interpretation of that provision that Evatt and Rich JJ applied presumptions in favour of the rights of the states.

A consideration of other Australian authority reveals a division of opinion on whether a state enjoys the benefit of governmental immunity in relation to Commonwealth legislation. In one of its early cases, *R* v *Sutton*[11] (the *Wire Netting* case), the High Court held that the importation of goods by a state was subject to Commonwealth customs legislation though the latter did not draw in the crown particularly as the subject of regulation. It was said that governmental immunity is only enjoyed by the crown as representing the community whose laws are being considered.[12] Consequently the general words of the customs statute were capable of binding the states. It is unclear whether the construction given the Commonwealth Act depended at all on the fact that the constitutional power, pursuant to which it was enacted, was exclusive rather than concurrent in nature.[13]

The court felt that it could distinguish the crown in its state capacity so as to deny it immunity in that regard, while at the same time admitting that governmental immunity from the Commonwealth statute was enjoyed by the crown in its federal capacity. In this context it was thought that the crown should be treated as functioning as separate juristic entities in line with the federal division of authority in the constitution.[14] The power of the Commonwealth parliament to impose duties of customs on the states was affirmed in *Attorney General of New South Wales* v *Collector of Customs for New South Wales*,[15] which was decided at the same time.

The issue presented by the *Wire Netting* case came before the High Court again several years later. This further confrontation with the question, in *Minister for*

11 (1908), 5 C.L.R. 789
12 Ibid, at 796–7 *per* Griffith CJ, at 801–2 *per* Barton J, at 806 *per* O'Connor J, & at 817 *per* Higgins J
13 Griffith CJ and Barton J stressed the exclusive character of the Commonwealth's power in relation to customs (constitution, ss. 52(ii), 86 & 90), see (1908), 5 C.L.R. 789, at 797–8 & 801–4, but O'Connor and Higgins JJ advanced reasons which would support a similar result whether the legislation was based on an exclusive or concurrent power, see ibid, at 806–7 & 816–17. Isaacs J, the fifth member of the court, emphasized the importance of the constitutional power at issue and the ability of a state to frustrate its exercise by the claimed immunity, rather than the exclusiveness of the power, see ibid, at 814.
14 Ibid, at 797 *per* Griffith CJ, at 805 *per* O'Connor J, at 813 *per* Isaacs J, & at 817 *per* Higgins J
15 (1908), 5 C.L.R. 818. When the Privy Council came to decide that the Canadian parliament had power to subject a provincial government to duties on the importation of

Works (Western Australia) v *Gulson*,[16] produced a quite different answer. In that case a state government had brought proceedings for the recovery of premises which it had let to the defendant. But it had not complied with subordinate legislation of the Commonwealth, namely certain wartime regulations governing landlord and tenant matters. In the result the state was held, by a 3-2 majority, to be free of the restriction of those regulations.

Both Rich and Williams JJ said that the regulations could not bind the state in the absence of an express mention of the crown or a necessary implication that it was to be bound. This requirement was thought to be consistent with an intimation to this effect in the revered, but sometimes obscure, majority judgment in *Amalgamated Society of Engineers* v *Adelaide Steamship Co.*[17] It was also viewed as in accord with *Re Silver Brothers Ltd*[18] and as demonstrating proper regard for the unity and indivisibility of the crown.[19] These considerations were taken to effectively undermine the authority of the *Wire Netting* case. Thus, in the view of these two judges, the benefit of governmental immunity from statute was not confined to the crown in right of the legislating government.[20] Latham CJ and McTiernan J, dissenting, said that the authority of the *Wire Netting* case was not diminished by the factors catalogued by Rich and Williams JJ.[21] Nor was its outcome dependent on the circumstance that the legislation from which immunity was unsuccessfully asserted was passed pursuant to a constitutional power that was exclusive of the authority of the states.[22] Therefore the *Wire Netting* case was considered to be directly in point and was followed by the dissenters. Starke J, the third majority judge, treated the rule of governmental immunity as apposite and recognized a need for stating in 'the most explicit and the clearest words'[23] that the regulations were intended to govern relationships between the

goods, in *A. G. of B.C.* v *A.G. of Can.*, [1924] A.C. 222 (P.C.), any argument that the federal legislation should not be construed as binding the crown in right of a province was precluded to the province concerned since the legislation specifically stated that it was to bind Her Majesty in right of a province (see an Act to amend the Customs Act, S.C. 1917, s 1(3), and an Act to amend the Special War Revenue Act, S.C. 1923, c 70, s 8).

16 (1944), 69 C.L.R. 338
17 (1920), 28 C.L.R. 129, ref'd to in *Gulson's* case (1944), 69 C.L.R. 338, at 367
18 (1944), 69 C.L.R. 338, at 365–6
19 Ibid, at 356–7 & 366–7
20 This opinion was adopted by Herron J, dissenting, in *Public Curator of Qd* v *Morris* (1951), 51 S.R. (N.S.W.) 402, at 419 (F.C.).
21 Owen J in *Public Curator of Qd* v *Morris*, ibid, came to the same view. The other majority judge, Street CJ, reached the conclusion that the crown in the right of the state of Queensland was bound by a New South Wales Act without reference to any presumption.
22 (1944), 69 C.L.R. 338, at 359–61 *per* McTiernan J. See also at 365 *per* Williams J.
23 Ibid, at 358

crown and its subjects and not simply relationships between subjects. Only then would they operate against the state. He concluded that these Commonwealth regulations failed to satisfy that criterion.[24] Thus a majority was prepared to accord a preferred position to the crown in right of the state in relation to Commonwealth legislation.

In *Essendon Corporation* v *Criterion Theatres Ltd*,[25] the principal proponents of the two opposing views concerning entitlement to the benefit of the presumption had occasion to reaffirm their positions.[26] And the fifth member of the court, this time Dixon J rather than Starke J, dismissed the argument that the general words of a state rating act bound the Commonwealth on the basis of an intergovernmental immunity. Having dismissed the state legislation as inapplicable on a constitutional ground, he declined to pass upon the relevance of governmental immunity from statute.

Some comfort was taken by one member of both the majority and the minority in *Gulson*[27] from *Pirrie* v *McFarlane*,[28] which had been decided in the interval since the *Wire Netting* case. But that decision is not particularly revealing on the point at issue. The basis for the finding, in that case, in favour of liability on the part of a Commonwealth servant under state highway traffic legislation, is not at all clear. The conclusion may have turned on the specific extension of the state legislation to servants of the crown[29] or on the appropriateness of the general words of the legislation, unaffected by any presumption, to the crown and its servants. Only Higgins J, giving one of the three majority judgments, opted clearly for the latter construction, affirming the more limited immunity established in

24 And see the interpretation given to this judgment by Taylor J in *Commonwealth* v *Bogle* (1953), 89 C.L.R. 229, at 278–9.

25 (1947), 74 C.L.R. 1

26 Ibid, at 12, 15, 28, & 30, *per* Latham CJ, Rich, McTiernan & Williams, JJ, respectively. Williams J also reasserted his preference for the broader scope of prerogative immunity, that is as having an interjurisdictional operation, in *Re Richard Foreman & Sons Pty; Uther* v *Federal Comm'r of Taxation* (1947), 74 C.L.R. 508, at 537–8, and in *Bogle's* case (1953), 89 C.L.R. 229, at 254. In the latter case he also secured the support of Taylor J, at 279, and may have influenced some modification by McTiernan J in his opposing view (consider the final paragraph of the latter's judgment, at 251, and note also the subsequent concurrence of McTiernan J with the reasons of Barwick CJ in *Commonwealth* v *Rhind* (1966), 119 C.L.R. 584, at 598–600).

27 (1944), 69 C.L.R. 338, at 349–50 *per* Rich J. And see the *Essendon* case (1947), 74 C.L.R. 1, at 12 *per* Latham CJ.

28 (1925), 36 C.L.R. 170. This case is discussed further infra, at 94–5.

29 See the judgment of Starke J, ibid, at 228, Knox CJ apparently agreeing, see ibid, at 179–80. Isaacs J, dissenting, seemed to think that the majority was deciding the case on this, to him, questionable basis, see ibid, at 185. It would have been, *inter alia*, inconsistent with *Gauthier* v *The King* (1918), 40 D.L.R. 353 (S.C.C.), see infra.

the *Wire Netting* case.[30] The burden of the argument against liability in *Pirrie* v *McFarlane* had been that it would be unconstitutional to apply the state statute against a servant of the Commonwealth and not that it was inapplicable to him as a matter of construction.

When it comes to the effect of the general words of state legislation upon the crown in other than its state capacity the decisions, apart from *Pirrie* v *McFarlane* which is of doubtful relevance, generally[31] support the extension of immunity to the crown in that other capacity whether that of the Commonwealth,[32] another state government,[33] or the imperial government.[34]

It is thus seen on review that the weight of authority is, on balance, in favour of the larger form of immunity, capable of operating in an interjurisdictional context. The immunity is one, therefore, that benefits the states when confronted with Commonwealth legislation and the Commonwealth when confronted with state legislation. The latter situation, however, may be resolved in favour of immunity on another ground, namely that the constitutional principle of intergovernmental immunity applies.[35] By comparison, authority in Canada is even more clearly weighted in support of the extension of governmental immunity to the crown in right of the non-legislating level of authority in the federal system, though the other view has found some expression as well.[36]

The Limits of Immunity in an Interjurisdictional Context

If governmental immunity works in favour of the crown in rights other than that

---

30 (1925), 36 C.L.R. 170, at 218
31 The exceptions are *Public Curator of Qd* v *Morris* (1951), 51 S.R. (N.S.W.) 402, judgment of Owen J (F.C.), and *Johnson* v *Lavender*, [1952] S.A.S.R. 267.
32 *Roberts* v *Ahern* (1904), 1 C.L.R. 406; *Commonwealth* v *N.S.W.* (1906), 3 C.L.R. 807, see esp. at 813–14, 818 & 821; *Re Keep, McPherson Ltd* (1931), 48 W.N. (N.S.W.) 180; *Commonwealth* v *Bogle* (1953), 89 C.L.R. 229, at 259 *per* Fullagar J, Dixon CJ, Webb & Kitto JJ concurring; *Marshall* v *Commonwealth Hostels Ltd*, [1953] V.L.R. 503, at 507; *Commonwealth* v *Rhind* (1966), 119 C.L.R. 584, at 598–9 *per* Barwick CJ, McTiernan, Taylor & Menzies JJ concurring
33 *Public Curator of Qd* v *Morris* (1951), 51 S.R. (N.S.W.) 402, judgment of Herron J, dissenting (F.C.)
34 *Broken Hill Associated Smelters Pty* v *Collector of Imposts (Vict.)* (1918), 25 C.L.R. 61
35 See *Commonwealth* v *Cigamatic Pty* (1962), 108 C.L.R. 372, considered infra at 114–15.
36 See *Reid* v *Canadian Farm Loan Bd*, [1937] 4 D.L.R. 248, at 252 (Man. K.B.), appr'd in *Majestic Mines Ltd* v *A.G. of Alta*, [1941] 2 W.W.R. 353, at 356 (Alta S.C.), aff'd without reference to this point at [1942] 1 D.L.R. 474 (Alta C.A.) and [1942] 4 D.L.R. 593 (S.C.C.). And cf *Independent Order of Foresters* v *The King*, [1939] 2 D.L.R. 53, at 56 (Alta S.C.), appr'd on this point on appeal at [1940] A.C. 513, at 536 (P.C.).

of the legislating authority, as has been suggested, then a further question needs to be explored. That is, in what circumstances will the crown in any or all of those other rights be treated as bound by statutes of the enacting jurisdiction? Is it sufficient to establish that the crown, in a general sense, is included expressly or by necessary implication? Or must the legislation meet the test that the crown, more specifically in right of the government which claims immunity, has been included expressly or by necessary implication?

If the burden on the legislature, if it is to include the crown in that other right, is of the latter order then it may be expected that there will be greater opportunities for successful claims to governmental immunity in an interjurisdictional situation than otherwise. While legislation may well provide for its operation against the crown generally, it will often be no more particular than this. The special treatment of the crown's position will often fail to carry the necessary implication that it is comprehensive of the crown in a right other than that of the legislating government. This may result then in an immunity which might appear to be excessive in practice and to unduly favour 'foreign' governments. But, on the other hand, the peculiar circumstances of a federal system are such that it does not seem unreasonable to insist that a legislature demonstrate its concern to include the crown specially in right of the other level of authority in the federation as a condition to its enactments affecting the crown in that capacity. The crown in that other right is a juristic entity functioning within the territorial jurisdiction of the enacting legislature and it is only to be anticipated that the question of whether it is subject to that legislature's statutes is apt to arise. Therefore it may be appropriate to expect the special inclusion of the crown in right of the other level of political authority before concluding that that authority is subject as a matter of interpretation to the legislation in question. In fact the construction given state or provincial provisions, making local enactments binding upon the crown, suggests that those enactments will extend to the federal crown only if they are express or carry a necessary implication in that particular regard.

In *Gauthier* v *The King*,[37] a case that was to assume fundamental importance for its recognition of a constitutional form of immunity,[38] the Supreme Court of Canada decided that a provision applying the terms of a provincial act to His Majesty ought not to be taken as subjecting the crown in the right of the dominion to the restrictions of the act. Anglin J put that conclusion on the basis that 'it may be accepted as a safe rule of construction that a reference to the Crown in a provincial statute shall be taken to be to the Crown in right of the province only,

37 (1918), 40 D.L.R. 353 (S.C.C.)
38 See infra, at 34–6.

unless the statute in express terms or by necessary intendment makes it clear that the reference is to the Crown in some other sense.'[39] 'This,' he said, 'would seem to be a corollary of the rule that the Crown is not bound by a statute unless named in it.'[40] By offering this explanation he may be taken to have limited the operation of the foregoing presumption to the interpretation of provincial enactments which mention the crown for the particular purpose of making their terms binding in that respect.[41] He also said that provincial legislation is incompetent to take away or abridge, of its own force, a privilege of the federal crown. But this consideration was put as a discrete ground for interpreting the provincial legislation as not applying to the crown in the dominion right.[42]

The Australian case of *Re Richard Foreman & Sons Pty; Uther* v *Federal Commissioner of Taxation*[43] (*Uther's* case) presented a question of interpretation that was similar to that in the *Gauthier* case. A state Companies Act specified that the crown was bound by its prescription of priorities in a winding up. And, in ranking various debts of a company in liquidation, it gave a preference to certain kinds of taxes assessed under any state or Commonwealth act. The Commonwealth as a creditor of the Foreman Company, which was in liquidation under the state act, insisted upon first payment. It asserted priority over the other unsecured creditors on the basis of the prerogative and claimed not to be affected by the provisions of the Companies Act ranking the claims of creditors.

The High Court construed the state legislation as intended to govern the priority to be accorded debts owed to the Commonwealth. Latham CJ proceeded to this conclusion from the starting point that the section of the act which subjected the crown to the statutory ranking scheme should be taken as referable only to the crown in the right of the state in the absence of any clear indication that the Commonwealth was included.[44] But he discovered such an indication in the spec-

---

39 (1918), 40 D.L.R. 353, at 365–6, Fitzpatrick CJ & Davies J concurring on this point. This rule of construction has been applied in *Montreal Trust Co.* v *The King*, [1924] 1 D.L.R. 1030, at 1032 (B.C.C.A.); *Towers* v *M.N.R.* (1954), 10 T.A.B.C. 347, at 351; *Re Mendelsohn* (1959), 22 D.L.R. (2d) 748, at 754 (Ont. S.C., Master), rev'd on consent at (1960), 25 D.L.R. (2d) 778 (Ont. H.C.). And see *R* v *Hamilton* (1962), 37 D.L.R. (2d) 545, at 555–6 (Man. Q.B.). The rule was quoted with approval in *Essendon Corp.* v *Criterion Theatres Ltd* (1947), 74 C.L.R. 1, at 11 *per* Latham CJ & at 26 *per* Dixon J.
40 (1918), 40 D.L.R. 353, at 366
41 Though it was taken to have a larger operation in the *Essendon* case (1947), 74 C.L.R. 1.
42 But see the treatment of the *Gauthier* case in *R* v *Jones*, [1962] 3 S.A.L.R. 1, at 7–8 *per* Claydon CJ (Fed. S.C. of Rhodesia & Nyasaland).
43 (1947), 74 C.L.R. 508
44 Ibid, at 515. The invocation of this presumption, in such a context, finds further support in the *obiter* remarks of Fullagar J in *Commonwealth* v *Bogle* (1953), 89

ification elsewhere in the statute of some Commonwealth debts among the preferred claims. Dixon J, though finding it unnecessary to go back to any presumption in view of that specification, also agreed that the expression 'the Crown' in the state act ought not to be taken as referring to the crown in right of the Commonwealth.[45] None of the other members of the court[46] made direct reference to any such rule of construction. And the two that did apparently relied upon a general rule that a reference, for whatever purpose, to the crown in a state statute means *prima facie* the crown in right of the state.[47] Thus the presumption was not specifically founded upon the dictates of the rule of governmental immunity as it might operate in an interjurisdictional setting, as it seems to have been in *Gauthier*. However, there would have been no need to consider the precise meaning of the provision of the state statute subjecting the crown to its ranking scheme had the rule of governmental immunity not been assumed to favour the Commonwealth in the face of a state statute[48] and had a provision extending such a statute to the crown been enough in any event to overcome that immunity.[49]

In view of the court's unanimous conclusion in *Uther's* case that the act purported to control the relative position of the Commonwealth as a creditor in a liquidation, the constitutional question of whether the state Parliament could bind the Commonwealth in this respect had to be faced. The decision that it could, Dixon J dissenting, was later to be overruled in *Commonwealth v Cigamatic Pty.*[50]

In deciding that the expression 'the Crown' in a 'Crown is bound' provision in a state or provincial statute is presumed to mean the state or provincial government, these judgments indicate, then, that to affect the federal government local legislation must be clear about its inclusion of the federal authority.[51] Presum-

C.L.R. 229, at 259, Dixon CJ, Webb & Kitto JJ concurring. But cf *Minister for Works (W.A.) v Gulson* (1944), 69 C.L.R. 338, at 356 *per* Rich J.

45 (1947), 74 C.L.R. 508, at 527, cited and foll'd in *Re Young's Horsham Garage Pty*, [1969] V.R. 977, at 978

46 Rich, Starke, McTiernan, & Williams JJ

47 Since they relied upon *Essendon Corp. v Criterion Theatres Ltd* (1947), 74 C.L.R. 1, which concerned the meaning of 'the Crown' in a statutory provision exempting the crown.

48 Though Latham CJ had always taken the view that governmental immunity is only enjoyed by the crown in right of the legislating authority, see supra.

49 The judgment of Williams J, in focusing on the meaning of the 'Crown is bound' provision (see (1947), 74 C.L.R. 508, at 537–8), carries the latter assumption as well. Consider also the judgment of McTiernan J, at 535.

50 (1962), 108 C.L.R. 372, considered infra, at 114–15

51 And see *Montreal Trust Co. v The King*, [1924] 1 D.L.R. 1030, at 1031 (B.C.C.A.), which is even more explicit on the latter point.

ably a similar requirement would have to be satisfied by federal legislation if it is to affect state or provincial governments.[52]

INTERGOVERNMENTAL IMMUNITY: ITS NATURE AND GENERAL SCOPE

In a federal state the several governments may require a degree of immunity from the legislative action of other political units within the system. The starting point for such a claim is that each government, within its own sphere, ought to be free to pursue the policies and programs which it decides upon, within the statutory framework, of course, that has been supplied by the legislature to which it is responsible. The statutes of another political authority within the federation may, if applicable, embarrass or inhibit the government in the realization of its goals. At the extreme there could conceivably be an interference with the central process of government itself, threatening the separate existence of a component part of the federal state. On the other hand, each legislature has a measure of jurisdiction which is assured to it by the constitution and the effectiveness of its exercise may be significantly impaired if exceptions are to be carved out of its statutes in favour of other governments. Even if the recognition of exceptions is necessary it need not be automatic but might be accorded so far as a government has been granted immunity from the kind of statute in question by an enactment of the legislature to which it is answerable. That is, it might be immune only in the event of a positive and particular assertion by the appropriate legislature of the need for immunity. These then are the competing considerations, briefly stated, that bear upon the protection each government might properly be accorded from the legislation of another political entity within a federation.

Naturally it will be unusual for a state or provincial government to be faced with the possible application to it of the legislation of another state or province because of the territorial constraint upon governmental and legislative activity at this level.[53] But confrontations between the central or federal government and local legislation and between state or provincial governments and federal legislation are to be expected. Here there is a form of territorial correspondence in the responsibility of the governments and legislatures of the two levels of authority since each state and province comes within a national or federal jurisdiction. It is

52 See *Minister for Works (W.A.)* v *Gulson* (1944), 69 C.L.R. 338, at 367 *per* Williams J, sed contra at 356 *per* Rich J.
53 There has never been any understanding that the federal constitution of Australia or Canada supports a general immunity of a state or province from the legislation of another state or province; see, as to Australia, *Public Curator of Qd* v *Morris* (1951), 51 S.R. (N.S.W.) 402, at 408 *per* Street CJ (F.C.).

in these situations, then, that an insistence upon some kind of intergovernmental immunity is likely to be forthcoming.

The constitution may be explicit in resolving the competing factors in favour of immunity in particular circumstances. This is the case in Australia and Canada, in that governments are expressly freed from the burdens of property tax statutes of the other level of authority in the federation.[54] But so far as legislation of other varieties is concerned the matter is largely untouched by the specifics of the relevant constitutional instruments. It was left to the courts, therefore, to develop appropriate general principles of intergovernmental immunity from such implications as might properly be drawn from the two constitutions.

In Canada recognition of the doctrine of intergovernmental immunity that was to secure acceptance fell to the Supreme Court without any imprint being imposed by the Privy Council which, during the relevant period, was the final court of appeal for Canada. This is remarkable since most of the fundamental principles of Canadian constitutional law came from the Judicial Committee. The seminal decision was *Gauthier* v *The King*.[55] It presented a question of the ability of the federal crown to revoke a submission to arbitration when the statute law of the province in which the matter arose proscribed any such unilateral withdrawal. The Supreme Court viewed that section of the provincial statute which purported to make the legislation binding upon the crown as not intended to restrict the crown in the right of the dominion. One of the reasons for arriving at this construction was, as put by Anglin J on behalf of himself and Davies J, that otherwise the provincial legislation would be *pro tanto ultra vires* for, '[p]rovincial legislation cannot *proprio vigore* take away or abridge any privilege of the Crown in right of the Dominion.'[56] Fitzpatrick CJ agreed in the narrow construction of the provincial act for the reasons given by Anglin J and added, in his own statement of the pertinent immunity, that, 'in any event the provinces have ... neither executive, legislative nor judicial power to bind the Dominion Government.'[57]

This, then, was the bare enunciation of a form of intergovernmental immunity which operated in favour of the federal authority. There was no consideration of the reason behind it, the need for it, or the possibility of a reciprocal immunity of provincial governments from federal legislation.

54 By s 125 of the British North America Act, 1867, 30 & 31 Vict. c 3 (Imp.) (hereinafter sometimes referred to as the BNA Act), and s 114 of the Australian constitution, enacted as s 9 of the Commonwealth of Australia Constitution Act, 63 & 64 Vict. c 12 (Imp.). These two constitutional provisions are considered at length infra, at 137–43.
55 (1918), 40 D.L.R. 353 (S.C.C.). An earlier Exchequer Court decision, *Powell* v *The King* (1905), 9 Ex. C.R. 364, turned on an intergovernmental immunity which was apparently of the kind recognized in *Gauthier*, see the former decision, at 374–5.
56 (1918), 40 D.L.R. 353 (S.C.C.), at 365
57 Ibid, at 356. Idington J wrote a further judgment and Duff J concurred in the result.

The 'privilege' of the crown in the federal right which Anglin J conceived to be beyond the reach of provincial legislation might have been the privilege of revoking a submission to arbitration, which was not peculiar to the crown but was enjoyed by all subjects at common law. Alternatively he may have been referring to the privilege, that was obviously exclusive to the crown, of standing outside legislation in which the sovereign is not specially included. That privilege has often been described as being of a prerogative nature.[58] The Chief Justice certainly thought that it was the former which was threatened by the provincial legislation.[59] But Anglin J and Idington J, who wrote a further judgment, suggested that a royal prerogative of the dominion crown was in jeopardy.[60] This can only have been that of governmental immunity. While the provincial legislation in question did purport to bind the crown, it did not indicate expressly or by necessary implication that that extension was to include the crown in the federal right. And Mr Justice Anglin assumed this to be essential to avoid governmental immunity, as he seems to have understood its operation in favour of the central authority in the Canadian federal setting.[61] The federal crown could be seen, therefore, to enjoy a prerogative which would be impaired if the provincial statute were to be applied against it.

It can be argued, then, that the Supreme Court simply held that the provincial legislature was incapable of binding the federal crown in the exercise of one of its prerogatives. Consequently other 'rights' of the federal crown would not necessarily be protected by the intergovernmental immunity first recognized in this decision. Several subsequent cases have put the immunity as one that operates in favour of the federal crown in the exercise of its prerogatives.[62] But other cases speak more generally of the inability of the provinces to bind the federal crown or to affect its rights or privileges.[63] Their results would not have been altered,

58 See supra, at 3.
59 See (1918), 40 D.L.R. 353, at 356.
60 Ibid, at 360 *per* Idington J & at 363 *per* Anglin J
61 See supra, at 30-1.
62 *Toronto & Toronto Electric Comm'rs* v *Wade*, [1931] 4 D.L.R. 928, at 929 (Ont. S.C.), aff'd on other grounds at [1932] 3 D.L.R. 509 (C.A.); *R* v *Star Kosher Sausage Mfg Co.*, [1940] 4 D.L.R. 365, at 367 (Man. K.B.); *Re Mendelsohn* (1959), 22 D.L.R. (2d) 748, at 754 (Ont. S.C., Master), rev'd on consent at (1960), 25 D.L.R. 778 (Ont. H.C.); *Ottawa Public School Bd* v *Ottawa*, [1953] 1 D.L.R. 692, at 695 (Ont. C.A.); *Emerson* v *Simpson* (1962), 32 D.L.R. (2d) 603, at 607 (B.C.S.C.); *Re Sternschein* (1965), 50 D.L.R. (2d) 762, at 763 (Man. Q.B.); *R* v *City of Montreal* (1972), 27 D.L.R. (3d) 349, at 355 (F.C.T.D.). And cf *Crowther* v *A.G. of Can.* (1959), 17 D.L.R. (2d) 437, at 441 (N.S.S.C. in banco).
63 *R* v *Lithwick* (1921), 57 D.L.R. 1, at 2 (Exch.); *R* v *Powers*, [1923] Ex. C.R. 131, at 134; *Re Adams Shoe Co., ex p. Town of Penetanguishene*, [1923] 4 D.L.R. 927, at 931 (Ont. S.C.); *Bowers* v *Hollinger*, [1946] 4 D.L.R. 186, at 196 (Ont. H.C.); *Palmer*

however, had the protection only extended to federal prerogative rights, if we include within that category governmental immunity from statutes, federal or provincial.

In Australia, *Commonwealth* v *Cigamatic Pty*[64] was the vehicle for the adoption of a form of intergovernmental immunity benefiting the Commonwealth. At issue was the right of the central government to stand outside an administration, pursuant to state statute, of the assets of an insolvent company and thus to secure priority for the debts it was owed by the company. The state act purported to bind the Commonwealth by its scheme of distribution. Therefore there was no possibility of governmental immunity saving the Commonwealth from the operation of the scheme which the act introduced for the ranking of creditors. But the Commonwealth did continue to enjoy another prerogative, that of priority for crown debts over the debts of a subject which are of equal degree, which it was found not to have waived by participating in the winding-up proceedings.[65] That prerogative was held to be beyond the reach of the state statute. Dixon CJ considered the state to be incapable of controlling a Commonwealth prerogative or fiscal right of government, as he preferred to label the priority of the crown in contemporary terms.[66] But he also spoke more generally of the state's inability to control the legal rights between the Commonwealth and its people.[67] Menzies J, Owen J concurring, put the immunity as one in relation to the prerogative. But, at the same time, he subscribed to the dissenting opinion of Dixon J, as he then was, in *Uther's* case.[68] That case had presented similar facts to *Cigamatic* and was of necessity overruled in the latter case.[69] The earlier opinion of Sir Owen Dixon had suggested that the Commonwealth enjoyed a very wide immunity from state legislation though the author of that view was not then forced into the closeness of reasoning that a majority decision requires. Windeyer J, giving another of the judgments in *Cigamatic*, adhered to the Dixonian position in both cases, while Kitto J concurred in the result and McTiernan and Taylor JJ dissented.

In two other earlier decisions[70] Dixon J had advanced descriptions of the in-

---

v *The King*, [1952] 1 D.L.R. 259, at 268 (Exch.); *A.G. of Can.* v *Rhode* (1957), 8 D.L.R. (2d) 89, at 90 (Sask. Dist. Ct); *Directeur de la Loi sur les terres* v *Home Ins. Co.*, [1959] C.S. 490, at 492; *R* v *Breton* (1967), 65 D.L.R. (2d) 76, at 79 (S.C.C.). And cf *R* v *Lamothe*, [1958] O.R. 207, at 210 (H.C.).
64 (1962), 108 C.L.R. 372
65 Ibid, at 378–9 *per* Dixon CJ
66 Ibid, at 377–8
67 Ibid, at 377
68 (1947), 74 C.L.R. 508
69 See (1962), 108 C.L.R. 372, at 389.
70 *Federal Comm'r of Taxation* v *Official Liquidator of E.O. Farley Ltd* (1940), 63 C.L.R. 278, and *Essendon Corp.* v *Criterion Theatres Ltd* (1947), 74 C.L.R. 1

tergovernmental immunity enjoyed by the Commonwealth, with neither the concurrence nor the disapproval of any of the other presiding judges,[71] which might not limit it to situations in which governmental rights of a prerogative order were in question. But his observations were made in relation to fact situations in which there was arguably a federal prerogative involved, namely priority as a creditor in the one case and governmental immunity in the other.

Also in *Commonwealth* v *Bogle*,[72] which gave warning of the High Court's later stance in *Cigamatic*, Fullagar J had said in a judgment that had the approval of the majority that the state had no power to legislate so as to bind the Commonwealth.[73] This comment was made *obiter*, for the corporate plaintiff which had asserted immunity from a state rental control statute, in proceedings to recover rent due, was held not to be an agent of the crown entitled to the benefit of immunity. And the immunity of the federal crown that was contemplated was qualified by the remark that the Commonwealth might be affected by some state laws, such as a sale of goods act, when it contracts within a state.[74] It is maintained in a later chapter that it is possible to view the central provisions of that kind of enactment as effective in relation to crown contracts because there is no interference with the right of the crown to contract on its own express terms.[75] That, it will be suggested, is the limited right which is protected by the prerogative of governmental immunity when legislation concerns the terms and effect of contracts. If state legislation would interfere with that right, as it would have in *Bogle* had the plaintiff been the Commonwealth or one of its agents, then governmental immunity would operate in the absence of an express or implied extension of the legislation to the crown. If the doctrine of intergovernmental immunity is taken to protect the Commonwealth in the enjoyment of that prerogative from state interference, then it can indeed be said that the state had no power to bind the Commonwealth in the matter of the rent it could extract by agreement.

At a minimum, it can be said that the state of authority in both Australia and Canada does not foreclose a restriction of the intergovernmental immunity of the federal crown to circumstances in which a state or provincial statute would otherwise prejudice a prerogative right.

71 Though Rich J in *Farley's* case (1940), 63 C.L.R. 278, at 291, suggested that a state legislature might be incompetent to take away the Commonwealth's prerogative priority as a creditor and Latham CJ in the *Essendon* case (1947), 74 C.L.R. 1, at 14, spoke rather tentatively of a general intergovernmental tax immunity pertaining in a federal system.

72 (1953), 89 C.L.R. 229

73 Ibid, at 259

74 Ibid, at 260. See also *Farley's* case (1940), 63 C.L.R. 278, at 308 *per* Dixon J, and *Uther's* case (1947), 74 C.L.R. 508, at 528 *per* Dixon J.

75 See infra, at 103–4.

There is much to be said for the narrower view of the intergovernmental immunity that is enjoyed by the federal crown. First of all it preserves a greater degree of latitude to the states and provinces in the exercise of their legislative roles in that they can effectively extend most of their statutory provisions to the federal crown. It is simply a question of being explicit in this respect. If the federal crown is unable to rely on any of its prerogatives, then it will be bound by express words. But those governmental interests which have a claim to be most jealously guarded because they inhere in the prerogative will in fact be secure from state or provincial interference.

It should be noted that other federal governmental interests which are central to the exclusive powers of the national parliament under the two constitutions are unaffected by state or provincial legislative changes by virtue of exclusive power immunities, described below, and do not require the aid of a larger form of intergovernmental immunity. And it is open to the federal parliament to create governmental immunities, which are further to those already considered, by legislation that would take priority on paramountcy principles over state or provincial legislation purporting to bind the federal crown.[76]

Secondly, with this approach we are left with less, or possibly no, discrepancy between the immunity of the federal crown from state or provincial legislation and the immunity of the state or provincial crown from federal legislation. As we shall see shortly, the latter immunity has been held to be considerably narrower than the larger of the possible versions of the intergovernmental immunity of the federal crown. It is difficult to discover a constitutional warrant for any difference in these two situations. It is true, of course, that federal legislation is paramount to state or provincial legislation in the event of a conflict, but in other major respects the two levels of authority are thought to be co-ordinate. One manifestation of this occurs in the very matter of the exercise of governmental powers, for the prerogative of priority may be exercised, absent a controlling statute, by both levels of government against a common debtor. First position is not given to the federal privilege in the event of insufficient assets to satisfy both governmental claims.[77] While precedent may now preclude perfect symmetry in the immunities operating each way between national and state or provincial political entities, to the extent that there is room for manoeuvre, the least distortion between the two privileges is to be preferred.

Thirdly, an immunity tied to federal crown prerogatives will necessarily contract with statutory restriction or judicial confinement of those prerogatives. Of

---

76 See *Great West Saddlery Co.* v *The King*, [1921] 2 A.C. 91, at 100 (P.C.), and *Melbourne Corp.* v *Commonwealth* (1947), 74 C.L.R. 31, at 50 *per* Latham CJ. And see Sawer, 'State Statutes and the Commonwealth' (1962), 1 *U. of Tasmania L. Rev.* 580, at 584.
77 See infra, at 119–24.

course it will also expand should the legislative or judicial thrust be to widen those prerogatives. But, by and large, that is not the evident direction of contemporary courts and legislatures. The trend is to reduce the differences in the position of the subject and that of the crown so as to minimize the prejudice that subjects are likely to suffer if room has to be accorded for the operation of special privileges of the crown. This is a sensible development as governmental activity expands, with a consequent increase in the opportunities for prerogative rights working to the detriment of private interests, and as awareness of the need to safeguard the civil rights of individuals becomes more acute. If a prerogative enjoyed by the federal crown is confined as the result of these underlying considerations, then it makes good sense similarly to confine the special position of the federal crown when it comes up against the régime of state or provincial law, for the need to protect the position of subjects will normally be just as compelling in that situation. Thus, in the absence of some overriding factor, there is considerable merit in equating the status of the federal crown under state or provincial law so far as possible to that which it enjoys in relation to federal law.

Fourthly, if the intergovernmental immunity of the federal crown can be explained as a device to protect the crown in the exercise of prerogatives, then a number of otherwise perplexing Canadian decisions denying an immunity claim fall into line. These decisions, the most notable of which is *Dominion Building Corporation* v *The King*,[78] held the federal crown bound by provincial legislation simply on the basis of the absence of any governmental immunity from statute in the circumstances at hand. In none of these cases was the crown able to rely on any other form of the prerogative. But no consideration at all was given, in the judgments, to the possibility of an intergovernmental immunity saving the federal authority from provincial regulation. That is explicable only on the basis of an implicit rejection of the notion of intergovernmental immunity, a totally inadequate argument on the part of counsel, an assumption that the scope of intergovernmental immunity is no greater than that of governmental immunity or an appreciation that it is only federal crown prerogatives, none of which were available in any of these cases, which cannot be reached by provincial legislation. The first two explanations must be rejected since intergovernmental immunity on the part of the federal crown is too firmly entrenched in Canadian jurisprudence to be treated as swept aside by inference and too notorious for a series of cases to be regarded as *per incuriam*. The third explanation equating the reach of the two forms of immunity suffers from the defect that the analogy has a serious

78 [1933] A.C. 533 (P.C.). The other cases are *R* v *McLeod*, [1930] 4 D.L.R. 226 (N.S.S.C. in banco), and *R* v *Stradiotto*, [1973] 2 O.R. 375 (C.A.). See also *R* v *Murray* (1967), 60 D.L.R. (2d) 647 (S.C.C.), considered infra, at 83–5.

imperfection, since the limits of governmental immunity are exceeded in the event that legislation binds the crown expressly or by necessary implication. That is a circumstance in provincial legislation that cannot be taken invariably to avoid the intergovernmental immunity of the federal crown. If it did, the latter would have no more effect than governmental immunity operating in a federal context. The final possibility, that of confining the federal crown's intergovernmental immunity to cases in which it enjoys a prerogative, is to be preferred, by comparison.

In sum, these various considerations support the narrower definition of the intergovernmental immunity of the federal crown, that is that local legislation will not be taken to affect the prerogative rights enjoyed by the central government authority.[79] This conclusion is consistent with judicial statements to the effect that a state could not have made the Commonwealth liable for torts committed within the state in the event that tort liability had not been imposed generally upon the Commonwealth by the federal Judiciary Act.[80] Such action on the part of a state, if sustained, would abrogate the prerogative of immunity in tort enjoyed by the Commonwealth. Therefore the case for intergovernmental immunity, in the sense to which we have preferred to confine it, would be established. The conclusion also accommodates various indications that the federal crown is subject to local legislation when it takes advantage thereof,[81] a familiar basis for the avoidance of governmental immunity.[82] In those circumstances the federal crown would be unable to insist upon governmental immunity so that, in the absence of any other prerogative, it would be subject to state or provincial legislation. On the approach which we have adopted here, the federal crown enjoys no special position, apart from that inherent in the prerogative, in the face of such legislation.

79 A somewhat different prerogative related explanation of intergovernmental immunity, in Australia, is given by Evans in 'Rethinking Commonwealth Immunity' (1972), 8 *M.U.L.R.* 521, at 547–57.

80 *Uther's* case (1947), 74 C.L.R. 508, at 529 *per* Dixon J, and *Commonwealth v Bogle* (1953), 89 C.L.R. 229, at 259–60 *per* Fullagar J, Dixon CJ, Webb & Kitto JJ concurring. It is notable that the inability of the state to affect Commonwealth liability is confined to the matter of tort liability, the crown enjoying no prerogative immunity from other forms of liability such as that in contract, though the special procedure of petition of right had traditionally to be used in these latter situations. As to the imposition of tort liability upon the Commonwealth pursuant to the Judiciary Act, 1903–73, see infra, at 47.

81 See *Commonwealth v N.S.W.* (1918), 25 C.L.R. 325, at 348 *per* Higgins J; *Bartlett v Osterhout*, [1931] 3 D.L.R. 609 (Ont. S.C.); *Reid v Canadian Farm Loan Bd*, [1937] 4 D.L.R. 248 (Man. K.B.), consid'd infra, at 110–11; *A.G. of Can. v Tombs*, [1946] 4 D.L.R. 516 (Ont. Co'y Ct), decision rev'd on other grounds, ibid, at 519 (Ont. C.A.). The *Reid* decision, however, also contains an assertion that governmental immunity has no interjurisdictional operation, at 252.

82 See supra, at 10–14.

In dividing legislative power between a central and local parliaments, a federal constitution may import a form of intergovernmental immunity which is a function of the exclusive nature of some legislative powers. For example, the exclusive power of the national parliament to legislate in respect of federally acquired public places in Australia[83] or federal public property in Canada[84] prevents the states or provinces from legislating on many important matters in regard to such places or property.[85] It is not likely that local legislation would single out those particular governmental interests for special treatment. The more usual situation will be that a state or province will have passed an enactment applicable generally throughout the jurisdiction and the relevant grant of constitutional power to the central Parliament will not invalidate the local act in its entirety but will only exclude its operation in relation to federal public places or property. Looking at the resulting situation from the point of view of the amenability of the federal government to statutory regulation by the states or provinces we may say, quite accurately, that the federal government is immune from the local enactment. This immunity derives directly from the division of legislative authority under the written federal constitution and may be usefully described as an exclusive power immunity.[86]

It is sometimes suggested that the intergovernmental immunity of the federal crown in Canada is simply a form of exclusive power immunity.[87] However, there are only two constitutional powers in the British North America Act that might permit legislation in relation to the various prerogatives, or other rights for that matter, of the federal crown. These are the general power, enabling parliament to enact laws for the peace, order, and good government of Canada[88] and that authority found in section 91(1A) in relation to the public debt and property. Yet the former rarely operates, except in its purely residual role, to preclude provin-

---

83 Australian constitution, s 52(i)

84 BNA Act, s 91(1A)

85 See, for example, *Worthing* v *Rowell & Muston Pty* (1970), 123 C.L.R. 89; *R* v *Phillips* (1970), 125 C.L.R. 93; *A.G. of N.S.W.* v *Stocks & Holdings (Constructors) Pty* (1970), 124 C.L.R. 262; *Deeks McBride Ltd* v *Vancouver Associated Contractors Ltd*, [1954] 4 D.L.R. 844 (B.C.C.A.); *Ottawa* v *Shore & Horwitz Constr. Co.* (1960), 22 D.L.R. (2d) 247 (Ont. H.C.), but cf *Cardinal* v *A.G. of Alta* (1973), 40 D.L.R. (3d) 553, at 560 (S.C.C.).

86 A third variety of constitutional immunity might be identified, that is the immunity enjoyed by the federal government from local legislation in the presence of a federal enactment applying to the central government which is inconsistent with local legislation and therefore takes paramountcy over it. Unlike the other forms of constitutional immunity this one is not automatic but depends upon legislative action by the central parliament.

87 See Abel (ed) *Laskin's Canadian Constitutional Law* (4th ed rev. 1975), at 527.

88 S 91, opening clause

cial legislation.[89] And the latter provision is inapt to comprehend legislation on matters of prerogative concern except so far as particular prerogatives confer rights or immunities in relation to property. Moreover, this rationalization of the intergovernmental immunity of the federal crown would mean that parliament could not effect a surrender of immunity for in so acting it would alter the division of powers under the BNA Act, a change which would require a constitutional amendment.[90] But, as will be seen, it is arguable that parliament can in fact surrender the immunity of the federal crown from provincial legislation by the device of a simple statute which is explicit in this respect.[91] That facility can be justified on the basis of the general principles of a distinct doctrine of implied intergovernmental immunity though not on the assumption that the immunity is of an exclusive power variety.

The state or provincial governments are entitled to a measure of immunity from federal legislation that may be more limited than that enjoyed by the central government from local legislation. The basic position is that the crown in the right of a state or province is bound by federal legislation.[92] This appears to be so even in relation to its prerogatives.[93] The argument may still be open that the states and provinces ought to enjoy an immunity from federal statutes interfering with their prerogatives, for that issue has yet to be squarely faced by a full appellate bench. The acceptance of this claim would have the merit of putting the states and provinces in the same position vis-à-vis federal legislation as the federal authority is arguably in vis-à-vis local legislation. As indicated earlier, any

89 *Johannesson* v *Rural Municipality of West St Paul*, [1952] 4 D.L.R. 609 (S.C.C.), is exceptional in this regard. And cf the judgment of Pigeon J, Martland & Beetz JJ concurring, in *Interprovincial Co-operatives Ltd* v *The Queen* (1975), 53 D.L.R. (3d) 321 (S.C.C.).

90 See the BNA Act, s 91(1) for the extent of the power of the central parliament to amend the constitution.

91 See infra, at 146–55.

92 Consider *R* v *Sutton* (1908), 5 C.L.R. 789; *A.G. of N.S.W.* v *Collector of Customs for N.S.W.* (1908), 5 C.L.R. 818; *Amalgamated Soc'y of Eng'rs* v *Adelaide Steamship Co.* (1920), 28 C.L.R. 129; *A.G. of B.C.* v *A.G. of Can.*, [1924] A.C. 222 (P.C.); *Re Silver Brothers Ltd*, [1932] A.C. 514, at 521 (P.C.); *Independent Order of Foresters* v *The King*, [1939] 2 D.L.R. 53, at 56 (Alta S.C.), appr'd on this point on appeal at [1940] A.C. 513, at 536 (P.C.).

93 *Re Cardston U.F.A. Co-operative Ass'n Ltd, ex p. The King*, [1925] 4 D.L.R. 897 (Alta S.C.); *Re Standard Pharmacy Ltd*, [1926] 2 D.L.R. 300 (Alta S.C.); *Re Hardy*, [1928] 3 D.L.R. 255 (Ont. S.C.), aff'd on other grounds at [1929] 1 D.L.R. 300 (Ont. S.C., App. Div.); *R* v *Trustee of Leach* (1929), 11 C.B.R. 214 (N.B.S.C.); *Federal Comm'r of Taxation* v *Official Liquidator of E.O. Farley Ltd* (1940), 63 C.L.R. 278, at 313–14 *per* Dixon J & at 322–3 *per* Evatt J; *Re Richard Foreman & Sons Pty; Uther* v *Federal Comm'r of Taxation* (1947), 74 C.L.R. 508, at 529 *per* Dixon J, dissenting; *Re Clemenshaw* (1962), 33 D.L.R. (2d) 524 (B.C.S.C.)

discrepancy in the privileges of the two levels of government in the face of legislation of the other does not appear to have any firm constitutional basis.

An important qualification to the general subjection of state governments to Commonwealth statute law was established in *Melbourne Corporation* v *Commonwealth.*[94] The Commonwealth had passed a Banking Act provision prohibiting private banks from conducting any banking business for a state or local or state authority without the permission of the Commonwealth Treasurer. The Treasurer had indicated that banks would be required under this section to cease doing business with the City of Melbourne. The municipal corporation was, therefore, in the position of being obliged to bank with the central banking agency, the Commonwealth Bank, in the absence of any state bank in Victoria at the time. The city successfully challenged the validity of this Commonwealth initiative in the High Court. The majority of the court considered the Banking Act section unconstitutional because it singled out or was aimed at the exercise by the states of one of their constitutional or sovereign powers, namely the control of state funds.[95] The element of discrimination against the states which the legislation evidenced was thus an important feature of the case. But three members of the court also said that a Commonwealth law even if general and non-discriminatory would be invalid if it were to interfere substantially with the exercise by a state of its governmental functions.[96] In fact Starke J pitched his judgment solely on the understanding that this was the effect of the Commonwealth banking legislation.[97]

Though the alternative criterion might be thought to involve a substantial immunity on the part of the states from federal control, it has not been applied to produce that result.[98] Thus, for example, the states have been held subject to the payment of a general Commonwealth pay-roll tax on the wages and salaries paid state government employees, though this might have a significant impact on the state in the performance of its governmental role.[99] And it has been assumed that the Canadian parliament could competently subject the provincial public service to a national wage control program.[100] In point of fact the magnitude of interference with state or provincial governmental functions which is likely to prove fatal

94 (1947), 74 C.L.R. 31
95 Ibid, at 60–2 *per* Latham CJ, at 66 *per* Rich J, at 78–84 *per* Dixon J, & at 99–100 *per* Williams J. McTiernan J dissented and Starke J put his decision on a different basis, see infra.
96 Ibid, at 60 *per* Latham CJ, at 66 *per* Rich J, & at 74 *per* Starke J
97 Ibid, at 74–5
98 See *Wenn* v *A.G. of Vict.* (1948), 77 C.L.R. 84; *Ex p. Professional Eng'rs' Ass'n* (1959), 107 C.L.R. 208; *Vict.* v *Commonwealth* (1971), 122 C.L.R. 353.
99 *Vict.* v *Commonwealth* (1971), 122 C.L.R. 353
100 See *Reference re Anti-Inflation Act* (1976), 68 D.L.R. (3d) 452, esp. at 501–2.

to the application of a general federal statute to the states or provinces would probably have to be such as to pose a serious threat to the independence which those political units enjoy from the central authority under the federal scheme.

A local legislature may have the exclusive constitutional power of making appropriations from the state or provincial consolidated revenue fund. When that is the case the central parliament is unable to impose financial burdens directly upon that revenue, a matter that will be considered subsequently at greater length.[101] This presents a further, but limited, inhibition upon the national parliament in the exercise of its legislative powers so as to bind the states or provinces.

No doubt these forms of immunity which favour the states or provinces operate to the benefit of the federal government as well, since the apparent rationale in each case equally supports an immunity of the federal crown from any local legislation that demonstrates the relevant characteristics. If the federal crown is free of the burdens of all state or provincial legislation then the above situations are comprised within the general intergovernmental immunity of the federal crown. But if that immunity only isolates the prerogatives of the crown from the reach of state or provincial legislation, as has been argued, then these circumstances in which there is an immunity of a reciprocal kind must be separately specified so far as they signify a special privilege of the federal crown as well as of the crown in right of a state or province.

The various governments in the two federal systems are clearly subject to the common law in the sense of non-statutory law.[102] The Canadian government has thus been restricted by common law principles. This has been so even though those principles happen to fall, as subjects for legislative attention, within the exclusive constitutional authority of the provincial legislatures.[103] To the extent that such principles in fact remain unaffected by local statute they are capable of operating to the detriment of the federal crown.

The attention given to the general principles of governmental and intergovernmental immunity in these initial chapters forms a foundation for the consideration hereafter of the effect of statutes upon governments in the course of differ-

---

102 This follows from the principle that the crown is subject to the general law (see *Eastern Trust Co.* v *Mackenzie, Mann & Co.*, [1915] A.C. 750, at 759 (P.C.)), which law is the same for the crown as the law applying between subjects except as modified by prerogative rules (see Mundell, 'Legal Nature of Federal and Provincial Executive Governments: Some Comments on Transactions between Them' (1960), 2 *O.H.L.J.* 56, at 58–9). This principle is not demonstrably altered by the Australian and Canadian constitutions.

103 Consider *Montreal Trust Co.* v *The King*, [1924] 1 D.L.R. 1030 (B.C.C.A.); *R* v *Plamondon*, [1965] 1 Ex. C.R. 778; *R* v *Sylvain* (1964), 52 D.L.R. (2d) 607 (S.C.C.).

ent kinds of contact which they are likely to have with the legal system. Specifically, the focus of the subsequent chapters is upon the immunity, of either variety, which governments enjoy, variously, in tort proceedings, when their criminal or contractual liability is in issue, when they are in the role of creditor, and when they are called upon to pay a tax.

3

Statute Law in
Tort Proceedings by and
against the Crown

THE CROWN AS DEFENDANT

The Imposition of Crown Liability in Tort

At common law the crown was not liable in tort.[1] The only exception, which may be offered in hindsight, was in the case of certain claims for the invasion of property rights, which would now be considered as sounding in tort.[2]

This special position of the crown was altered by legislation in all of the Australian colonies, except Victoria,[3] before federation in 1901.[4] Typical of the most common form of colonial statute was that of New South Wales, which provided that anyone having a claim against the government could bring suit against a nominal defendant, representing the crown. This facility might have been taken as referable to contract and property claims which could always have been advanced through the device of a petition of right, and not as intended to alter the prerogative of immunity in tort which the crown traditionally enjoyed. However, such an interpretation was firmly rejected by the Privy Council in the 'cataclas-

---

1 *Tobin v The Queen* (1864), 143 E.R. 1148
2 Street *Governmental Liability* (1953), at 1–2
3 The crown in right of the state of Victoria was not made liable in tort until 1955, see the Crown Proceedings Act, 1955. The legislation currently in effect in Victoria is the Crown Proceedings Act, 1958, see esp. ss 23 & 25.
4 See the Claimants Relief Act, 1853 (S.A.); Claims against Government Act, 1857 (N.S.W.); Claims against Government Act of 1866 (Qd); Crown Remedies Act 1891 (Tas.); Crown Suits Act, 1898 (W.A.). The legislation currently in force in the successor states is as follows; Crown Proceedings Act, 1972 (S.A.); Claims against the Government and Crown Suits Act, 1912 (N.S.W.), see esp. ss 3 & 4; Claims against the Government Act of 1866 (Qd), see esp. ss 2 & 5; Supreme Court Civil Procedure Act 1932 (Tas.), see esp. ss 64(1) & 66(1); Crown Suits Act, 1947–54 (W.A.), see esp. s 5.

mic case'[5] of *Farnell* v *Bowman*.[6] That decision established that the New South Wales legislation[7] had the effect of rendering the government liable in tort.

Shortly after the creation of the Commonwealth of Australia the new parliament enacted the Judiciary Act 1903.[8] Section 56 of that act enabled tort and contract actions against the Commonwealth to be brought in the Supreme Court of the state in which the claim arose[9] or the High Court of Australia. Jurisdiction was conferred in any event on the latter court by section 75 of the constitution in all suits involving the Commonwealth. In *Baume* v *Commonwealth*,[10] the High Court held that section 56 together with section 64, equating the rights of parties in crown proceedings to those in a suit between subjects, imposed a liability in tort upon the Commonwealth.[11] These provisions of the Judiciary Act were said not to be materially different from the legislation in question in *Farnell* v *Bowman*. But some High Court judges were later to express the view that it is the constitution itself, in section 75, which makes the Commonwealth liable in tort though this is quite clearly a minority opinion.[12]

In British North America none of the colonial legislatures was moved to abolish or curtail the crown's immunity in tort. Indeed, after confederation tortious liability was not imposed upon the crown in the right of the common law provinces until the period after 1950, three provinces having undertaken this reform as recently as 1973-4.[13] In the province of Quebec a form of crown proceedings

5 *Per* Windeyer J in *Downs* v *Williams* (1971), 126 C.L.R. 61, at 80
6 (1887), 12 App. Cas. 643 (P.C.). See also *A.G. of the Straits Settlement* v *Wemyss* (1888), 13 App. Cas. 192 (P.C.); *Theodore* v *Duncan*, [1919] A.C. 696, at 705 (P.C.); *Welden* v *Smith*, [1924] A.C. 484, at 494 (P.C.).
7 In its 1876 form, the Claims against the Colonial Government Act, 1876
8 A temporary statute, the Claims against the Commonwealth Act 1902, was replaced by the Judiciary Act. The 1903 enactment remains in force with amendments.
9 Jurisdiction has since been extended to other state and some territorial courts, see the Judiciary Act 1960. For the text of s 56 in its current form see infra, at 72.
10 (1906), 4 C.L.R. 97
11 See s 78 of the Australian constitution for the necessary authority of the Commonwealth Parliament to legislate to this effect. It has also been held that a state is liable in tort for the purpose of suits brought against it in the federal jurisdiction, see *Commonwealth* v *N.S.W.* (1923), 32 C.L.R. 200.
12 The relevant cases are considered and this conclusion is reached by Hogg in *Liability of the Crown* (1971), at 216, and by Pryles and Hanks in *Federal Conflict of Laws* (1974), at 184-6.
13 The original statutes were as follows; Proceedings against the Crown Act, S.M. 1951, c 13; Proceedings against the Crown Act, S.N.S. 1951, c 8; Proceedings against the Crown Act, S.N.B. 1952, c 10; Proceedings against the Crown Act, 1952, S.S. 1952, c 35; Proceedings against the Crown Act, 1952, S.O. 1952, c 78 (which was never proclaimed in force, however, and was replaced by a similar Act, S.O. 1962-3, c 109);

legislation was adopted in 1883.[14] But it was not until 1935 that it was established as having the effect of subjecting the crown to delictual and quasi-delictual responsibility, the approximate civil law equivalent of tort liability.[15]

At the dominion level a statute of 1887[16] granted exclusive original jurisdiction to a federal tribunal, the Exchequer Court,[17] over a variety of claims against the crown in right of Canada, including damage actions arising out of the negligence of crown officers and servants.[18] A substantial limitation was imposed, however, in that the damage had to occur in connection with a public work,[19] a restriction that underwent later modification in its detail[20] but was not finally removed until 1938.[21] The procedure for suing the crown in this and other causes was the petition of right.[22] In a series of cases the Supreme Court of Canada came to espouse the view that the Exchequer Court Act, the name later given to the 1887 statute,[23] had the effect of subjecting the crown to liability for the negligence of its subordinates.[24] It was concluded, therefore, that the act was not merely a vehicle for conferring jurisdiction on the federal court whenever such liability might be imposed upon the crown independently.

Proceedings against the Crown Act, S.A. 1959, c 63; Proceedings against the Crown Act, S.Nfld 1973, c 59; Crown Proceedings Act, R.S.P.E.I. 1974, c C-31; Crown Proceedings Act, S.B.C. 1974, c 24. The principal enactments currently in force in these provinces may be found at R.S.M. 1970, c P140; R.S.N.S. 1967, c 239; R.S.N.B. 1973, c P-18; R.S.S. 1965, c 87; R.S.O. 1970, c 365; R.S.A. 1970, c 285; S.Nfld 1973, c 59; R.S.P.E.I. 1974, c C-31; S.B.C. 1974, c 24.

14 The Quebec Petition of Right Act, S.Q. 1883, c 27, see esp. s 2, subsequently incorporated as art. 1011 of the Code of Civil Procedure, given force of law by S.Q. 1897, c 48. Art. 1011 became art. 94 of the Code of Civil Procedure, S.Q. 1965, c 80, and was altered by S.Q. 1966, c 21, s 5.

15 In R v Cliche, [1936] 1 D.L.R. 195 (S.C.C.)

16 An Act to amend the Supreme and Exchequer Courts Act, S.C. 1887, c 16

17 Originally established by the Supreme and Exchequer Courts Act, S.C. 1875, c 11

18 See s 16(c) of S.C. 1887, c 16. A good deal of the jurisdiction conferred on the Exchequer Court by this act was formerly exercised by the Official Arbitrators, see s 1 of S.C. 1870, c 23, which statute was repealed by the 1887 enactment.

19 A similar limitation existed under the Western Australia legislation (see the Crown Suits Act, 1898 (W.A.)), which was not removed until 1947 (by the Crown Suits Act, 1947 (W.A.)).

20 See S.C. 1917, c 23, s 2.

21 By S.C. 1938, c 28, s 1

22 See S.C. 1887, c 16, s 23. The only exception was in the case of a reference made to the court by a department head, see ibid. For the detail of the then existing petition of right procedure see the Petition of Right Act, R.S.C. 1886, c 136, as amended by S.C. 1887, c 16.

23 The 1887 statute and an amending act of 1889 were styled the Exchequer Court Act by the latter act, see S.C. 1889, c 38.

24 Que. v The Queen (1894), 24 S.C.R. 420, see esp. the judgment of Strong J, dissenting; R v Filion (1895), 24 S.C.R. 482; R v Armstrong (1908), 40 S.C.R. 229.

Choice of Law in Tort Actions against the Federal Crown

The surrender of immunity in tort effected by the two federal statutes, the Judiciary Act of Australia and the Exchequer Court Act of Canada, only went some of the way towards creating a régime of liability on the part of the federal crown. There had to be some body of tort law with reference to which crown liability could be determined. In the absence of an available federal law of tort, or any appreciation of the notion that it might be for the courts to evolve such a law from whole cloth, a choice of law rule was required.

The Australian statute appears, at first blush, to be much more helpful about the proper resolution of the choice of law question in this kind of case than its Canadian counterpart. In cases within the federal jurisdiction, which includes tort actions against the Commonwealth,[25] section 79 directs the application of the laws of the state in which the court hearing the matter exercises jurisdiction.[26] The state laws which are thus applied embrace private international law, which may direct the court to yet another legal system.[27] The impact of section 79 is fully appreciated only if one bears in mind that the High Court is peripatetic and may sit to decide a matter in any of the six states. The direction of section 79 does not operate, as the section itself indicates, if another Commonwealth law or the constitution provides a different choice of law rule. And there is a good deal of authority to the effect that in actions in tort and contract against the Commonwealth, section 56, which featured in *Baume v Commonwealth*[28] as a basis for Commonwealth liability in tort, does provide such a rule by impliedly directing choice of law as the place where the claim arose.[29] This position, however, has not gone unchallenged.[30]

25 The High Court can be said to exercise federal jurisdiction, at least in acting in its original rather than appellate jurisdiction, see *Huddart Parker Ltd v The Ship 'Mill Hill'* (1950), 81 C.L.R. 502, at 507–8 *per* Dixon J; *R v Oregan* (1957), 97 C.L.R. 323, at 330 *per* Webb J. The state or territorial courts exercise federal jurisdiction when invested with it as, for instance, under ss 39 and 56 of the Judiciary Act 1903, which concern proceedings against the Commonwealth. For an extended consideration of the concept of federal jurisdiction in Australia see Cowan *Federal Jurisdiction in Australia* (1959).

26 See also s 80, which has been given a very limited role to play; Hogg *Liability of the Crown* (1971), at 217. Section 80A makes ss 79 and 80 applicable to proceedings against the Commonwealth in a territorial court.

27 *Deputy Comm'r of Taxation (N.S.W.) v Brown* (1958), 100 C.L.R. 32, at 39 *per* Dixon CJ

28 (1906), 4 C.L.R. 97

29 *Musgrave v Commonwealth* (1937), 57 C.L.R. 514, at 547–8 *per* Dixon J & at 550–1 *per* Evatt & McTiernan JJ; *Washington v Commonwealth* (1939), 39 S.R. (N.S.W.) 133, at 143 (F.C.); *Suehle v Commonwealth* (1967), 116 C.L.R. 353, at 355–6

The Exchequer Court Act contained no explicit choice of law rule of a general character appropriate for negligence actions against the federal crown. It did contain one specific direction about provincial law in proceedings against the crown, namely that the laws relating to prescription and limitation of actions of the province in which a cause of action arose were to apply.[31] As to provincial legislation on other matters, a judicial assumption seems to have been made that the liability in negligence imposed was that which would result in accordance with the law of the province in which the claim arose.[32] Crown liability in tort – no longer simply in negligence – is now the subject of a separate statute, the Crown Liability Act, introduced in 1953.[33] The new statute does not appear, however, to have necessitated any change in this assumption as to the determination of the applicable law.[34]

The choice of law rule in tort actions against the crown in right of Canada is illustrative of a more general proposition that in suits in the Exchequer Court and in its successor tribunal, the Federal Court of Canada, the law to be applied is the law of the province in which the cause of action arose, in the absence of an appropriate federal law.[35] It may be objected that in invoking provincial law in this way the Exchequer or Federal Court would be exceeding its constitutionally permitted mandate as a court 'for the better administration of the laws of Canada.'[36] This latter phrase describes the kind of courts, additional to the Supreme Court, which the central parliament has authority to establish under section 101 of the British North America Act. An effective answer to this criticism is that the federal court in resorting to provincial law does so only secondarily and in reliance primarily upon a law of Canada, that is, a federal choice of law rule. In any event it may be enough to satisfy section 101 that the cause of action, in the course of which provincial law is applied, is itself founded on relevant and exist-

---

per Windeyer J. But cf *Parker* v *Commonwealth* (1965), 112 C.L.R. 295, at 306–7 *per* Windeyer J.

30 See Pryles and Hanks *Federal Conflict of Laws* (1974), at 192–200.

31 S.C. 1887, c 16, s 18, numbered s 31 in the general revision of federal statutes in 1927, see R.S.C. 1927, c 34. This provision has been carried forward in s 19 of the Crown Liability Act, S.C. 1952–3, c 30, now R.S.C. 1970, c C-38. See also s 38 of the Federal Court Act, R.S.C. 1970, c 10 (2d Supp.).

32 See, for example, *R* v *Armstrong* (1908), 40 S.C.R. 229.

33 S.C. 1952–3, c 30, now R.S.C. 1970, c C–38

34 See *Gaetz* v *The Queen*, [1955] Ex. C.R. 133, at 186; *Schwella* v *The Queen* (1957), 9 D.L.R. 137, at 141 (Exch.).

35 See, for example, *Black* v *The Queen* (1899), 29 S.C.R. 693; *Ross* v *The King* (1902), 32 S.C.R. 532; *R* v *Richardson & Adams*, [1948] 2 D.L.R. 305, at 306 *per* Kerwin J (S.C.C.); *Stein Estate* v *The Ship 'Kathy K'* (1975), 62 D.L.R. (3d) 1, at 16–17 (S.C.C.).

36 Cf Abel (ed) *Laskin's Canadian Constitutional Law* (4th ed rev 1975), at 796–7, and the argument advanced, unsuccessfully, by the applicants in *Schwella* v *The Queen* (1957), 9 D.L.R. (2d) 137 (Exch.).

ing federal law.[37] No similar question can arise in suits involving the Commonwealth of Australia since the exercise of federal jurisdiction in that situation has a constitutional basis in the character of the parties, as including the Commonwealth, rather than in the character of the law to be administered.[38]

Justification for the Application of State or Provincial Statutes against the Federal Crown

The selection of the laws of a particular state or province through the relevant choice of law rule is not always decisive of their applicability in proceedings against the federal crown. If the laws are of a statutory character and their invocation to the prejudice of the crown is being urged, immunity questions arise. Governmental and intergovernmental immunity, if unaltered in their operation by the relevant federal crown liability legislation, will clearly limit the possibilities for resort to state or provincial laws in this situation. The legislation making the federal crown accountable in tort may have the effect, however, of displacing or modifying the usual impact of those immunity principles. Thus local statutes may apply generally or in some circumstances against the federal crown when it is sued in tort. There are several possible bases for attributing such a result to federal crown liability legislation.

Implied Consent to the Application of Existing State or Provincial Statutes

As indicated earlier, federal crown liability legislation created a new form of governmental responsibility in a field largely unoccupied by federal enactment. In the absence of any specific provision that might be thought to determine the import of state or provincial statutes, an implication might be drawn, in these circumstances, that the content of liability was intended to be worked out in accordance with any such statutes that were appropriate to a given case. In other words it may be assumed that local statute law was envisaged as part and parcel of the new rights created against the federal crown. A mere inference, however, seems a totally inadequate basis for a surrender by the crown of its constitution-

---

37 Consider *Quebec North Shore Paper Co* v *Canadian Pacific Ltd* (1976), 71 D.L.R. (3d) 111 (S.C.C.), and *McNamara Constr. (Western) Ltd* v *The Queen* (1977), 13 N.R. 181 (S.C.C.).

38 See s 75 of the Australian constitution. There is a good deal of confusion about the appropriate limitations upon the operation of a federal choice of law rule which brings in state laws in proceedings in a federal court or a court exercising federal jurisdiction, see *Commissioner of Stamp Duties (N.S.W.)* v *Owens (No. 2)* (1953), 88 C.L.R. 168, *Pedersen* v *Young* (1964), 110 C.L.R. 162; *John Robertson & Co.* v *Ferguson Transformers Pty* (1973), 129 C.L.R. 65. And see Pryles and Hanks *Federal Conflict of Laws* (1974), at 177–82, and Nygh *Conflict of Laws in Australia* (2d ed 1971), at 781–4.

ally based immunity, that is that of an intergovernmental variety.[39] But any direct interference with that immunity is avoided if the local statutes applied are only those in existence at the time liability was imposed by the central parliament. The federal statute, then, only brings about the application of an existing set of rules and no special consequence need be attached to the fact that they were originally established by a state or province and could not have affected the federal crown of their own force. Therefore, an implied consent to the application of local statutes, when that provides the justification under federal crown liability legislation for resorting to such statutes, ought properly to be limited to those statutes in force when tort liability was imposed upon the federal crown.

Ambulatory Incorporation by Reference of State or Provincial Statutes

Federal crown liability legislation may bear the interpretation that it incorporates as federal law state or provincial statutes, whenever enacted, that are relevant to the determination of tort liability. There is no constitutional impediment to federal legislation effecting an ambulatory incorporation by reference of state or provincial statutes. It does not constitute an objectionable interference with the exercise of the powers of the states or provinces[40] nor does it involve an improper delegation of legislative authority to those constituent units of the federation.[41] Consequently federal legislation, if appropriately worded, may operate to adopt pertinent state or provincial statutes, existing from time to time, as part of the federal law of crown liability in tort.

In these circumstances the federal crown can no longer maintain that governmental immunity protects it from the burdens of state or provincial statutes which do not specially include the crown. The reason for this is that those statutes have become, for a limited purpose, federal statutes which are impliedly binding upon the crown.[42] There is a necessary implication that the rules embodied in the local legislation bind the crown since that legislation has been adopted simply with reference to the matter of crown liability. It must, therefore, bind the crown if the purpose of the legislation in its 'federalized' form is not to be totally frustrated. The same conclusion, that the federal crown is bound, is

---

39 That such an immunity can be surrendered in specific terms by federal statute is demonstrated in a later chapter, see infra, at 146–55.
40 *Hooper* v *Hooper* (1955), 91 C.L.R. 529, at 537
41 *Commonwealth* v *District Ct of the Metropolitan Dist. Holden at Sydney* (1954), 90 C.L.R. 13, esp. at 22; *Coughlin* v *Ont. Highway Transport Bd* (1968), 68 D.L.R. (2d) 384 (S.C.C.)
42 See *Hooper* v *Hooper* (1955), 91 C.L.R. 529, at 536–7; *R* v *Isaac* (1973), 38 D.L.R. (3d) 349 (Ont. C.A.); *Cardinal* v *A.G. of Alta* (1973), 40 D.L.R. (3d) 553, at 576–7 *per* Laskin J, dissenting (S.C.C.); *Natural Parents* v *Superintendent of Child Welfare*

reached if the federal legislation can be taken as incorporating state or provincial statutes as they apply to subjects. If that is a proper interpretation it makes no difference that the local legislation may not purport to bind the crown or even that it is clearly expressed not to bind the crown for it is only picked up as it would apply in proceedings between subjects.

The fact that state or provincial legislation takes on a federal character has the further consequence that the federal crown is unable to benefit from its constitutional immunity. There is no intergovernmental character to the question of the effect of the legislation upon the federal crown in these circumstances. It is simply a matter of the federal authority being potentially subject to the burdens of federal legislation. There is no constitutional significance to the fact that that legislation employs the shorthand device of incorporating state or provincial statutes rather than spelling out afresh a complete régime of tort law for federal purposes.

Federal crown liability legislation may adopt federal statutes as well. The result is that such enactments will apply, to the same extent as relevant state or provincial statutes, in tort proceedings against the federal crown.

Submission to State or Provincial Law applying as between Subjects

Federal crown liability legislation may equate the position of the crown as a defendant in a tort action to that of a subject similarly situated. Subjects of the crown, of course, may be reached by the general words of statutes, whether federal or provincial, for they enjoy no special position in the face of legislation by virtue of either the prerogative or the constitution. Therefore, if the federal crown is deemed to be a subject, for the purpose of ascertaining its tort liability, it would appear to be bound by any relevant state or provincial, and also federal, statutes in the same way that a subject would be bound. Governmental and intergovernmental immunity have no role to play. Even if a statute specifically excepts the crown from its operation, that ought not to change the result, for the crown loses its sovereign character for the limited purpose of the federal crown liability legislation.[43] It cannot, therefore, come within the terms of the exception.

Surrender of Immunity from State or Provincial Statutes

Legislation might attempt a surrender of that immunity which the crown, in its central role, enjoys from state or provincial statutes so far as those statutes relate to the determination of tort liability. To date, though, this does not seem to have

(1975), 60 D.L.R. (3d) 148, at 152–3 (S.C.C.); *R* v *Willoughby*, [1975] W.A.R. 19, at 21 (C.C.A.).
43 *Re Mar-Lise Industries Ltd* (1968), 5 D.L.R. (3d) 487 (Ont. C.A.), discussed infra, at 110.

been the thrust of any of the federal crown liability provisions which have been adopted in Australia and Canada. The central parliament appears, however, to possess the constitutional capability of making a statutory surrender of intergovernmental immunity and, moreover, state or provincial enactments are apparently competent to bind the federal crown in that event. Support for these propositions is demonstrated in a later chapter.[44]

It is convenient, at this point, to direct attention to the cases which have had to decide upon the relevance of particular statutes, other than from a purely choice of law perspective, in tort proceedings against the crown. Most of the decisions concern the applicability of state or provincial statutes against the federal crown and can be considered in the light of the alternative bases which have been introduced in this section for invoking such statutes in this way.

The Canadian Position

The Canadian decisions which have dealt with the tort liability of the federal crown under provincial enactments do not usually separate two rather different questions. The first, which has already been addressed, is what provincial legal system provides the appropriate law. The second question is what particular statutes, within that system, apply against the federal crown, having in mind the scope that may have been left by the federal crown liability provisions for the operation of governmental and intergovernmental immunity. Judicial attention has been directed primarily to the formulation and application of principles for deciding what kind of provincial statutes can be invoked and only incidentally, within those principles, to choice of law.

Before 1953

The Exchequer Court Act, from 1938 through to 1953,[45] read in section 19(c)[46] as follows:

---

44 See infra, at 146–55.
45 That is after the amendment effected by S.C. 1938, c 28, s 1, removing the public work limitation, and before the Crown Liability Act, S.C. 1952–3, c 30, came into force on 14 May 1953 (ss 3(1) (b) & 8–14 were not proclaimed in force until 15 Nov. 1954).
46 The provision was renumbered s 18(1) (c) in the general revision of the federal statutes in 1952, see R.S.C. 1952, c 98.

19. The Exchequer Court also has exclusive original jurisdiction to hear and determine the following matters:
(c) every claim against the Crown arising out of any death or injury to the person or to property resulting from the negligence of any officer or servant of the Crown while acting within the scope of his duties or employment ...

The office that has been ascribed to this provision is staggering in its proportions. It fulfills the obvious role of conferring jurisdiction in the matters in question on the Exchequer Court. It also imposes a new substantive liability upon the crown, as has been noticed. And, finally, it has been held to render applicable the law of negligence of the province in which the negligence occurred, including any such law that takes statutory form, if in force at the time liability was imposed upon the federal crown.[47] This restricted resort to provincial statute law appears to have been justified on the theory that the Exchequer Court Act evidenced an implied consent by parliament to the application of existing local statutes.[48]

Provincial statute law bearing upon the resolution of federal crown liability has not, in fact, been completely frozen at 1887, the date when tort liability was first imposed on the crown, albeit in very narrow circumstances. The precise question for the courts has been what was the law of the province at the time the crown became accountable for the particular kind of tort liability alleged in a given case.[49] It was not until 1938 that the public work limitation was removed from section 19(c) of the Exchequer Court Act.[50] Most of the recent proceedings under that act have been of a type which, because of that limitation, could not have been brought until 1938 and consequently the relevant cut-off date for provincial statute law has been the latter year. By that time the doctrine of common employment (as a defence to a tort action) had been abolished,[51] wrongful death statutes allowing tort actions by personal representatives of a deceased had been

---

47 See, for example, *R* v *Armstrong* (1908), 40 S.C.R. 229, at 248 *per* Davies J, McLennan J concurring; *Tremblay* v *The King*, [1944] 2 D.L.R. 338, at 344 (Exch.).
48 See especially *Gauthier* v *The King* (1918), 40 D.L.R. 353, at 356–7 *per* Fitzpatrick CJ.
49 See *Tremblay* v *The King*, [1944] 2 D.L.R. 338 (Exch.); *Snell* v *The King*, [1946] 1 D.L.R. 632 (Exch.), aff'd at [1947] 2 D.L.R. 81 (S.C.C.); *Workmen's Compensation Bd of Sask.* v *The King*, [1947] 3 D.L.R. 7 (Exch.); *McDevitt* v *The Queen*, [1954] Ex. C.R. 296.
50 By S.C. 1938, c 28, s 1
51 In the early case of *Ryder* v *The King* (1905), 36 S.C.R. 462, this doctrine in fact prevented recovery against the crown, though it has never presented an impediment to a successful action in Quebec, where the doctrine has no place, see *R* v *Filion* (1895), 24 S.C.R. 482; *R* v *Grenier* (1899), 30 S.C.R. 42; *R* v *Armstrong* (1908), 40 S.C.R. 229; *R* v *Desrosiers* (1908), 41 S.C.R. 71.

passed,[52] as had apportionment statutes allowing distribution of liability and removing contributory negligence as a complete defence to a negligence claim.[53] But any amendments to such legislation and any new provincial statutes, since 1938, which might have some bearing upon tort liability have been excluded from consideration in section 19(c) proceedings.[54]

The suppliant in a proceeding against the federal crown might wish to rely upon a provincial regulatory statute as disclosing the appropriate standard of care to be observed by a servant of the crown, whose conduct was the basis of the claim against the federal government. However, in this case as well, the Exchequer Court has said that it ought not to have regard to provincial statutes – in fact it was motor vehicle statutes which were in question – which post-date the imposition of liability upon the federal crown.[55] If the action were essentially one for breach of statutory duty this might be a defensible application of the general principle.[56] But since a subject had relied upon a regulatory statute and its violation by a servant of the federal crown in a proceeding under section 19(c) of the Exchequer Court Act then it must, of necessity, have been in the context of a negligence claim given the limitations of that provision, and not simply a claim for breach of statutory duty.[57] In a negligence proceeding a court is entitled, as a matter of common law, to consider any relevant statutory standards of care in ascertaining whether there is a duty of care in a given situation which may have been breached. And in that event the violation of a statute may be utilized by a court, if at all, simply as evidence of negligence and not as indicative of negli-

---

52 Consider *R* v *Armstrong* (1908), 40 S.C.R. 229; *R* v *Desrosiers* (1908), 41 S.C.R. 71; *Arial* v *The King*, [1946] Ex. C.R. 540.

53 *R* v *Murphy*, [1948] 3 D.L.R. 1 (S.C.C.). In the earlier case of *C.N.R.* v *St John Motor Line Ltd*, [1930] 3 D.L.R. 732 (S.C.C.), a 1925 provincial contributory negligence statute was held inapplicable. In Quebec apportionment of damages was always the proper course under the doctrine of *faute commune*, see *R* v *Armstrong* (1908), 40 S.C.R. 229; *Sabourin* v *The King* (1911), 13 Ex. C.R. 341; *Lapointe* v *The King* (1913), 14 D.L.R. 394 (Exch.); *R* v *Laperrière*, [1946] S.C.R. 415.

54 See *McDevitt* v *The Queen*, [1954] Ex. C.R. 296. And cf *Tremblay* v *The King*, [1944] 2 D.L.R. 338, and *Shpur* v *The King*, [1955] 2 D.L.R. 368 (Exch.).

55 See *Tremblay* v *The King*, [1944] 2 D.L.R. 338 (Exch.), and *Shpur* v *The King*, [1955] 2 D.L.R. 368 (Exch.). But cf *Gibson* v *The King*, [1947] 4 D.L.R. 39 (Exch.), where some reliance was placed on provincial legislation in a manner prejudicial to the federal crown without consideration of its date of enactment.

56 Consider *Downs* v *Williams* (1971), 126 C.L.R. 61.

57 The Canadian courts are not inclined, in any case, to speak in terms of a civil cause of action for breach of statutory duty which is distinct from a cause of action in negligence; Alexander, 'The Fate of Sterling Trusts v Postma' (1968), 2 *Ottawa L. Rev.* 441, at 445–6.

gence *per se*.[58] Thus breach of a statute is not necessarily determinative of civil liability. These factors suggest that the Exchequer Court should have considered itself entitled to attach some weight at least to the breach of a provincial regulatory statute, whenever enacted, if called in aid by a claimant in a negligence action against the federal crown. It is the provincial common law which would then be given a binding effect upon the federal crown, which is of course unobjectionable, and not the provincial statute in any direct or decisive way.[59]

An important qualification was made in the application of provincial law in negligence actions against the federal crown. Such law, it was said, had no place in so far as it was 'repugnant to the terms of the statute by which the liability of the Crown was imposed or seeks to impose a liability different from that imposed by Parliament.'[60] This limitation goes to provincial common law as well as statute law and has nothing to do with governmental or intergovernmental immunity. Since the accountability of the crown in tort was entirely dependent upon the federal crown liability provision, the crown being otherwise free of tort liability, it was thought that any provincial law which was inconsistent therewith could have no application. In particular, provincial laws introducing a legal presumption of negligence were to be disregarded in suits pursuant to section 19(c)[61] because the crown's liability thereunder was vicarious[62] and the onus rested upon the suppliant to show negligence on the part of an officer or servant of the crown, while acting within the scope of his duties or employment, and that the loss or injury complained of resulted from such negligence.[63]

58 Indeed there is a judicial preference for the latter approach if, as in these cases, the statute in question is a motor vehicle act, see Alexander, 'Legislation and the Standard of Care in Negligence' (1964), 42 *Can. Bar Rev.* 243, at 271-2.
59 Compare *R v Nord-Deutsche Versicherungs-Gesellschaft*, [1969] 1 Ex. C.R. 117, aff'd at (1971), 20 D.L.R. (3d) 444 (S.C.C.), which is considered in the next section of this chapter. And cf *Wasney v Jurazsky*, [1933] 1 D.L.R. 616 (Man. C.A.), in which Trueman J A suggested, at 627, that though a Criminal Code provision could not constitutionally confer a civil cause of action yet it was relevant in determining the standard of care in a negligence action.
60 *Tremblay v The King*, [1944] 2 D.L.R. 338, at 344-5 (Exch.)
61 *Labelle v The King*, [1937] Ex. C.R. 170; *Tremblay v The King*, [1944] 2 D.L.R. 338 (Exch.); *Gibson v The King*, [1947] 4 D.L.R. 39 (Exch.); *Diano v The Queen*, [1952] Ex. C.R. 209. However, an inference of fact, such as that which arises under the doctrine of *res ipsa loquitur*, could operate; *Gauthier & Co. v The King*, [1945] 2 D.L.R. 48, at 60, appl'd in *Duncan & Duncan v The Queen*, [1966] Ex. C.R. 1080, at 1108 (and cf *Leadbetter v The Queen* (1970), 12 D.L.R. (3d) 738, at 744 (Exch.)). But see, as to the limits of the applicability of this doctrine in proceedings in negligence against the crown, *Alexander, Kelly & Kelly v The Queen* (1960), 23 D.L.R. (2d) 369, at 375 (S.C.C.).
62 See *R v Anthony*, [1946] 3 D.L.R. 577 (S.C.C.).

The federal crown could always take advantage of a provincial statute when sued in tort, independent of any enabling federal provision,[64] for that situation is unaffected by governmental or intergovernmental immunity. In proceedings against the federal crown this facility was specifically provided to the sovereign, as far as statutes creating defences were concerned, under the terms of section 8 of the Petition of Right Act,[65] which read as follows:

8. The statement of defence or demurrer may raise, besides any legal or equitable defences in fact or in law available under this Act, any legal or equitable defences which would have been available if the proceeding had been a suit or action in a competent court between subject and subject; and any grounds of defence which would be sufficient on behalf of [Her] Majesty may be alleged on behalf of any such person as aforesaid.

The federal crown, in relying upon a provincial statutory defence, was not then governed by the 1938 date, which generally limited the suppliant in the provincial statutes which he might rely upon in the very same proceeding.[66] The apparent anomaly in this situation did not escape judicial notice.[67]

Provision was also made in section 31 of the Exchequer Court Act for the application, subject to any act of parliament, of the laws relating to prescription and limitation of action in force between subjects in the province where a cause of action against the crown arose. Under this section as well the crown was held entitled to rely upon provincial statutes, of the variety mentioned, which had come into force after 1938.[68] But if the crown chose to counterclaim it would seem that a provincial limitation statute would not preclude its claim because of the governmental or intergovernmental immunity of the federal crown[69] which, in this situation, was not avoided by any provision of federal legislation. Once again a considerable disparity between the position of the crown and a subject in a single proceeding is evident.

The comparative advantages, in terms of access to the benefits of provincial

63 *Tremblay* v *The King*, [1944] 2 D.L.R. 338 (Exch.); *Laberge* v *The Queen*, [1954] Ex. C.R. 369; *Harris* v *The Queen*, [1955] Ex. C.R. 75; *Meredith* v *The Queen*, [1955] Ex. C.R. 156

64 *Schwella* v *The Queen* (1957), 9 D.L.R. (2d) 137 (Exch.)

65 R.S.C. 1927, c 158. The section in this form was first introduced by S.C. 1876, c 27. The Petition of Right Act was repealed by the Federal Court Act, R.S.C. 1970, c 10 (2d Supp.), s 64(1).

66 *Shpur* v *The King*, [1955] 2 D.L.R. 368 (Exch.)

67 Ibid, at 374–5

68 *Zakrzewski* v *The King*, [1944] 4 D.L.R. 281 (Exch.)

69 Cf *A.G. of Can.* v *Rhode* (1957), 8 D.L.R. (2d) 89 (Sask. Dist. Ct)

statutes, in tort proceedings against the federal crown were not all on the side of the crown rather than the subject. While the crown could take advantage of provincial legislation, as could the subject if the legislation was of the appropriate vintage, it apparently could not secure the benefit of any provincial statute which stated specifically that it was inapplicable to the crown. Such an exception in a statute would not of course foreclose reliance by a subject. This disparity is evident from the Privy Council decision in *Nisbet Shipping Co.* v *The Queen*,[70] which actually concerned the applicability of a federal rather than a provincial statute in favour of the federal crown. In that case the crown in right of Canada sought to limit its liability as a shipowner in a negligence action against it, in accordance with the Canada Shipping Act. But that act included a section to the effect that the act did not, except where specially provided, apply to ships belonging to His Majesty. It was held by the Privy Council that this exclusion related to any provision of the act whether creating an obligation or conferring a benefit. Viscount Simonds concluded as follows:

There is no sufficient justification for saying that, because the Exchequer Court in the exercise of its jurisdiction applies to proceedings between subject and the Crown the law which it applies between subject and subject therefore it should apply that law which by the terms of the statute enacting it is expressly excluded from application to the Crown.[71]

The result was that statutory limits upon civil liability that benefited a subject were of no avail to the crown. That conclusion would not have altered had the statute limiting liability been a provincial rather than a federal enactment. The actual outcome of the *Nisbet* case would have been different, however, had the events taken place after passage of the Crown Liability Act, which now enables the crown to take advantage of the limitation of liability provisions of the Canada Shipping Act.[72]

The general principle in *Nisbet* is difficult to justify given that section 8 of the Petition of Right Act in fact permitted the crown to raise any defences that would be available if the proceeding were an action in a competent court between subjects. This appears to provide the very opportunity that was denied the crown in this case, that is to insist upon a 'defence' that a subject would be entitled to raise if sued in a competent court. Unless a claim to limit liability is not a de-

70 [1955] 4 D.L.R. 1 (P.C.)
71 Ibid, at 5
72 S.C. 1952–3, c 30, s 3(4). And see *Canadian Fishing Co.* v *The Queen*, [1960] Ex. C.R. 303. If the situation is reversed and the Crown is suing a subject it has since been held that the subject may limit his liability under the Canada Shipping Act and preclude full

fence, a doubtful proposition,[73] the only way to justify the *Nisbet* result in the face of this section is to construe the section as serving the limited purpose of authorizing the crown to rely upon defences which, while appropriate in an ordinary action, would not fit the situation of a proceeding by petition of right.[74] That interpretation does receive some retroactive support from the fact that there was evidently no recognized need for any similar provision in respect of proceedings against the crown by ordinary claim in the new Federal Court.[75]

From 1953

It remains to consider whether the principles for determining the applicability of provincial statutes in tort proceedings against the federal crown are altered by the Crown Liability Act of 1953[76] and, if so, in what respects. That act provides as follows:

3. (1) The Crown is liable in tort for the damages for which, if it were a private person of full age and capacity, it would be liable
   (a) in respect of a tort committed by a servant of the Crown, or
   (b) in respect of a breach of duty attaching to the ownership, occupation, possession or control of property.
   (2) The Crown is liable for damage sustained by any person by reason of a motor vehicle, owned by the Crown, upon a highway, for which the Crown would be liable if it were a private person of full age and capacity.

2. In this Act ...
   "tort" in respect of any matter arising in the Province of Quebec, means delict or quasi-delict.

recovery by the crown; *Gartland Steamship Co.* v *The Queen* (1960), 22 D.L.R. (2d) 385 (S.C.C.); *R* v *Murray* (1967), 60 D.L.R. (2d) 647 (S.C.C.); *B.C. Telephone Co.* v *Marpole Towing Ltd* (1970), 17 D.L.R. (3d) 545 (S.C.C.). This situation is not one that comes within the scope of either governmental or intergovernmental immunity so as to free the crown from the limitation of the Canada Shipping Act.

73 See *Wahlberg* v *Young* (1876), 45 L.J.C.P. 783, which treated a limitation of liability claim under the Merchant Shipping Act 1862 as properly pleaded by way of defence. And cf *Croswell* v *Daball* (1921), 58 D.L.R. 572 (Ont. S.C., App. Div.).

74 Consider *Tylee* v *The Queen* (1877), 7 S.C.R. 651, at 676, and *McQueen* v *The Queen* (1887), 16 S.C.R. 1, at 60, 80, 97, 113, & 118. And cf *De Rossi* v *Walker* (1902), 2 S.R. (N.S.W.) 249 (F.C.).

75 Though there remains a comparable provision, oddly enough, in the Crown Liability Act applicable to proceedings against the crown in provincial courts, see R.S.C. 1970, c C-38, s 11, as amended by the Federal Court Act, R.S.C. 1970, c 10 (2d Supp.), s 65.

76 S.C. 1952–3, c 30, now R.S.C. 1970, c C-38

Section 3(1) was adopted, with minor modifications, from the English Crown Proceedings Act of 1947.[77] That act also provided the model for the crown proceedings statutes of the common law provinces abolishing crown immunity in tort. It will be noticed that the crown is now subject to tortious,[78] and in Quebec delictual, liability and is no longer simply accountable in negligence. While the liability is vicarious under section 3(2)[79] and paragraph (a) of section 3(1),[80] the latter provision, in paragraph (b), imposes a direct liability upon the crown.[81] Jurisdiction in proceedings against the federal crown was retained by the Exchequer Court,[82] which was succeeded in 1971 by the Federal Court of Canada.[83] Proceedings against the federal crown must now be commenced in the trial division of this new court, by ordinary claim rather than petition of right.[84] The Crown Liability Act, however, confers concurrent original jurisdiction on provincial courts in negligence claims against the federal crown involving sums not in excess of one thousand dollars.[85] It also recognizes that suits in tort against agencies of the federal crown may be pursued in provincial courts, in so far as such agencies are made suable in a competent court by their constitutive statutes.[86]

The Crown Liability Act may be thought to envisage the application of provincial statutes in an unrestricted manner or limited by consideration of their date of enactment in relation to that of federal crown proceedings provisions, as

77 10 & 11 Geo. VI, c 44
78 The pattern of the provincial acts is a more immediate reflection of the Model Act respecting Proceedings against the Crown recommended by the Conference of Commissioners on Uniformity of Legislation in Canada in 1950. For the text of the Model Act see Conference of Commissioners on Uniformity of Legislation in Canada *Model Acts Recommended from 1918 to 1961 inclusive* (1962), at 244–51. In drafting the Model Act the Commissioners relied, to a considerable extent, upon the English statute of 1947.
79 See s 4 (3).
80 A fact that is further emphasized by s 4(2). And see *Meredith* v *The Queen*, [1955] Ex. C.R. 156.
81 *Deslauriers-Drago* v *The Queen*, [1963] Ex. C.R. 289, at 300–1
82 Per s 7(1)
83 See the Federal Court Act, R.S.C. 1970, c 10 (2d Supp.).
84 Federal Court Act, R.S.C. 1970, c 10 (2d Supp.), ss 17(1) & 48
85 R.S.C. 1970, c C-38, ss 7(2) & 8(2)
86 S 23. However, if injunctive relief is sought against a federal crown agency which can be described as 'a federal board, commission or other tribunal' it would seem that the action must be brought in the Trial Division of the Federal Court in accordance with s 18(a) of the Federal Court Act, R.S.C. 1970, c 10 (2d Supp.). The kinds of federal entities referred to in that provision are not just those exercising judicial or quasi-judicial functions, see *Hamilton* v *Hamilton Harbour Comm'rs* (1972), 27 D.L.R. (3d) 385 (Ont. C.A.), but compare *Canada Metal Co.* v *C.B.C. (No. 2)* (1975), 65 D.L.R. (3d) 231 (Ont. C.A.).

was the case under section 19(c) of the Exchequer Court Act. The latter option would leave the permitted scope for provincial enactments in tort actions against the federal crown to be determined by the principles evident from the pre-1953 jurisprudence. But there would be this difference in result that the cut-off date for the application of provincial statutes in some, if not all, proceedings would now be as recent as 1953, at which time the crown was first subjected to a considerably extended form of liability in tort.

The decision in *Lamoureux* v *Le Procureur Général du Canada*[87] takes this general approach. This was a proceeding against the federal crown arising out of a road accident. The driver of the crown vehicle involved was found to be acting outside the course of his duties for the crown. Therefore liability could attach to the crown only if a case could be established in the terms of section 3(2) of the Crown Liability Act. That provision makes the crown liable for the damage caused by its vehicles on the highway as if it were a subject. Under the law of Quebec, the jurisdiction in which the accident occurred, the owner of a vehicle is responsible, with limited exceptions, for damage caused by his vehicle unless he can establish that the driver was not at fault. But this law takes the form of a statute, the Highway Victims Indemnity Act, which came into effect in 1961 subsequent to the Crown Liability Act. Noël J, of the Exchequer Court, dismissed the claim on the ground that the statutory responsibility of a vehicle owner under Quebec law did not apply.[88] He relied upon the cases under section 19(c) of the Exchequer Court Act limiting the effect of provincial statute law, in negligence actions against the federal crown, to that in force when crown liability was imposed. He found no cause to alter this principle in the language of section 3(2) of the new act although that provision imposes liability as if the crown were a private person. To render applicable provincial statute law in force when a cause of action arose would, he felt, require express words to that effect.[89]

The action in *Lamoureux* was of a variety which could not have been brought against the crown until 1953 with the enactment of section 3(2) of the Crown Liability Act. Consequently, on the traditional view which the court took, the latter date would be the crucial one in terms of defining the applicable provincial statutes. But in many cases, namely those put on the ground of negligence on the part of a crown officer or servant, relief would have been available in respect of the kind of claim advanced ever since 1938. Is this then the important date in a case of that nature or does the introduction in 1953 of a new scheme of crown

---

87 [1964] Ex. C.R. 641
88 But compare *Schmitz* v *The Queen*, [1974] 2 F.C. 898, in which Walsh J applied the same Quebec statutory provision against the federal crown without giving consideration to any possible immunity.
89 [1964] Ex. C.R. 641, at 648

liability mean that the latter date is controlling in all circumstances? It may be noted that no date more recent than this could be pertinent since there are no amendments to the Crown Liability Act which enlarge or alter the general basis of responsibility in tort. Thurlow J, without addressing himself to any possible alternative, mentioned the 1953 date as determinative in *Schwella* v *The Queen*,[90] a case which presented a fact situation of a kind that could have given rise to a claim against the crown under the 1938 wording of the Exchequer Court Act.

The most recent decision to shed light upon the role of provincial statutes under the Crown Liability Act is *R* v *Nord-Deutsche Versicherungs-Gesellschaft*.[91] That case involved a claim against the crown for damages arising out of a ship collision and for interest, on the damages awarded, from the date of the deposit of the petition. Article 1056c, added in 1957 to the Civil Code of Quebec, in which province the accident occurred, provides for the award of interest on delictual or quasi-delictual damages from the time of commencement of the action. At common law, however, no interest is allowable except as it may be payable by the terms of a statute or a contract. Noël J, who had sat in the earlier *Lamoureux* case, presided at the trial of the action.[92] He found the crown solely to blame for the collision. In awarding damages he acceded to the claim for interest principally on the ground that the law of Quebec, unlike the common law, has long been that interest is payable on an award of damages. Article 1056c of the code, therefore, created no new right but simply specified the manner of giving effect to a recognized right.[93] Consequently, in awarding interest, the court was not relying upon a right created by a provincial statute passed after liability was imposed upon the crown. But the court did rely upon the code, rather than the pre-existing law, to determine the applicable rate of interest as 'the legal rate,' then five per cent. This approach suggests that any limitation upon the use of provincial statutes by reference to date of enactment, in proceedings against the federal crown, may be subject to a general qualification to the effect that resort may be had to provincial statutes passed after the relevant date if they do not create a new right but simply specify the manner of giving effect to a right established apart from statute.[94] But that distinction is bound to be an elusive one in practice.

Noël J also took an alternative position on the interest point, that even if the relevant law of Quebec were that interest could only be allowed in accordance

90 (1957), 9 D.L.R. (2d) 137, at 141 (Exch.)
91 (1971), 20 D.L.R. (2d) 444 (S.C.C.)
92 The trial decision is reported at [1969] 1 Ex. C.R. 117.
93 Ibid, at 235
94 But see *McDevitt* v *The Queen*, [1954] Ex. C.R. 296, as to the limits of any such qualification.

with a statute or an agreement, the Crown Liability Act, in imposing the tortious or delictual responsibility of a private person upon the crown, satisfied that requirement in relation to crown proceedings.[95] This does not mean that he would treat the Crown Liability Act as avoiding the immunity of the federal crown from provincial legislation generally. But that act was taken to satisfy the common law, or assumed civil law, insistence upon a statute envisaging an award of interest. Thus reliance was placed primarily upon the 'common law' as the source of the right, upon the federal statute secondarily as the satisfaction of the common law criterion for the existence of the right, and upon the provincial statute, only in a tertiary sense, as the source of the liabilities of a private person deemed pertinent by the federal statute.

The Supreme Court of Canada, on appeal, did not agree that the crown was solely to blame for the accident and accordingly apportioned liability. Though allowing the appeal in that respect the court affirmed the 'careful reasoning' of the trial judge concerning the crown's liability to pay interest on the damages for which it was responsible.[96] But Pigeon J, dissenting as to the appropriate apportionment of damages between the crown and a third party, considered the crown subject to the award of interest against it on a quite different basis than that taken in the court of first instance and affirmed by the other members of the Supreme Court. His opinion was that article 1056c changed the law of Quebec with regard to damages in delicts and quasi-delicts but that section 3 of the Crown Liability Act referred to the law in force at the time and place where the injury complained of occurred.[97] Therefore article 1056c applied as part of that law notwithstanding that it was enacted after the relevant delictual or quasi-delictual responsibility was first imposed upon the crown.

The conclusion that the Crown Liability Act applies provincial statutes in force when the cause of action arose is to be preferred to that given expression in the *Lamoureux* and *Schwella* cases in the Exchequer Court. In those decisions resort to provincial statutes was limited by consideration of their date of enactment in the same way as under the earlier legislation. But liability imposed upon the crown in tort is now framed in terms of that to which it would be subject as if 'a private person of full age and capacity.' And such a person would doubtless be governed in his civil responsibilities by any pertinent provincial as well as federal statutes. Consequently the crown should be similarly restricted by the process of identification which the federal enactment requires us to make. The Crown Liability Act would seem to involve a submission to provincial law applying between

---

95 [1969] 1 Ex. C.R. 117, at 238
96 (1971), 20 D.L.R. (3d) 444, at 454
97 Ibid, at 470–1

subjects which, as indicated in an earlier section, removes any possibility of the federal crown relying successfully upon its governmental or intergovernmental immunity to escape the burdens of provincial legislation.[98]

There is a complicating factor, however, to this analysis in that the Crown Liability Act[99] also provides, in section 20, as follows:

20. Except as otherwise expressly provided in this Act, nothing in this Act affects any rule of evidence or any presumption relating to the extent to which the Crown is bound by an Act of Parliament.

This clause finds its origin in a similar section of the English Crown Proceedings Act,[100] which of course was devised for a jurisdiction without potential federal complications to immunity questions. It has no counterpart in contemporaneous crown proceedings statutes of the provinces. Such statutes, in most cases, were and remain quite explicit about subjecting the provincial crown to the liability in tort of a private person *notwithstanding* that section of the provincial Interpretation Act embodying the presumption of governmental immunity.[101] Under that statutory scheme of civil liability it is reasonably clear that the crown is bound by any other pertinent statutes of the legislating jurisdiction which were in force when the cause of action arose.

While the Crown Liability Act, through section 20, purports to leave governmental immunity from federal statutes unaffected by its terms this is subject to any express provision otherwise in the act. The act does contain two provisions, namely section 3(4) and (5), which subject the crown particularly to the apportionment and limitation of liability sections of the Canada Shipping Act, though that act does not purport to bind the crown.[102] By comparison section 3(1) and (2) of the act, in imposing the liability of a subject upon the crown, do not seem sufficiently specific about affecting governmental immunity so as to come within the exception to section 20.[103] The only escape from section 20 is to say that since the crown is deemed to be a subject, for the purposes of tort liability, that section has no bearing for there is no potential for governmental immunity fav-

98 See supra, at 53.
99 R.S.C. 1970, c C-38
100 10 & 11 Geo. VI, c 44, s 40(2) (f)
101 See the Proceedings against the Crown Acts of Manitoba, S.M. 1951, c 13, s 5; Saskatchewan, S.S. 1952, c 35, s 5; Ontario, S.O. 1952, c 78, s 5 (never proclaimed in force).
102 Indeed, s 714 of the Canada Shipping Act, R.S.C. 1970, c S-9, states that the act does not apply to ships belonging to Her Majesty except where specially provided in the act.
103 Cf Treitel, 'Crown Proceedings: Some Recent Developments,' [1957] *Public Law* 321, at 324, but compare Williams *Crown Proceedings* (1948), at 55–8.

ouring the defendant in those circumstances for it enjoys no higher status than that of a subject. But this seems to rob section 20 of any role whatsoever.

The failure of the Crown Liability Act to speak to the matter of the federal crown's immunity from provincial statutes is probably of no significance in indicating whether the operation of that immunity was to be preserved or curtailed. It is quite probable that the draftsman simply followed the English model without any conscious attention to the immunity questions that are thrown up by a federal system but are not apt to arise in a unitary state.

It has been suggested then that the Crown Liability Act may be treated as involving a submission of the federal crown, as if it were a subject, to provincial statute law existing from time to time for the purposes of determining tort liability. But it is not clear, because of section 20, that federal statute law would also apply if it did not expressly bind the crown. If it doesn't apply then the assimilation of the position of the crown to that of a subject for tort liability purposes may have totally different effects in terms of enabling federal and provincial statutes to operate. That seems anomalous to say the least. The matter is one that needs clarification by parliament and, with that in mind, reforms are suggested in a later section of this chapter.

The Supreme Court of Canada in *R* v *Breton*[104] has taken a restrictive view of the kinds of provincial statutory provisions which can be applied in proceedings against the crown under section 3(1) (b) of the Crown Liability Act. That provision, it will be recalled, imposes civil liability upon the crown as if it were a private person in respect of 'a breach of duty attaching to the ownership, occupation, possession or control of property.' In *Breton* the claimant sought damages from the crown under section 3(1) (b) to compensate her for injuries suffered in a fall occasioned by the defective condition of a sidewalk in Quebec City which fronted on property owned by the government of Canada. The Quebec City Charter, an enactment of the province of Quebec, made the repair and maintenance of sidewalks the responsibility of adjoining proprietors.

In determining whether this Quebec statute imposed a duty of the kind contemplated by the Crown Liability Act, the court felt that a strict interpretation of the latter act was in order since it affects the rights and prerogatives of the crown.[105] The conclusion was then reached that the provincial statute was inapplicable because it did not impose 'a clearly identified and well-known duty established by the general law, and common in all territorial jurisdictions.'[106] Nor did it, significantly in the court's view, fix a duty upon persons in relation to

104 (1967), 65 D.L.R. (2d) 76 (S.C.C.)
105 Ibid, at 79
106 Ibid, at 79

property which they actually owned or occupied as distinct from property simply adjoining that which was owned or occupied.[107] These were thought to be requisites to the existence of a duty of the kind envisaged by section 3(1) (b) of the Crown Liability Act on its proper construction. An alternative, constitutional ground was also offered for the decision.[108]

The effect of this case is not simply to confine the delictual and quasi-delictual responsibility of the federal crown to that of a subject under the law of Quebec. It is clear that a subject who was a proprietor would have been responsible, under article 1053 or article 1054 of the Civil Còde, for damages resulting from his breach of the Quebec City Charter though the latter created no specific cause of action.[109] As a matter of common law that result would be much more doubtful.[110] A possible difference in outcome under the two legal systems is no reason, however, for denying scope for the law of Quebec to operate in this situation when the federal crown is sued. Variations in the relief available under the Crown Liability Act in matters arising in the several provinces are both common and inevitable.

In the absence of any valid underlying premises for the decision all that can be said is that the court was simply disposed to take an exceedingly narrow view of the kinds of statutory duties, violation of which would give rise to civil liability under section 3(1) (b) of the Crown Liability Act. The ·decision, therefore, suggests that we might expect a similarly restrictive approach on the part of the final appellate tribunal to the application of provincial statutes generally in proceedings under section 3(1) and (2), which would leave only those in force when liability was imposed on the crown to operate to its prejudice. But of the Supreme Court justices, Pigeon J, in the *Nord-Deutsche* case, has already rejected such a limitation in favour of a general application of provincial statutes. That result has considerable textual justification and is one which, it is argued above and in a later section,[111] is to be preferred. No very confident prediction can be made that a Supreme Court majority would in fact resolve the question, unaided by any further legislative direction on the matter, as Mr Justice Pigeon has done.

It has sometimes been said that a presumption of fault existing under provin-

107 Ibid, at 80
108 The court relied upon s 125 of the BNA Act, a provision which is considered at some length infra, at 137–43.
109 *Caron* v *Forgues*, [1944] 2 D.L.R. 201. See also *Nadeau* v *Valcourt*, [1952] B.R. 558. And see generally as to 'Breach of Statute as the Basis of Responsibility in the Civil Law' an article of that title by Newman in (1949), 27 *Can. Bar Rev.* 782.
110 Consider *Commerford* v *Board of School Comm'rs of Halifax*, [1950] 2 D.L.R. 207 (N.S.S.C.), and *Tzogas* v *Ont. Housing Corp.*, unreported decision of the Ontario Court of Appeal dated 3 March 1976.
111 See infra, at 77–80.

cial law cannot apply in proceedings under section 3(1) (a) of the Crown Liability Act consistently with the restricted nature of the crown's liability.[112] The onus of proof to establish tortious conduct on the part of a servant or agent of the crown was thought to be inflexibly fixed by the federal statute upon the claimant in the same way as under the predecessor provision. The role of the Crown Liability Act in bringing in provincial law in this respect has thus been viewed narrowly, as it was in other contexts in the *Lamoureux, Schwella*, and *Breton* decisions. However, if there is no place for presumptions under provincial law there is an impediment, in section 3(1) (a) actions arising in Quebec,[113] to the application of a key section of the Civil Code, namely article 1054. That article, in imposing liability for damage caused by things upon the owner or custodian who has them under his care, raises a presumption of responsibility.[114] In the *Nord-Deutsche* case Noël J, at trial, was prepared to apply that article in an action supportable under section 3(1) (a) as well as under section 3(1) (b). The ground for doing so was that it was consistent with the new form of crown liability which corresponds to the liability to which a private person would be subject in delict and quasi-delict as well as in tort.[115] There was no dissent from this comparatively liberal construction of the Crown Liability Act on the appeal to the Supreme Court of Canada.[116]

Since the crown is now liable in tort as if it were a private person then it ought to be entitled to raise whatever defences would be open to a subject in response to a tort claim against it. The fact that the governmental immunity of the crown is deemed to be unaffected by the Crown Liability Act has no bearing on the matter for the right of the crown to take advantage of a statute is outside that rule. Nor is there any reason for construing the Crown Liability Act restrictively against the crown. The crown's responsibility, therefore, ought not to go beyond that of a subject given the modern basis of liability. That will indeed be the case only if it can rely upon any pertinent legislation, provincial or federal, to the same extent as a subject, that is notwithstanding that that legislation may indicate that it does not extend to the crown. Consequently the *Nisbet* case,[117] which

112 *Gaetz v The Queen*, [1955] Ex. C.R. 133; *Meredith v The Queen*, [1955] Ex. C.R. 156; *Deslauriers-Drago v The Queen*, [1963] Ex. C.R. 289, at 297
113 Though perhaps not in s 3(1) (b) actions since liability thereunder is direct rather than vicarious.
114 See Immarigeon, 'La responsabilité de la puissance publique,' in Barbe (ed) *Droit administratif canadien et québécois* (1969), 631, at 660.
115 [1969] Ex. C.R. 117, at 169–71. And see Immarigeon *La responsabilité extracontractuelle de la Couronne au Canada* (1965), at 133–6, and Dussault *Traité de droit administratif* (1974), at 1455.
116 See (1971), 20 D.L.R. (3d) 444 (S.C.C.).
117 [1955] 4 D.L.R. 1 (P.C.), considered supra, at 59–60.

was decided under the earlier legislation and would dictate a different conclusion, can no longer be taken as decisive of the limits of the crown's right to rely on legislation as a defendant in a tort action given the different form in which liability is now cast upon the federal crown.[118]

The Australian Position

It will be remembered that in *Farnell* v *Bowman*[119] a colonial statute of New South Wales was interpreted as imposing a liability in tort upon the crown. That statute, the Claims against the Government and Crown Suits Act (hereinafter the Claims Act), has been continued in substantially the same form[120] and was the subject of judicial attention in the recent case of *Downs* v *Williams*.[121] The Claims Act, as well as enabling any just claim or demand against the state government to be brought by way of proceedings against a nominal defendant, also provides, in section 4, as follows:

4. The petitioner may sue such nominal defendant at law or in equity in any competent court, and every such case shall be commenced in the same way, and the proceedings and rights of the parties therein shall as nearly as possible be the same, and judgment and costs shall follow or may be awarded on either side as in an ordinary case between subject and subject.

Downs v *Williams* concerned a claim against a nominal defendant for personal injuries sustained by the plaintiff while operating machinery in a technical college. The machinery was allegedly without the protective fencing required by the Factories, Shops and Industries Act of New South Wales (hereinafter the Factories Act), a statute which did not expressly bind the crown. The action was framed both in terms of negligence and breach of statutory duty. An application was made by the defendant to strike out the counts based on the latter ground. For the purposes of that interlocutory proceeding it was assumed that the technical college was under the care and control of the government of New South Wales and that it was a factory within the meaning of the Factories Act. The application was dismissed and this disposition was affirmed on appeal. A further appeal to the High Court was successful. That tribunal decided by a bare 3-2 majority that the Claims Act, section 4 of which was particularly relied on by the respon-

118 Cf *Re Mar-Lise Industries Ltd* (1968), 5 D.L.R. (3d) 487 (Ont. C.A.).
119 (1887), 12 App. Cas. 643, considered supra, at 46–7.
120 See the Claims against the Government and Crown Suits Act, 1912 (N.S.W.).
121 (1971), 126 C.L.R. 61

dent, did not have the effect of making the crown liable for breach of a duty imposed by an act that was not itself binding on the crown.

The disparate majority opinions disclose major differences of emphasis. McTiernan J and Menzies J did take a similar tack in that they both proceeded to give a restrictive interpretation to section 4 of the Claims Act. But for McTiernan J a distinction between 'the rights of the parties,' a concern of section 4 of the act, and the law to be applied in any proceeding against the crown assumed particular importance.[122] The general law had first to be considered, he said, to determine whether a statutory duty was imposed on the crown. And in this case the rule of governmental immunity precluded a finding of a duty under the statute in question. Only in the event of the disclosure of a duty was it necessary to have regard to the rights pertaining between subjects, similarly situated, to ascertain the rights between the parties in a crown proceeding. On the other hand, Menzies J declined to give section 4 of the Claims Act the role contended for it because he felt that it could not be construed as amending or modifying the operation of other acts of parliament. That would be to give those other acts, *ex post facto*, an effect upon the crown which they didn't have when the events occurred and before the Claims Act was invoked by the commencement of an action against the crown.[123] Owen J, the third majority judge, treated section 4 of the Claims Act as positively securing the defence of the crown in that the crown was entitled, in reliance on that provision, to insist upon the rights which any subject would have if sued for breach of duty. That would include, in his view, the general right to maintain that the statute imposed no obligation at all on the defendant for whatever reason.[124]

Windeyer J dissented because he felt that the Factories Act bound the crown by necessary implication. This was a prerequisite to its application in this proceeding, in his opinion, only because it was passed after the Claims Act.[125] Gibbs J, also dissenting, decided that section 4 of the Claims Act effectively applies the substantive law as between subjects, including subsequent statute law if the latter is not inconsistent in the sense that it is explicitly stated not to bind the crown. He relied upon *Farnell* v *Bowman* and several cases which had construed a similar federal provision, namely section 64 of the Judiciary Act.

The decision that the regulatory act, not binding the crown, cannot be ap-

---

122 Ibid, at 65–6. He relied, particularly, on a remark of Dixon CJ in *Commonwealth* v *Anderson* (1960), 105 C.L.R. 303.
123 (1971), 126 C.L.R. 61, at 68
124 Ibid, at 92. But see *Sydney Harbour Trust Comm'rs* v *Ryan* (1911), 13 C.L.R. 358, esp. at 372, a decision which was ignored by the majority in *Downs*.
125 Support for this approach may be found in *Washington* v *Commonwealth* (1939), 39 S.R. (N.S.W.) 133, at 138 (F.C.).

plied 'at one remove' as it were by virtue of the Claims Act[126] is based upon reasoning that, by and large, would equally preclude the application of other kinds of acts, not binding upon the crown, which might affect liability in other ways than the imposition of a statutory duty.[127] Yet to give it this larger implication is, as will be seen, to invite difficulties in reconciling the decision with other cases under both section 4 of the Claims Act and the comparable provision of the federal Judiciary Act.

The judgments in *Downs* all but ignore a much earlier Privy Council decision, *Jamieson* v *Downie*,[128] in which it was held that the general language of section 4 of the Claims Act is sufficient to displace the operation of the crown's prerogative immunity from discovery in proceedings pursuant to that act. Yet governmental immunity from statute which also has its source in the royal prerogative is, according to *Downs*, unaffected by that same section. There is no suggestion in the *Downs* case that section 4 is referable only to procedural rights. And absent such a limitation there does not appear to be any rational basis for concluding that the section should have an effect which is dramatically more far-reaching with respect to a prerogative relating to a procedural matter than with respect to one relating to a substantive matter. This is especially apparent when it is remembered that governmental immunity from statute, while resulting in an immunity from a provision of substantive law in *Downs*, may well afford the basis for a claim to immunity from legislation or rules dealing with procedure, most procedural rights now having their source in such instruments.

If the state government is not fettered, in terms of tort liability, by state statutes which do not bind it, then the Commonwealth ought also to be similarly free of regulation by state statute since its liability in tort is governed by legislation which, in the relevant provisions, is substantially on the model of the New South Wales Claims Act. Indeed once the federal dimension is introduced we no longer have a situation which simply requires an exercise in reconciling two statutes of a single legislature. Intergovernmental immunity considerations are also introduced. And one might expect that it would require language at least as clear to avoid the effect of the latter immunity given its constitutional basis. If the assimilation of the rights of the parties in crown proceedings to those in proceedings between subjects is incapable of avoiding the operation of governmental immunity it ought to be no more effective in relation to the operation of intergovernmental immunity. The latter is an *a fortiori* case. Unfortunately the matter of

126 Compare Williams *Crown Proceedings* (1948), at 55–6.
127 But consider the judgment of McTiernan J.
128 [1923] A.C. 691 (P.C.). And cf *Commonwealth* v *Miller* (1910), 10 C.L.R. 742; *Heimann* v *Commonwealth* (1935), 54 C.L.R. 126; *Naismith* v *McGovern* (1953), 90 C.L.R. 336.

Commonwealth tort liability and state statutes cannot be disposed of this easily because there is a good deal of pre-*Downs* v *Williams* jurisprudence on section 64 of the federal Judiciary Act, which reflects the language of section 4 of the New South Wales Claims Act, that must be taken into account. But the use of that case as the beginning of analysis may be justified on the basis that it represents the most recent expression of opinion by the High Court on the general question at issue and that it deals with the least complicated form of the general question.

The Judiciary Act, first enacted in 1903, now contains the following provisions:[129]

56. (1) A person making a claim against the Commonwealth, whether in contract or in tort, may in respect of that claim bring a suit against the Commonwealth –
   (a) in the High Court;
   (b) in the Supreme Court of the State or Territory in which the claim arose; or
   (c) in any other court of competent jurisdiction of the State or Territory in which the claim arose.

   ...

57. Any State making any claim against the Commonwealth, whether in contract or in tort, may in respect of the claim bring a suit against the Commonwealth in the High Court.

58. Any person making any claim against a State, whether in contract or in tort, in respect of a matter in which the High Court has original jurisdiction or can have original jurisdiction conferred on it, may in respect of the claim bring a suit against the State in the Supreme Court of the State, or (if the High Court has original jurisdiction in the matter) in the High Court.

59. Any State making any claim against another State may in respect of the claim bring suit against the State in the High Court.

64. In any suit to which the Commonwealth or a State is a party the rights of parties shall as nearly as possible be the same, and judgment may be given and costs awarded on either side, as in a suit between subject and subject.

Several differences between section 64 and section 4 of the Claims Act may be noted but none seems material to the matter under discussion. Section 64 is more extensive than section 4 in that it covers proceedings in which the crown is plaintiff and not just actions against the crown. And suits of the latter variety under the federal act are brought directly against the Commonwealth or a state without the need for inserting the name of a nominal defendant to represent the

129 The act continues to be styled the Judiciary Act 1903.

crown as required by the state act. Finally, the kinds of proceedings against the crown to which section 64 is potentially applicable are ostensibly only those in tort and contract,[130] and not 'any just claim or demand' which may be the basis of proceedings to which section 4 of the Claims Act might apply. But the respects in which section 64 differs from section 4 do not make for any stronger case under the former for applying statute law against the crown when it is sued in tort.

Yet state statutes altering the principles of tort liability have been applied, from time to time, against the Commonwealth when sued in tort. There are only two reported decisions applying a state statute against the Commonwealth, in this context, in which the specific authority for doing so is explained.[131] In both cases the act was the New South Wales Compensation to Relatives Act, imposing liability for wrongful death. That act was passed in 1897 before the creation of the Commonwealth and naturally, therefore, before the imposition of tort liability on that political authority. The basis for subjecting the Commonwealth to the act was said, in *Pitcher* v *Federal Capital Commission*[132] and *Washington* v *Commonwealth*,[133] to be sections 56 and 64 of the Judiciary Act, though in the second case section 56 was mentioned as the preferred vehicle.

In the *Washington* case Jordan CJ, for the New South Wales Full Court, placed considerable reliance on the Canadian decisions concerning section 19(c) of the Exchequer Court Act in concluding that the Commonwealth was subject to the law of torts in the states at 1903 when the Judiciary Act came into operation.[134] Subsequent state legislation must be disregarded, he said, except so far as it might be capable of binding the crown of its own force. The latter was an *inter se* matter involving the boundaries between state and Commonwealth constitutional powers which only the High Court could decide.[135] This approach, like that in the early Canadian cases, seems to be based upon the theory that the federal crown liability provisions involved an implied consent to the application of existing local statute law.[136]

Of course in *Downs* v *Williams* a similar result, that is that the statute in question applied against the crown, could not have been reached on this narrow basis because the statute in that case was subsequent to the crown liability legislation.

---

130 But see Hogg *Liability of the Crown* (1971), at 142–3.
131 In *Moore* v *Commonwealth* (1958), 99 C.L.R. 177, the issue did not have to be reached.
132 (1928), 41 C.L.R. 385
133 (1939), 39 S.R. (N.S.W.) 133 (F.C.)
134 Or possibly at 1901, when the Commonwealth came into existence, or 1902, the date of the Claims against the Commonwealth Act, which was replaced the next year by certain of the provisions of the Judiciary Act; see ibid, at 144.
135 See s 38A of the Judiciary Act 1903.
136 See supra, at 51–2.

On reasoning similar to that in the *Washington* case it could only apply of its own force and it did not do so but for prerogative rather than constitutional reasons in that it did not purport to bind the crown.

But this possible rationalization of the case law loses considerable appeal when two more recent cases which came before the same single judge of the High Court, sitting in the exercise of its original jurisdiction, are taken into account. In *Suehle* v *Commonwealth*,[137] Windeyer J said, in an *obiter* remark, that notwithstanding the *Washington* decision 'the references in the Judiciary Act to the laws of the States (e.g. in s. 64) are now regarded as having an ambulatory effect.' 'They are not tied to State law as it was in 1903.'[138] The basis of the dictum was no doubt *Parker* v *Commonwealth*[139] in which the same judge had applied state legislation, abolishing the defence of common employment, which was passed subsequent to the Judiciary Act so as to give the plaintiff a remedy in tort against the Commonwealth.[140] The quotation from the *Suehle* case suggests that it is section 64, rather than section 56, which brings in state statute law. If the state legislation that applies is, as it appears to be on this recent view, that in force when the cause of action arose then the language of section 64 is indeed more appropriate to realize this result. But how can section 64 have this effect if section 4 of the Claims Act, in similar terms to section 64, has no like effect when governmental immunity considerations alone are at work without the added possibility of a claim of intergovernmental immunity?

To what extent, and on what theory, may section 64 be treated as avoiding the consequences of the immunity which the Commonwealth enjoys from state legislation? Some light is shed on this matter by the judgments in *Asiatic Steam Navigation Co.* v *Commonwealth*.[141] The issue there was whether the Commonwealth was entitled as a shipowner to the benefit of a limitation of liability provision in the imperial Merchant Shipping Act of 1894, notwithstanding that that statute provided that it did not generally apply to ships belonging to Her Majesty. The case, on its facts, bears a strong resemblance to the Canadian case of *Nisbet Shipping Co.* v *The Queen*,[142] which was considered by the court and distinguished by the majority in deciding that the federal crown could take advantage of the limitation provision. In a joint judgment, Dixon CJ, McTiernan and Williams JJ said that section 64 of the Judiciary Act, alone or together with section 56 and

---

137 (1967), 116 C.L.R. 353
138 Ibid, at 356–7. See also *Downs* v *Williams* (1971), 126 C.L.R. 61, at 100 *per* Gibbs J, dissenting.
139 (1965), 112 C.L.R. 295
140 See Hogg *Liability of the Crown* (1971), at 230.
141 (1956), 96 C.L.R. 397
142 [1955] 4 D.L.R. 1 (P.C.), discussed supra, at 59–60.

the constitution itself, covers the limitation of liability section of the imperial act as part of the private law which it gathers in and incorporates as governing the delictual responsibility of the Commonwealth.[143] The crown exception in the imperial act was, therefore, irrelevant. Kitto J, in a separate judgment, asserted that section 64 takes up and enacts the whole body of law, statutory or otherwise, which would govern the rights of the parties if the Commonwealth were a subject. Therefore, in this case, the limitation of liability provision of the imperial statute would apply by the independent force of section 64.[144] The requirement of that section, he said, was that any special position of the crown was to be put out of account. Fullagar J, dissenting, took the position that a general enactment in the form of section 64 of the Judiciary Act cannot override any special enactment made applicable or inapplicable to the crown by its express terms.[145] If section 64 had this large a role it would presumably also operate to bring in state statutes from which the Commonwealth enjoyed an intergovernmental immunity, a proposition which he could not espouse.[146]

The statute applied through the terms of the Judiciary Act in the *Asiatic Steam Navigation* case was in force before the imposition of liability in tort upon the Commonwealth. Consequently it might have operated as the result of a limited application, through the Judiciary Act, of the existing statute law pertaining between subject and subject. That was the basis of the *Washington* case, though reliance there was placed primarily on section 56 of the act rather than section 64, which featured in the *Asiatic Steam Navigation* decision. But no such point was made and the judgment of Kitto J, if not the joint judgment, indicates that section 64 involves an adoption of statute law applying between subjects of such a general scope as to embrace legislation whenever enacted. In other words the section effects an ambulatory incorporation by reference of any relevant statutes as they may operate between subjects.[147]

However, the function which Kitto J ascribed to section 64 has not gone unchallenged. In two later cases, *Commonwealth* v *Anderson*[148] and *Downs* v *Williams*,[149] Menzies J expressed reservations.[150] And in the latter case he indicated a definite preference for what Fullagar J had said about section 64 in the *Asiatic*

---

143 (1956), 96 C.L.R. 397, at 419–20
144 Ibid, at 427–8
145 Ibid, at 424
146 Ibid. And see *N.S.W.* v *Bardolph* (1934), 52 C.L.R. 455, at 459–60 *per* Evatt J, decision aff'd by the Full Court, at 493.
147 See supra, at 52–3.
148 (1960), 105 C.L.R. 303
149 (1971), 126 C.L.R. 61
150 See (1960), 105 C.L.R. 303, at 317–18, and (1971), 126 C.L.R. 61, at 69.

Steam Navigation case. The dissenting opinion of Fullagar J received further support in *Commonwealth* v *Lawrence*.[151] In that case Else-Mitchell J, of the New South Wales Supreme Court, refused to apply a state landlord and tenant provision against the Commonwealth. The federal authority was the claimant in an ejectment action and the state statute would have required it to follow a special procedure for terminating leases of 'prescribed premises.' Every state law which limits legal rights, the court said, does not, 'bind the Commonwealth ... with no waiver of constitutional immunity other than the general words of s. 64 of the Judiciary Act.'[152]

And section 64 did not affect the outcome of another suit which was to become a landmark in the recognition of an intergovernmental immunity of the Commonwealth from state statutes, namely *Commonwealth* v *Cigamatic Pty*.[153] In that case the Commonwealth as a creditor of the Cigamatic company was held to be unaffected by the priority provisions of state winding-up legislation. No mention was made by the High Court of any possible impact of section 64 as removing the Commonwealth's immunity from state legislation. That action, however, was one by the Commonwealth in the federal jurisdiction to which that section was ostensibly applicable.[154]

A particular limitation upon the kinds of state statutes which section 64 is capable of applying in proceedings by or against the Commonwealth is evident from *Commonwealth* v *Anderson*.[155] The state act in question there prescribed a form of termination notice which had to specify one or more enumerated grounds as a pre-condition to proceedings by a landlord for the recovery of leased premises. In *Anderson* the Commonwealth was suing tenants of crown land in ejectment to recover possession and the state act in question had not been complied with. Dixon CJ, whose opinion attracted the most support,[156] noted that it was fundamental to the state scheme for the regulation of landlord and tenant relations that jurisdiction be exercised by inferior tribunals, designated to replace the courts usually entrusted with comparable matters, and that they bring to bear a wide discretion on the issues brought before them including the adequacy of grounds for termination. Consequently the state act did not provide 'the source of definite rights between subject and subject capable of appropriation under s. 64

---

151 (1960), 77 W.N. (N.S.W.) 538
152 Ibid, at 541
153 (1962), 108 C.L.R. 372, considered supra, at 36, and infra, at 114–15.
154 And cf *Re Young's Horsham Garage Pty*, [1969] V.R. 977. See also *Commonwealth* v *Bogle* (1953), 89 C.L.R. 229.
155 (1960), 105 C.L.R. 303
156 McTiernan, Kitto, & Windeyer JJ concurred in the opinion of Dixon CJ on the issue ; under discussion.

of the Judiciary Act ... '[157] Indeed, section 64 was thought to presuppose that a suit could be properly brought were the matter at issue one between subjects. But in fact the state act denied the right to launch proceedings in ejectment in the ordinary courts. The case having been disposed of on this basis it was not necessary to enter the larger question of whether section 64 was capable of avoiding, generally, the Commonwealth's immunity from state statutes.

There are, then, several cases and individual judicial opinions, the cumulative effect of which is to raise doubts about the attribution of a very large role to section 64 such as would enable it to provide an escape from the impact of the Commonwealth's intergovernmental immunity. This despite the fact that state statutes, sometimes subsequent to the assumption of liability by the Commonwealth, have been considered to be applicable against the Commonwealth when sued in tort as the result of either section 64 or section 56 of the Judiciary Act and that section 64 has been held to make the Commonwealth amenable to discovery orders pursuant to state procedural rules.[158] The latter class of case might be regarded as representing the only legitimate role for section 64 as one in relation to procedural rights. But while there is some isolated support for this position[159] it is hardly consistent with many of the decided cases.[160]

The matter is complicated further when we return to *Downs* v *Williams* and bring it into the balance in so far as it may be regarded as indicative of the function of section 64 in terms of avoiding possible immunity claims, intergovernmental as well as governmental. To treat that decision as simply excluding regulatory statutes imposing a duty of care from the assimilation of the rights of subjects effected by section 4 of the Claims Act hardly seems justified. In any case, that would not resolve all the apparent inconsistencies in the jurisprudence. The state of the law in Australia, as in Canada, is confused and is ripe for reform.

Suggested Legislative Reform

The liability of the federal crown in tort should be determinable in accordance with any state or provincial statutes, whenever enacted, that would govern the liability of a subject similarly placed. This would accord with the original philo-

---

157 (1960), 105 C.L.R. 303, at 311
158 See *Commonwealth* v *Miller* (1910), 10 C.L.R. 742; *Heimann* v *Commonwealth* (1935), 54 C.L.R. 126. And cf *Naismith* v *McGovern* (1953), 90 C.L.R. 336.
159 See *Commonwealth* v *Baume* (1905), 2 C.L.R. 405, at 418 *per* O'Connor J; *Griffen* v *S.A.* (1924), 35 C.L.R. 200, at 204 *per* Isaacs ACJ.
160 For example, *Asiatic Steam Navigation Co.* v *Commonwealth* (1956), 96 C.L.R. 397; *Parker* v *Commonwealth* (1965), 112 C.L.R. 295. And cf *Farnell* v *Bowman* (1887), 12 App. Cas. 643 (P.C.).

sophy of crown liability legislation – to give the subject a complete remedy in tort against the crown[161] or, to put it another way, to place the crown in the same position as a private person for the purposes of the law of torts.[162] This salutary objective was understood to be difficult of realization in that there are situations in which the crown performs functions which have no counterpart in the private sector. But that, of course, is no reason for limiting the application of state or provincial statutes, as has often been done or suggested, when the federal crown or its servants are acting in a role which does have a close private analogy. Certainly the trend since the assumption of tort liability by the federal crown has been for government to engage more and more in the kinds of activities that are pursued by private persons. The result is to add further significance to the differences between the position of the crown and that of a subject. This together with the increase in state or provincial legislation affecting liability in tort contributes to an even greater shortcoming in the realization of the objective of crown liability legislation than was originally the case.

To subject the federal crown to local statute law is to introduce discrepancies in the extent of federal crown liability in tort from state to state or province to province. There would certainly be nothing new about that phenomenon in Canada. The civil responsibility of the federal crown in Quebec has always differed markedly from its responsibility in other jurisdictions because of the civil law system which is peculiar to that province.[163] And, of course, a limited application of local statute law by reference to the date of imposition of tort liability upon the federal crown, which was the effect attributed to crown liability provisions in both Australia and Canada at one time or another, results in considerable differences between jurisdictions given the inevitable variation in the degree of modernization of tort law at the crucial date.

On balance it would seem better to bring the liability of the federal crown in a given state or province into line with that of private persons and remove the anomaly in that regard, even though it may be at the expense of accentuating the already existing differences in the liability of the crown from jurisdiction to jurisdiction in the federation. This should present no great hardship for the federal crown for, in other respects, it has already come to live with the obligation to take state or provincial law as it finds it. Moreover the planning of its affairs in a consistent manner throughout the country is prejudiced less by statutes affecting

161 See *Farnell* v *Bowman* (1887), 12 App. Cas. 643, at 648 (P.C.).
162 See the Explanatory Memorandum to the English Crown Proceedings Bill, quoted in Street *Government Liability* (1953), at 26.
163 Compare, for instance, *R* v *Filion* (1895), 24 S.C.R. 482, with *Ryder* v *The King* (1905), 36 S.C.R. 462, and *Lapointe* v *The King* (1913), 14 D.L.R. 394 (Exch.), with *C.N.R.* v *St John Motor Line Ltd*, [1930] 3 D.L.R. 732 (S.C.C.).

tort liability than by other kinds of statutes on the basis of which formal engagements are entered into. From the point of view of the injured party it is largely fortuitous that the perpetrator of the harm suffered may have been the crown or one of its servants. For him, of course, it can represent a very real hardship if recovery is denied or diminished because his defendant happens to be the federal crown.

Since there is considerable doubt, at present, as to the general applicability of state or provincial statutes against the federal crown, when sued in tort, remedial legislation is called for. That legislation should make it clear that local statutes can indeed operate indifferently, either in favour of the crown or a subject, in this situation. The lesson of the cases is that crown liability legislation must be very explicit or it is likely to fail in achieving this result when submitted to judicial scrutiny.

The crown ought also to be subject to statutes passed by the legislature of that political level in right of which it is sued if it is to approach the position of a subject for the purposes of tort liability. That is, the legislation of the central parliament should apply against the federal crown and local legislation against the crown in right of a state or province in tort proceedings to establish governmental liability. The latter is presently the case in the Canadian provinces which have followed the Model Crown Proceedings Act promulgated in 1950 by the Commissioners for the Uniformity of Legislation.[164] Under the Model Act liability is imposed in tort notwithstanding the particular section of the Interpretation Act of the enacting jurisdiction which declares that the rights of Her Majesty are not affected by legislation in which Her Majesty is not expressly mentioned.[165] Because the rule of governmental immunity takes statutory form in Canada its effect in tort actions against the crown may be circumvented by the neat device of a short *non obstante* clause referring simply to the relevant section of another act. Governmental immunity from statute could be similarly subordinated to the imposition of tort liability upon the crown in right of Canada. This would represent a departure from what would appear to be the current legislative philosophy concerning governmental liability, which contemplates the preservation of 'any

164 For the text of the Model Act see Conference of Commissioners on Uniformity of Legislation in Canada *Model Acts Recommended from 1918 to 1961 inclusive* (1962), at 244–51. The crown proceedings legislation of all the provinces except Quebec was derived, to some extent, from this model.
165 See s 5(1) of the Model Act. There was no need for such a qualification in the British Columbia Crown Proceedings Act, S.B.C. 1974, c 24, because the rule of governmental immunity has been effectively abolished by statute, see the Interpretation Act, S.B.C. 1974, c 42, s 13. The Tasmanian crown proceedings provisions make some specific statutes, which might affect tort liability, binding upon the crown, see the Supreme Court Civil Procedure Act 1932 (Tas.), s 64(9).

presumption relating to the extent to which the Crown is bound by an Act of Parliament.'[166]

It may be that in tort proceedings against the state or provincial crown the claimant wishes to rely upon federal legislation which is in point. The intergovernmental immunity which works in favour of the state or province is a very limited one, as has been noticed, and does not normally provide protection absent a need to preserve the constituent units of the federation or to insulate them from discriminatory treatment.[167] Thus most federal legislation that might be relevant in a tort action against a state or province would apply of its own force. But on the view that governmental immunity operates in favour of the crown in these circumstances[168] there is a definite need to provide for the application of federal statutes if they are to bind the state or province even though they do not encompass the crown expressly or by necessary implication.

Of course the statutes of any jurisdiction which has abolished the rule of governmental immunity[169] will extend, as a matter of construction, to the crown in any right when it is sued in tort without special provision to that effect in the relevant crown proceedings legislation.

THE CROWN AS PLAINTIFF

When the federal crown is plaintiff in a tort action the defendant may seek to rely upon a state or provincial statute which, if applied, would operate to the detriment of the crown's claim. This final part of the chapter will deal with the extent to which the crown can insist upon immunity in this circumstance. This question has rarely troubled the courts in Australia though it has been a frequent subject of litigation in Canada. But it will be remembered that section 64 of the Australian Judiciary Act, assimilating the rights of the parties in crown proceedings to those in a suit between subjects, applies equally to proceedings by as against the Commonwealth. Consequently consideration of the effect of that section, which has already been undertaken with somewhat uncertain results, reveals the role of state statutes, and federal statutes for that matter, in tort proceedings by the Commonwealth which are brought in the federal jurisdiction. In Canada there is no federal provision which might arguably effect a general introduction of provincial statute law, applying between subjects, in tort proceedings by the federal crown.

166 Crown Liability Act, R.S.C. 1970, c C-38, s 20
167 See supra, at 43-4.
168 See supra, at 23-9.
169 This reform, which has already been adopted in the province of British Columbia, was suggested supra, at 21-2.

The related question of whether the crown in the right of a state or province, as plaintiff in a tort action, is subject to having its claim barred or curtailed by local legislation turns simply on the application of the general principles of governmental immunity. The matter is largely unaffected, in either Australia or Canada, by crown proceedings statutes, which generally concern actions against but not by the crown.

When the crown in right of Canada sues, it is obliged to take the cause of action as it finds it in the sense that if the law of the relevant province does not envisage such a cause of action the claim must be dismissed (assuming no federal law in point).[170] A particular kind of action may be unavailable in a province, however, not because of the absence of any common or statutory law providing for it but because of a statutory bar to such an action. In principle it would seem odd if, in this case, the crown could pursue its claim though it could not do so in the former case. Yet in the second situation, immunity, of an intergovernmental and possibly of a governmental variety, appears to be available to the crown as plaintiff as a reply to an insistence by the subject defendant on the provincial legislation. Nonetheless, the Supreme Court of Canada, in *Attorney General of Canada v Jackson*,[171] reached the common sense result that a federal crown claim is effectively precluded by a provincial statute removing civil liability in the circumstances giving rise to the proceedings.

But a distinction was suggested in later cases between a statute preventing any cause of action arising (such as in *Jackson*) and one that operates on causes of action which have already come into existence, the latter form of statute having no operation against the federal crown as plaintiff.[172] Certainly provincial statutory provisions which simply restrict tort proceedings, by introducing a time limitation upon actions or a requirement of notice before suit, have been held inapplicable to the federal crown.[173] The crown's immunity from this kind of provincial enactment has been put on either or both of the grounds of intergovernmental and governmental immunity. This state of the law unfortunately has the consequence of inviting forum shopping by the crown with a view to avoiding having an action dismissed as out of time. If suit is brought in the Federal Court, provincial limitation periods will apply by virtue of the explicit direction of sec-

170 *R v Plamondon*, [1965] 1 Ex. C.R. 778, and *R v Sylvain* (1964), 52 D.L.R. 607 (S.C.C.)
171 [1946] 2 D.L.R. 481 (S.C.C.). But cf *Bowers v Hollinger*, [1946] 4 D.L.R. 186 (Ont. H.C.).
172 *A.G. of Can. v Tombs*, [1946] 4 D.L.R. 519, at 523 (Ont. C.A.); *R v Richardson & Adams*, [1948] 2 D.L.R. 305, at 324 *per* Estey J (S.C.C.).
173 *R v Verdun*, [1945] 2 D.L.R. 429 (Exch.); *A.G. of Can. v Rhode* (1957), 8 D.L.R. (2d) 89 (Sask. Dist. Ct), and *R v City of Montreal* (1972), 27 D.L.R. (3d) 349 (F.C.T.D.). And cf *Re Young's Horsham Garage Pty*, [1969] V.R. 977.

tion 38 of the Federal Court Act.[174] But the crown is free to select its own forum[175] and, by choosing a provincial court, can avoid the effect of a provincial limitation section which, according to this line of cases, cannot apply against the federal crown. Such a discrepancy in the application of limitation periods has no apparent justification. The sensible way of removing it, if the federal crown is not to be subjected generally to provincial statutes, would be to extend the Federal Court Act provision to its logical limit so as to encompass proceedings in any court in which the federal crown is a party.

The principle of the *Jackson* case is seriously limited by the circumstance that the crown's action in that case was derivative in nature, being a claim for loss of the services of a servant (*per quod servitium amisit*).[176] Since the servant, a member of the armed forces, had no claim because of a provincial statute denying liability on the part of a host driver to a gratuitous passenger, the crown, it was said, could be in no better position. Its right of recovery depended upon its servant having suffered an actionable wrong at the hand of the defendant driver. Section 50A of the Exchequer Court Act, introduced in 1944,[177] provided that for the

---

174 R.S.C. 1970, c 10 (2d Supp.). S 17(4)(a) of that act gives the Trial Division of the Federal Court concurrent original jurisdiction in proceedings in which the crown or the attorney general of Canada claims relief. But it seems to follow from the recent Supreme Court of Canada decision in *McNamara Constr. (Western) Ltd* v *The Queen* (1977), 13 N.R. 181 (S.C.C.), that a common law tort action by the crown cannot be maintained, constitutionally, in the Federal Court since any such action would not normally be supported by an 'applicable and existing federal law.' A law of that nature must underlie an action in the Federal Court, according to the *McNamara* case, in order for that court to be engaged, in disposing of the action, in the 'administration of the laws of Canada.' That expression, which occurs in section 101 of the BNA Act, describes the function of the courts which the central parliament may create in addition to a general court of appeal for Canada. The judgment in the *McNamara* case specifically affirms that an action against the federal crown in tort, on the other hand, does involve an 'applicable and existing federal law,' namely federal common and statutory law relating to crown liability. Therefore jurisdiction in such an action is properly conferred on the Federal Court. See also *Quebec North Shore Paper Co* v *Canadian Pacific Ltd* (1976), 71 D.L.R. (3d) 111 (S.C.C.).
175 See the cases cited in note 52 of chapter 1.
176 While the English Court of Appeal has indicated that this action is confined to suits for the loss of the services of a member of the claimant's family or of a domestic servant (see *Inland Revenue Comm'rs* v *Hambrook*, [1956] 2 Q.B. 658 (C.A.)), the Australian and Canadian courts have rejected any such limitation (see *Commissioner for Rys (N.S.W.)* v *Scott* (1959), 102 C.L.R. 392, and *Genereux* v *Peterson Howell & Heather (Can.) Ltd* (1972), 34 D.L.R. (3d) 614 (Ont. C.A.)).
177 By S.C. 1943–4, c 25, s 1. The successor to this provision is s 37 of the Federal Court Act, R.S.C. 1970, c 10 (2d Supp.), which contains no reference to any particular date and deems members of the Royal Canadian Mounted Police, as well as members

purposes of determining liability in a proceeding by or against the crown a person who had been a member of the armed forces at any time since 1938 was deemed to be a servant of the crown at such time. This section was held simply to put the crown in a recognized common law relationship subject, therefore, to the provincial law as to the consequences of that relationship. It did not itself create a direct and specific right in the crown.

It would seem to follow from this reasoning that limitation provisions would also apply against the federal crown when attempting to pursue a *per quod* action in a provincial court, notwithstanding that such provisions normally have the effect of simply limiting the right to bring suit rather than extinguishing a liability. But this has been held to be an impermissible extension of the *Jackson* decision because of a long-standing common law rule that a limitation bar against a servant cannot be raised against the master in a *per quod* action. The theory is that for these purposes his claim is sufficiently different from that of the servant.[178] This, of course, is a general principle and any 'immunity' which the crown might be said to enjoy in this kind of a case is not a governmental or intergovernmental immunity at all.

In *Regina* v *Murray*[179] the issue was whether a provincial statutory provision which did not go so far as to totally preclude a particular kind of action could apply against the federal crown. Again the issue arose in the context of a *per quod* proceeding. But, unlike the *Jackson* situation, there was clearly an actionable wrong against the servant. The provincial legislation would have the effect, however, of restricting the amount of the servant's recovery had he sued. The question was whether the crown was fixed with the same limits in its action for loss of the services of its servant. The crown argued that it was not reached by the provincial legislation in view of either its governmental or its intergovernmental immunity and was therefore entitled to full recovery for its loss.

The Supreme Court of Canada rejected the crown's argument,[180] relying principally on an earlier decision in relation to a fact situation which did not present any interjurisdictional features at all. The authority invoked was *Gartland*

of the Canadian Forces, to be servants of the crown. In Australia the crown cannot bring a *per quod* action for the loss of the services of a member either of the armed forces or the police, see *Commonwealth* v *Quince* (1944), 68 C.L.R. 227, and *A.G. of N.S.W.* v *Perpetual Trustee Co.*, [1955] A.C. 457 (P.C.).

178 *R* v *Richardson & Adams*, [1948] 2 D.L.R. 305, esp. at 308 (S.C.C.), and *R* v *Lightheart*, [1952] Ex. C.R. 12

179 (1967), 60 D.L.R. (2d) 647 (S.C.C.)

180 The holding of this case is inconsistent with an earlier trial decision, *Crowther* v *Patterson* (1958), 13 D.L.R. (2d) 90 (N.S.S.C.), aff'd without reference to the point being considered here at (1958), 17 D.L.R. (2d) 30 (N.S.S.C. in banco).

Steamship Co. v *The Queen*,[181] in which the Supreme Court had held that the federal crown was restricted in the amount it could recover from a shipowner, for damage negligently occasioned to its property by the defendant's ship, as a result of the Canada Shipping Act's provisions limiting the extent of liability of shipowners. Locke J had said in that case that

[t]he fact that liability may not be imposed upon the Crown, except by legislation in which the Sovereign is named, or that any of the other prerogative rights are not to be taken as extinguished unless the intention to do so is made manifest by naming the Crown, does not mean that the extent of liability of a subject may be extended in a case of a claim by the Crown beyond the limit of the liability effectively declared by law.[182]

This statement was found to be equally applicable in the *Murray* situation[183] on the view that the language, 'limit of the liability effectively declared by law' meant, in a federal state, so declared by the legislature, whether provincial or national, having constitutional authority to declare such a limit.

The case of *Gauthier* v *The King*[184] was not considered by the Supreme Court to be inconsistent with the result arrived at in *Murray*. The earlier case had held, among other things, that the Exchequer Court Act, in giving a federal tribunal jurisdiction in contract claims against the federal crown, did not change the immunity of the crown from provincial legislation. But the opinion acknowledged the different result under section 19(c) of the act,[185] relating to negligence claims against the crown, in that the governing law in that case was to be taken as that applying between subject and subject in the province in which the cause of action arose. The role of section 50A of the Exchequer Court Act which was critical in *Murray* was equated by the court to that of section 19(c), that is it was said to bring in any relevant provincial law. But, section 19(c) had been treated as applying existing provincial statute law in negligence proceedings against the federal crown simply because it created a totally new kind of liability in a field

181 (1960), 22 D.L.R. (2d) 385 (S.C.C.)
182 Ibid, at 400, Martland J concurring. This view was also concurred in by the other members of the court, see 410.
183 The proposition was later held to apply as well to a case in which the crown in the right of a province argued for recovery against a subject in an amount in excess of the limits of liability declared by the Canada Shipping Act. The result was that the provincial crown was treated as limited in its recovery, in the same way as the federal Crown in *Gartland*, by virtue of the federal statute: *B.C. Telephone Co.* v *Marpole Towing Ltd* (1970), 17 D.L.R. (3d) 545, see 559 (S.C.C.).
184 (1918), 40 D.L.R. 353 (S.C.C.), considered in detail supra, at 34–6, and infra, at 95–8.
185 Then s 20(c) of the Exchequer Court Act, R.S.C. 1906, c 140

in which there was no available régime of federal law. That was not true at all of section 50A. That provision simply deemed a relationship to exist which had, among other effects, a consequential significance in relation to the already established accountability in negligence of the federal crown by extending the range of situations in which vicarious liability would attach to the crown. The analogy posed seems, therefore, to be inappropriate. It would have been even more obviously so had the Manitoba legislation in point been passed after the enactment of section 50A of the Exchequer Court Act for neither section 19(c) nor any other section of that act was ever taken to have applied subsequent provincial statute law (except, by specific provision, the section incorporating provincial limitation periods) in crown proceedings pursuant to the terms of the act.

If the *Murray* and *Gauthier* cases are to be conformed only in the manner suggested in *Murray* then the latter decision has a very limited impact indeed. It would not provide authority for applying provincial limitation of liability provisions against the federal crown whenever it commences proceedings of any kind against a subject. Rather it would be limited to applying such provisions when the crown brings an action for loss of the services of a member of the armed forces or of the Royal Canadian Mounted Police, having therefore to rely upon section 37 of the Federal Court Act, the successor to section 50A of the Exchequer Court Act.

The two cases can, however, be more satisfactorily reconciled if we treat the intergovernmental immunity of the federal crown, recognized in *Gauthier*, as simply securing prerogatives but not other crown 'rights' against the possible prejudicial effect of provincial legislation. It has been argued earlier that that is, in principle, a desirable limitation and one that does indeed have some respectable implicit judicial support.[186] On this assumption the *Murray* case does not evidence a situation in which the federal crown enjoyed a right of a sufficient order that would enable it to claim an intergovernmental immunity. It had been argued that the crown could insist upon governmental immunity from the provincial statute limiting an award of damages. But that prerogative had already been confined in the *Gartland* case so as to preclude the crown from recovering damages against a subject in an amount in excess of that declared recoverable by statute. And it was precisely such an excess which the federal crown laid claim to in the *Murray* case. There was no prerogative enjoyed by the federal crown, therefore, with which the provincial statute might be thought to interfere. In *Gauthier*, by comparison, the federal crown was in a position, in the circumstances, to assert the prerogative of governmental immunity, with which the provincial statute would have interfered if applied. On this basis, which is considerably more satisfactory

186 See supra, at 34–40.

than that advanced by the Supreme Court, the two cases are not inconsistent.

Federal legislation is wanted which will have the result of applying generally provincial statute law, whenever enacted, in proceedings by the federal crown in tort. This review of the cases has revealed a sporadic application of provincial statutes. Some nice distinctions are suggested between situations in which provincial enactments govern and those in which they don't, namely where the crown's action is derivative and where it is otherwise, where the crown takes advantage of section 37 of the Federal Court Act and where it does not, where the provincial statute bars a cause of action and where it simply affects a cause of action which has already arisen. These differences are not supportable on any general theory of the appropriate limits of governmental or intergovernmental immunity.

The differences could be effectively eliminated by federal legislation equating the position of the federal crown with that of a subject in proceedings by the crown in tort with sufficient precision to avoid either or both forms of immunity. In Australia section 64 of the Judiciary Act may be thought to do just that but, as indicated earlier, that section requires amendment if it is to be absolutely clear that it has this effect. The subjection of the federal crown to the general statute law, when suing in tort, is supportable by many of the same considerations that sustain the case for a similar subjection when the federal crown is sued in tort. For like reasons, when a state or province sues in tort it too should be subject to any legislation in point. But, as in the case of the legislative reform that was recommended to assure the application of any pertinent statutes in tort proceedings against the crown, the need for change in relation to the particular kind of crown proceeding under review would be substantially lessened in the event that governmental immunity were abolished generally.

Provincial statutes will, of course, apply under the existing régime to the benefit of the federal crown in tort proceedings which it may bring against a subject for that situation is not controlled by governmental or intergovernmental immunity.[187] Thus the crown has been able to take advantage of provincial apportionment of liability legislation so that its claim is not liable to be dismissed, as at common law, on a finding of contributory negligence.[188]

---

187 See, for example, *R* v *Richardson & Adams*, [1948] 2 D.L.R. 305 (S.C.C.), and *Algoma Central & Hudson Bay Ry* v *Man. Pool Elevators Ltd*, [1964] Ex. C.R. 505, aff'd without reference to this point at [1966] S.C.R. 359.

188 *Toronto Transport Comm'n* v *The King*, [1949] 3 D.L.R. 161 (S.C.C.); *R* v *Lightheart*, [1952] Ex. C.R. 12; *Gartland Steamship Co.* v *The Queen* (1960), 22 D.L.R. 385 (S.C.C.); *Fraser River Harbour Comm'n* v *The 'Hiro Maru,'* [1974] 1 F.C. 490.

4

Statutes affecting the Criminal and Contractual Liability of the Crown

CROWN LIABILITY FOR STATUTORY OFFENCES

One advantage which the crown might assert in a criminal prosecution, equally for a statutory as for a common law offence, is that it is inherently incapable of committing any offence. After all, a maxim of respectable antiquity has it that the king can do no wrong.[1] But the weight of authority is against the attribution of such absolute perfection to the sovereign.[2] The contemporary position is that the crown may indeed be held criminally responsible and subjected to those penalties which can be suitably imposed against it.

This is not to dismiss as irrelevant all consideration of the historical position of the crown under the criminal law in the determination of whether a statute creating an offence in fact binds the crown. The presumption that the crown is not bound by such a statute has been supported or reinforced by reference to the traditional absence of any court with authority to try the sovereign, the more modern version of the sense of the phrase, 'the king can do no wrong.'[3] This suggests that the presumption that the crown is not bound by legislation may be stronger in the case of a criminal statute, because of the existence of an extra factor to sustain it, than in the case of a non-criminal statute. In other words the inclusion of the crown may have to be more explicit in the former case if the crown is to be bound. This is not particularly remarkable if it means simply that a nec-

---

1 See *Blackstone's Commentaries* (1st ed 1769) vol. 4, at 254ff.
2 *Cain* v *Doyle* (1946), 72 C.L.R. 409, and *C.B.C.* v *A.G. of Ont.* (1959), 16 D.L.R. (2d) 609 (S.C.C.). And see the discussion of these cases, in this aspect, in Hogg *Liability of the Crown* (1971), at 176–9.
3 See *Cain* v *Doyle* (1946), 72 C.L.R. 409, at 424; *C.B.C.* v *A.G. of Ont.* (1959), 16 D.L.R. (2d) 609, at 617. See also *R* v *Marsh, ex p. Walker* (1909), 39 N.B.R. 329, at 335 (N.B.S.C., App. Div.).

essary implication that the crown is to be bound by a statute is less likely to be discovered in a criminal statute than in any other kind of statute. But that hardly explains the result in *Canadian Broadcasting Corporation* v *Attorney General of Ontario*.[4] In that case the CBC, a federal crown agency, was charged with broadcasting on Sunday contrary to the Lord's Day Act. That act makes it an offence for any 'person' to carry on business on Sunday and adopts the definition of 'person' in the Criminal Code which includes, among others, Her Majesty in relation to the acts and things she is capable of doing and owning. The Supreme Court of Canada, by a 4–3 majority, held that the business activities of the crown through its agent, the CBC, were not caught by the act.[5]

The reference to Her Majesty was explained as designed to include the crown as one of those against whom a crime might be committed rather than as one who might be a perpetrator.[6] But the Criminal Code uses the word 'person' indifferently to describe one who is responsible for and one who suffers from proscribed conduct. Therefore if the definition brings in Her Majesty for one purpose it should logically do so for the other. On that basis the statutory definition of the code and, by incorporation, of the Lord's Day Act as well would determine the meaning of the general term 'person' consistently for the various purposes for which it is used. In any case, the definition seems to be particularly concerned with the crown as an actor, rather than simply as a victim, for it draws in Her Majesty only in relation to the acts and things she is capable of doing and owning.[7]

It is difficult to escape the impression that in the Supreme Court's view the presumption that the crown is not bound by a criminal statute is not just a reflection of the rule of construction applying to statutes generally, but is a presumption of a different order, which is substantially more difficult to dislodge. But there is certainly no warrant for such a distinction in the various Interpretation Acts, which embody a rule of construction for all statutes without regard to their subject matter to the effect that the crown is not bound except by express mention.

The judgment of Dixon J in the Australian High Court in *Cain* v *Doyle*[8] also supports a special and particularly strong presumption that the crown is not bound by a statute if of a criminal character. Mr Justice Dixon's analysis of the issue in that case was principally in terms of the appropriateness of the criminal

4 (1959), 16 D.L.R. (2d) 609 (S.C.C.)
5 While a bare majority in the Supreme Court (4–3) upheld the position taken by the CBC the majority of the judges who heard the matter, at the several stages of the litigation, rejected the claim to immunity (7–4).
6 (1959), 16 D.L.R. (2d) 609, at 617 & 623 (S.C.C.)
7 A point that was emphasized by Taschereau J, dissenting, Abbott and Judson JJ concurring; ibid, at 612–13.
8 (1946), 72 C.L.R. 409

process and criminal penalties to the crown rather than in terms of considerations of governmental immunity from statute. His basic approach was that '[t]he principle that the Crown cannot be criminally liable for a supposed wrong ... provides a rule of interpretation which must prevail over anything but the clearest expression of intention.'[9] The question in *Cain* v *Doyle* was whether the manager of a munition factory operated by the Commonwealth government could be convicted of aiding and abetting the Commonwealth in the dismissal of a crown employee in violation of a provision of a federal statute for which the prescribed penalty was a fine. By a 3–2 majority the High Court held that the defendant could not be liable for the offence charged since the Commonwealth itself could not be guilty of the principal offence. The Commonwealth was considered to be immune from liability even though the prohibition was directed to employers generally and appeared in a division of the statute which defined employer as including the crown, 'unless a contrary intention appears.' Of the majority, Dixon J, with whom Rich J concurred, failed to find in the latter definition a sufficiently clear expression of intention to overcome the crown's *prima facie* immunity and Latham CJ held that the Commonwealth was simply incapable of committing any criminal offence. Williams J, dissenting, concluded that the Commonwealth as an employer could be guilty of the offence under the federal statute. Starke J agreed but voted with the majority to sustain the dismissal of the charge on the basis that the defendant was not shown as a factual matter to have been party to the improper dismissal by the Commonwealth.

While the crown seems to have been given a more privileged status in relation to criminal than to other statutes, Dixon J would apparently narrow the privilege to a presumptive immunity from criminal penalties. A statutory proscription might then be enforceable against officers or servants of the crown by mandamus or injunction, might give rise to a tort action for breach of statutory duty[10] and might, conceivably, have the effect of tainting a contract entered into by the crown with illegality and therefore rendering it unenforceable.[11] These consequences would be possible even though as a matter of construction neither the crown nor its officers or servants could be subjected to penalties for breach of the criminal prohibition. There is nothing particularly anomalous in one part of a statute applying to the crown and another not, even absent an explicit differentiation in the statute to this effect. But it does seem odd indeed that a single provision should apply in its directive aspect but not in its penal aspect to the crown.

9 Ibid, at 425
10 Ibid. See also the judgment of Windeyer J, dissenting, in *Downs* v *Williams* (1971), 126 C.L.R. 61, at 77.
11 But see *R* v *Pouliot* (1888), 2 Ex. C.R. 49, and *R* v *Marsh, ex p. Walker* (1909), 39 N.B.R. 329, at 334 (N.B.S.C., App. Div.).

This was a matter which troubled Williams J in dissent. If, for instance, the section of the federal act under consideration had impliedly conferred a civil right of action upon the discharged employee it would be difficult 'to discover in the Act, by which the Crown is expressly bound, an intention that its express duties should not be enforced against the Crown by the remedies expressly prescribed but only by some other remedy lurking in the Act by implication.'[12] Of course legislation making the crown liable in tort might subject it to the latter kind of remedy where the criminal statute or its penal provisions did not of their own force apply to the crown, but that is a different matter which has been dealt with previously.[13]

The distinction suggested by Dixon J between permissible and impermissible applications of a criminal provision against the crown does tend to remove much of the logical difficulty and some of the harshness to subjects of the crown inherent in the creation of a special rule of construction, more favourable to the crown, for criminal statutes. However, the problem with this, in a practical sense, is that sanctions embodied in regulatory statutes, of which we now have a multitude, are often of a hybrid nature possessing both a criminal and a civil aspect. Indeed this was the very situation in *Cain* v *Doyle* for in entering a conviction under the federal act in question the court was authorized to order payment to a dismissed employee of a portion of the fine imposed as well as to make an independent order for compensation. To deny the application of the statute to the crown in its criminal aspect would probably be to deny relief by way of damages to the employee. This would be so because compensation under the act was dependent upon a conviction being entered while any implication of a separate damage action for breach of the statute was likely precluded by the existence in the statute of specific provision for direct financial relief to an employee discharged in violation of the act.[14]

What is open to the most serious criticism, however, is that a penal statute should call for any special consideration at all except in two very limited respects. Such a statute may be less likely to reveal a necessary implication that the crown is bound by it and some penalties such as imprisonment obviously cannot be suitably imposed against the crown. But apart from these factors a penal statute and any other kind of statute should be approached in a similar fashion in ascertaining whether they may have an impact on the crown. A legislature may seek to secure the realization of the objectives of a regulatory scheme with the aid of the devices of civil sanctions, administrative controls, criminal sanctions, or some

12 *Per* Williams J; (1946), 72 C.L.R. 409, at 432
13 Supra, chapter 3
14 See the judgment of Williams J, dissenting, in *Cain* v *Doyle* (1946), 72 C.L.R. 409, at 430–2.

mixture thereof. If criminal sanctions should be the chosen control technique, there seems no reason in principle why the crown should be entitled to a greater immunity than would otherwise be the case.

THE LIABILITY OF SERVANTS AND AGENTS OF THE CROWN FOR STATUTORY OFFENCES

For a servant or agent to come under the shield of the crown it must be established that the application to him of the penal provision in question would adversely affect the performance of a crown function or, to put it another way, would frustrate crown business.[15] This is really just a particular manifestation of the general principle that the crown is only outside the reach of statutes, not purporting to bind it, which in fact would operate to its prejudice.[16]

If an individual is engaged in acting on behalf of the crown regard must be had to the task or responsibility he was performing or exercising on the occasion in which possible criminal liability was incurred. Was he, for example, under orders which if they were to be obeyed would necessitate a breach of the criminal statute? Or if not subject to explicit directions was he carrying out a duty for the crown which he could not perform within the limits of the discretion entrusted to him without abrogating the statute? If so, a claim to immunity can be successfully advanced for the application of the statute to the individual, acting on behalf of the crown, in these instances would result in an interference with the exercise of a crown function.[17] Otherwise there is no basis for governmental immunity, for it is not enough that the crown servant may have been acting in the course of his employment at the time of the alleged violation.[18]

While this may be an adequate description of the position in respect of subordinate officers of the crown, it cannot be exhaustive of the situations in which all crown servants enjoy immunity. Superior officers are bound to have considerable discretion conferred upon them so that particular conduct on their part is unlikely to be authorized by specific orders from above or dictated by any spec-

15 *Wynyard Investments Pty v Commissioner for Rys (N.S.W.)* (1955), 93 C.L.R. 376, at 394 *per* Kitto J, dissenting, and *R v Stradiotto*, [1973] 2 O.R. 375, at 379 (C.A.)
16 See supra, 8–10 and 14–15.
17 *R v Berriman* (1883), 4 O.R. 282, at 289 & 291 (H.C.J., Q.B.D.); *Cooper v Hawkins*, [1904] 2 K.B. 164, especially the judgment of Wills J; *R v Marsh, ex p. Walker* (1909), 39 N.B.R. 329 (N.B.S.C., App. Div.); *Chare v Hart* (1918), 88 L.J.K.B. 833; *R v Le Blanc* (1930), 1 M.P.R. 21, esp. at 28 (N.B.S.C., App. Div.); *R v Rhodes*, [1934] 1 D.L.R. 251 (Ont. S.C.); *R v Fattore*, [1972] 5 W.W.R. 636 (B.C. Prov. Ct); *R v Stradiotto*, [1973] 2 O.R. 375, at 379 (C.A.).
18 *Cooper v Hawkins*, [1904] 2 K.B. 164, at 173 *per* Wills J; *R v McLeod*, [1930] 4 D.L.R. 226 (N.S.S.C. in banco); *R v Stradiotto*, [1973] 2 O.R. 375 (C.A.)

ific prescribed duty. Yet such officials, so long as governmental immunity is not abolished entirely, would seem to deserve the benefit of immunity in the interests of the crown when acting within the limits of their discretion if their subordinate servants are to enjoy immunity when acting pursuant to their orders.[19] But we are then left with the problem of determining at what point in the hierarchy crown servants enjoy immunity as a matter of course and at what point they are limited by the necessity of establishing superior orders or duties which require a departure from the general statute law. That problem has never been faced squarely by the courts.

So far as a crown entity other than an individual is concerned the proper approach would seem to be to look to the powers conferred upon the entity to see if a breach of the criminal statute was a natural consequence of their proper execution.[20] Thus the majority judgments in the CBC case paid heed to the power, indeed the statutory mandate, of the Canadian Broadcasting Corporation to 'carry on a national broadcasting service within Canada' which, with a good deal of inference, was treated as envisaging broadcasting unlimited as to times.[21] Therefore to apply the prohibition of the Lord's Day Act against the CBC would have been to interfere unduly with the powers which it exercised as an agent of Her Majesty.

Persons acting under contract with the crown who are not servants or otherwise agents or agencies of the crown are sometimes in a position to assert immunity from statute on behalf of the crown, that is if the application of a statute to them would prejudice the sovereign.[22] However, the contract with the crown may require, not untypically, that the contractor comply with all applicable statutory regulations. What then is the position of an independent contractor charged with a breach of a statute in the course of performing his agreement with the crown? Is he ever entitled to assert crown immunity in the face of such a contractual term? The conclusion must be that he is, for a consensual arrangement ought not to be capable of altering the proper interpretation to be given to a statute which the rule of governmental immunity dictates.[23]

A question that has frequently arisen in the Canadian courts is whether a servant of the crown, acting in the course of his employment, can be guilty of a

19 See Williams *Crown Proceedings* (1948), at 51–2.
20 The corporate powers of a crown agency can certainly have the converse effect of denying to the corporation, in their exercise, an immunity from statute which might otherwise exist, see *Reid* v *Canadian Farm Loan Bd*, [1937] 4 D.L.R. 248 (Man. K.B.), and *Re Mar-Lise Industries Ltd* (1968), 5 D.L.R. (3d) 487 (Ont. C.A.), which are discussed infra, at 110–11.
21 (1959), 16 D.L.R. (2d) 609, at 618 & 621 (S.C.C.)
22 See supra, at 15.
23 Cf *Ottawa* v *Shore & Horwitz Constr. Co.* (1960), 22 D.L.R. (2d) 247 (Ont. H.C.) (an exclusive power immunity case).

traffic offence. The answer has been in the affirmative when the statutory offence is driving in a careless or unsafe manner,[24] always in the absence of superior orders requiring breach of the statute. But crown servants have been held immune from liability for the offence of driving without a driver's licence since their duties for the crown have required them to drive.[25] Were the charge that a crown servant was driving a vehicle that was unlicensed or in an unsafe condition once again the servant, if directed to drive, would generally enjoy immunity.[26] But he would be subject to the statutory prohibition if he had some discretion in the choice of the particular vehicle he was to use in carrying out his instructions and other available vehicles were in satisfactory order. Likewise he would be liable if he had the opportunity, without infringing his instructions, to remedy the deficiency in the state of the vehicle. There are limits, however, to the kinds of penal sanctions that may be imposed in the event that a crown servant is properly convicted of a motor vehicle offence. A statutory power to order the seizure of a vehicle used in the commission of an offence, for instance, could not be exercised in relation to a crown vehicle for that would constitute an objectionable interference with a crown property interest.[27]

All the traffic cases which have arisen have been in an interjurisdictional context, the issue being the applicability of a provincial highway traffic provision to a servant of the federal crown. The matter has been disposed of on the basis of either governmental or intergovernmental immunity considerations. The most recent case at the appellate level is *R v Stradiotto*[28] in which the Ontario court held that a federal crown servant could be liable for negligent driving under a provincial statute. To so apply the statute, the court held, did not 'affect the rights of Her Majesty' so as to come within the Ontario Interpretation Act's statement of the rule of governmental immunity from statute.[29] The crown right which was to be protected, in these circumstances, was that of commanding acts which would

24 *R v McLeod*, [1930] 4 D.L.R. 226 (N.S.S.C. in banco), and *R v Stradiotto*, [1973] 2 O.R. 375 (C.A.), the latter decision disappr'g *R v McInnes* (1962), 7 C.L.Q. 234 (Ont. Mag. Ct)
25 *R v Anderson*, [1930] 2 W.W.R. 595 (Man. C.A.), and *R v Rhodes*, [1934] 1 D.L.R. 251 (Ont. S.C.). And see *Johnson v Maryland* (1920), 254 U.S. 51.
26 *R v Fattore*, [1972] 5 W.W.R. 636 (B.C. Prov. Ct)
27 Consider *R v Justices of Kent* (1889), 24 Q.B.D. 181, at 185 *per* Mathew J; *R v L'Heureux* (1913), 14 D.L.R. 604 (Exch.); *G. Martinello & Co. v McCormick* (1919), 50 D.L.R. 799 (S.C.C.).
28 [1973] 2 O.R. 375 (C.A.)
29 The failure of the court to consider the possibility of any intergovernmental immunity saving the federal crown servant from the provincial statute is explicable if that immunity only protects the federal crown in the exercise of its prerogatives, see supra, at 34–40. The only prerogative that was potentially available here, that of governmental immunity, was of course held inapplicable by the court.

be in breach of the provincial statute. And to hold the accused servant liable did not interfere with that right. Had the servant been acting under orders which effectively required him to breach the statute then, admittedly, he could not have been held accountable for that would, indeed, amount to an interference with 'the rights of Her Majesty' in the pertinent sense. The scope of crown immunity is, on this analysis, rather limited when a penal statute is sought to be applied against a crown servant.

In the 1925 Australian case of *Pirrie* v *McFarlane*[30] a Commonwealth servant, acting in the course of his military duties, was held to be subject to a state driver's licence requirement. That result would seem, on first impression, to be out of line with Canadian authority. But the High Court simply decided, in that case, that the state legislation bound the Commonwealth so that there was no possibility of immunity on the ground that the crown servant was obliged to drive in order to comply with the directions of his commanding officer. In any case, the two possible constructional reasons that are suggested for the result, though not fully discussed, are not supportable in light of subsequent judicial opinion. These alternative possibilities, which are not entirely consistent, emerge from the various majority judgments; either the state legislation applied to the crown servant because, by its terms, it bound persons in the public service of the crown though no specific mention was made of the Commonwealth crown service,[31] or because the general language of the state prohibition was sufficient to comprehend Commonwealth servants, governmental immunity not operating in favour of other than the legislating government.[32] However, subsequent authority indicates, firstly, that a reference to the crown as bound by a state statute means *prima facie* the crown in right of the state[33] (and there seem to be no factors that might have overcome that presumption in *Pirrie*). Secondly, it is now established that governmental immunity does in fact have a wider scope of operation and is capable of favouring the Commonwealth in the face of state legislation.[34] Therefore, *Pirrie* v *McFarlane* is not now supportable except so far as, having rejected any governmental immunity, it decided against the central arguments for immunity that were advanced. The court did clearly and properly dismiss the principal claim that the Commonwealth servant had the benefit of an implied constitutional

---

30 (1925), 36 C.L.R. 170
31 This may have been the view of Starke J, see ibid, at 228, Knox CJ agreeing with Starke J on the issue of the proper construction of the state statute.
32 Higgins J took this position, see ibid, at 218. The two remaining judges, Isaacs & Rich JJ, dissented.
33 See supra, at 31–2.
34 See supra, at 25–9.

immunity and that the state act, if applied to him, would raise a conflict with Commonwealth defence legislation.[35]

In summary, the servants and agents of the crown are only entitled to the benefit of governmental immunity from a statutory prohibition if the sovereign would otherwise be prejudiced. And the sovereign will be so affected only if the statute interferes directly with the performance and fulfilment of the specific duties and orders imposed by a superior officer or by statute upon the servant or agent. The right of the crown which is secured in this situation is simply the right to direct conduct which would be in breach of the statute. The intergovernmental immunity of federal crown servants and agents from provincial penal legislation would seem in practice to be no more extensive than their governmental immunity.

THE EFFECT OF STATUTES UPON THE CONTRACTUAL LIABILITY OF THE CROWN

To the extent that it concerned contract actions the original federal crown proceedings legislation did not introduce a new kind of crown liability as it did in respect of tort.[36] Previously the crown had been amenable to contract claims through the vehicle of the petition of right.[37] The crown proceedings provisions served principally to confer jurisdiction on certain named courts to entertain contract actions against the crown and to provide a choice of law rule for those courts.

Because of this difference in the function of the legislation in respect of contract and tort claims Anglin J, Davies J concurring, concluded in *Gauthier* v *The King*[38] that the Exchequer Court Act of Canada did not subject the crown, if sued in contract, to the existing provincial law as between subject and subject as it would if the crown were sued in negligence. Rather in this class of case the crown was governed only by the general provincial law under which the federal crown enjoyed a position in relation to legislation superior to that of the subject. The act, he said, in simply recognizing an existing liability in contract, provided

35 The decision also remains an authority on the validity and operation of s 40A of the Judiciary Act under which causes involving questions concerning the limits *inter se* of the constitutional powers of the various federal units are to be removed to the High Court.

36 See *Gauthier* v *The King* (1918), 40 D.L.R. 353, at 363 (S.C.C.). And cf *Daly* v *Vict.* (1920), 28 C.L.R. 395.

37 *Thomas* v *The Queen* (1874), L.R. 10 Q.B. 31; *Windsor & Annapolis Ry* v *The Queen & the Western Co'ys Ry* (1886), 11 App. Cas. 607 (P.C.)

38 (1918), 40 D.L.R. 353 (S.C.C.). Fitzpatrick CJ and Idington J wrote separate judgments and Duff J simply agreed in the result reached by the other members of the court. This decision is also considered at some length supra, at 34ff.

'no ground for holding that the Crown thereby renounced whatever prerogative privileges it had theretofore enjoyed.'[39] Consequently the contractual liability of the federal crown was determinable in accordance with the common law except so far as modified by statute that was binding upon the crown in right of the dominion. Therefore, on this view, when contract claims are brought against the federal crown, governmental and intergovernmental immunity will operate to their full extent in favour of the crown. No modification is necessitated by federal crown proceedings provisions, which have not been significantly changed in relation to the matter of contractual liability since the date of the *Gauthier* case.

A different position on this point seems to have been taken by Chief Justice Sir Charles Fitzpatrick who, while agreeing in the main with Anglin J, delivered a separate opinion in *Gauthier*. He suggested that some provincial statutes would in fact bind the federal crown in contract matters, that is those in force in the province when the crown became liable in contract.[40] In *Bank of Nova Scotia* v *The Queen*[41] Thorson P of the Exchequer Court took the relevant date to be 1876,[42] at which time the first generally applicable Petition of Right Act[43] embodying a procedure for suing the crown in right of the dominion came into effect. Had 1876, or indeed any point in time after 1859, been the date which the Chief Justice had in mind in *Gauthier* he would have been led to dissent in that case rather than to join the majority as he did, for the provincial statute held inapplicable there had been, in effect, the law of Ontario since the latter date.[44] It is difficult, however, to pinpoint any particular earlier date as satisfying the criterion proposed by the Chief Justice. But whatever the cut-off point, colonial statutes which may be applicable, on this theory, must be so few in number as not to affect significantly the contractual liability of the federal crown.

In the *Bank of Nova Scotia* case the court was able to decide in favour of the subject in a contract proceeding against the federal crown by applying a provincial statute, in error it has been suggested, which came into force in 1875. But the court would have preferred to come to the same result by treating the applicable law as that in force between subjects in the relevant province at the time the agreement was entered into and the cause of action arose.[45] That law included a re-enactment of the 1875 statute. This is even more clearly inconsistent with au-

39 Ibid, at 363
40 Ibid, at 354, 355 & 356–7
41 (1961), 27 D.L.R. (2d) 120 (Exch.)
42 Ibid, at 147
43 S.C. 1876, c 27
44 See the judgment of Anglin J in *Gauthier* (1918), 40 D.L.R. 353, at 364.
45 (1961), 27 D.L.R. (2d) 120, at 149–51 (Exch.), apparently foll'd in *Crawford's Ltd* v *Wanhil Line Constr. Co.* (1970), 10 D.L.R. (3d) 497 (Sask. C.A.)

thority, however, in particular the *Gauthier* case and various other decisions in Exchequer Court matters declining to apply provincial statutes against the federal crown that were in existence when the cause of action arose.[46]

In Australia section 64 of the Judiciary Act has application to proceedings against the Commonwealth in contract as well as in tort. That section, it will be remembered, equates so far as possible the rights of parties in proceedings involving the crown that are taken in the federal jurisdiction to those in a suit between subjects.[47] This provision would seem to be capable of picking up all those state statutes which would be relevant in a contract action against a subject and applying them in a similar action against the crown. But, as has been seen in the previous chapter, there is some authority which gives cause to doubt the capacity of section 64 to avoid the operation of intergovernmental immunity, which would otherwise give some protection to the Commonwealth from the effect of state legislation.

There is, of course, the possibility that state or provincial statutes affecting contractual arrangements might apply against the federal crown, in some situations at least, independently of the operation of crown proceedings legislation. It has been maintained, in an earlier chapter, that the intergovernmental immunity of the federal authority is properly limited to securing crown prerogatives from the prejudicial effect of state or provincial statutes.[48] Even so, in the absence of any other prerogative, the federal crown can always rely upon its governmental immunity as entitling it to stand outside state or provincial legislation which does not bind the federal crown expressly or by necessary implication. But because of the limitations on the scope of governmental immunity there are very real opportunities for state or provincial legislation reaching the federal authority. For instance special inclusion of the federal crown in the local legislation will avoid immunity. And there are other circumstances as well in which federal governmental activity can be controlled by state or provincial statutes as we have seen in considering the liability of federal crown servants for statutory offences. When it comes to the contractual liability of the federal crown some state or provincial statutes have also been given scope for operation though others have not. The difficulty that will be evident is in discerning the appropriate criteria for making the distinction between those statutes which apply and those which do not.

The *Gauthier* case concerned an agreement, to which the dominion government was a party, that provided for the settlement by arbitration of the purchase

46 For example, *Powell* v *The King* (1905), 9 Ex. C.R. 364; *C.N.R.* v *St John Motor Line Ltd*, [1930] 3 D.L.R. 732 (S.C.C.); *Palmer* v *The King*, [1952] 1 D.L.R. 259 (Exch.)
47 The section is considered at length supra, at 72–7, and is set out in full at 72.
48 See supra, at 38–40.

price to be paid for certain fishing rights. The arbitration proceeded and an award was made though, by that time, the government had revoked the authority of the arbitrators. The result, at common law, would have been that the award was unenforceable since a submission to arbitration was always revocable before the award though the party withdrawing was liable in damages for breach of contract. This position was changed in the province of Ontario by the Arbitration Act, which provided that a submission to arbitration was to have the same effect as a rule of a provincial court. As such it was only revocable by order of that court. The dominion claimed that it was not bound by this provision when it came to defend a proceeding by the licensee of the fishing rights to enforce the arbitral award. [49]

A short answer to the suppliant's petition might have been that the provincial statute could not operate, in the circumstances, consistently with the conferral of exclusive jurisdiction on the Exchequer Court in claims arising out of dominion government contracts.[50] The provincial act would have subjected the contracting parties in important respects to the jurisdiction of another court, the Supreme Court of Ontario, in that its authorization was required to lawfully revoke a submission to arbitration. Indeed this point was taken by Anglin J in the course of his opinion as a reason for giving a narrow reading to the Arbitration Act so as not to affect the dominion government.[51] He did not rest his judgment on the point, however. The principal reason given by the Supreme Court for treating the Arbitration Act as not embracing the federal crown, when a party to an arbitration agreement, was that this would be to give it an operation that would be *ultra vires*. The dominion was thought to enjoy an intergovernmental immunity, so far as its 'privileges' were concerned, from provincial legislation.[52]

This decision appears to contrast sharply with that of the Privy Council in the later case of *Dominion Building Corporation* v *The King.*[53] A good deal of intellectual effort has been expended in attempting to reconcile this case with the *Gauthier* decision without any very satisfactory results.[54] The *Dominion*

49 Though it could, of course, have claimed the benefit of a provincial statute concerning arbitral agreements, see *R* v *McCarthy* (1919), 46 D.L.R. 456, at 458 (Exch.), decision aff'd by the Supreme Court, see Morse Ex. Ct Dig., at 15.
50 Exchequer Court Act, S.C. 1887, s 19
51 (1918), 40 D.L.R. 353, at 365 (S.C.C.)
52 Ibid, esp. at 365
53 [1933] A.C. 533 (P.C.). This decision is also considered supra, at 5.
54 See Mundell, 'Remedies against the Crown' in Law Society of Upper Canada *Special Lectures 1961, Remedies*, 149, at 155; *R* v *Murray*, [1965] 2 Ex. C.R. 663, at 675–8, decision aff'd at (1967), 60 D.L.R. (2d) 647 (S.C.C.); Garant, 'Contribution à l'Etude du Statut Juridique de l'Administration Gouvernmentale' (1972), 50 *Can. Bar Rev.* 50, at 81–2. See also *Bank of N.S.* v *The Queen* (1961), 27 D.L.R. (2d) 120, at 151–2

Building case arose out of a reference to the Exchequer Court[55] of a claim against the crown for damages for breach of a contract for the sale of land. The contract did not expressly provide that time was of the essence and a number of extensions had in fact been granted to the appellant corporation by the crown. At common law, time was deemed of the essence of a contract absent an expression of a contrary intention. But in equity time was not treated as of the essence unless the parties had so stated or it was a necessary implication of their agreement. An Ontario statute extended the equitable rule to matters arising in all courts exercising jurisdiction in law as well as in equity. The point was not taken, as it might have been, that the statutory change was directed to courts, which arguably meant provincial courts. If that position were accepted, then, as a matter of construction, the act could have no application in a matter such as this which was before a federal tribunal. In fact the crown simply claimed immunity from this provision and insisted that time must be regarded as of the essence of the contract in question pursuant to the common law rule. Therefore the appellant, being in default under the agreement because of its delay, could have no claim against the crown.

The Judicial Committee rejected this argument and in so doing dealt with the question, without reference to *Gauthier*, as if it were one involving the reach of governmental immunity from statute. The Board attached no special consequence to the interjurisdictional guise in which the immunity issue arose.[56] This was not, Lord Tomlin said, a situation in which 'the rights of [Her] Majesty' were affected by a statute within the meaning of the rule of construction concerning the effect of statutes upon the crown in the Ontario Interpretation Act. He read that phrase narrowly as referring to the accrued rights of Her Majesty but not rights which might accrue to Her Majesty under future contracts but for the change in the law represented by the statute in question.[57] This would seem to indicate that the only legislation affecting contracts from which there is governmental immunity, at least in its statutory form, is that which is subsequent to an outstanding agreement under which the crown has secured certain rights and which affects those rights.[58]

If the test in *Dominion Building* had been applied in *Gauthier* the result

(Exch.), and Gibson, 'Interjurisdictional Immunities in Canadian Federalism' (1969), 47 *Can. Bar Rev.* 40, at 51–2.

55 Pursuant to the Exchequer Court Act, R.S.C. 1906, c 140, s 38
56 For an explanation of this approach see supra, at 39–40.
57 [1933] A.C. 533, at 549 (P.C.). This definition was quoted and appl'd in *Bank of N.S.* v *The Queen* (1961), 27 D.L.R. (2d) 120, at 154 (Exch.), and *R* v *Board of Transport Comm'rs* (1967), 65 D.L.R. (2d) 425, at 429–30 (S.C.C.).
58 But compare *R* v *Pouliot* (1888), 2 Ex. C.R. 49.

would have been different, for the provincial Arbitration Act was not sought to be applied in a way that would affect the accrued rights of the crown. Accordingly the act ought to have been controlling on the *Dominion Building* approach though of course it was denied any role by the Supreme Court. Conversely, the latter case would have been decided the other way had the governmental immunity of the dominion from provincial legislation been viewed, as *Gauthier* would seem to indicate, as a privilege which the province could not withdraw. The decisions, taken at face value, cannot therefore be satisfactorily reconciled. If they are to co-exist it must be by attributing narrower explanations to one or both of the two results. That possibility will be explored after an examination of Australian authority.

In *Commonwealth* v *Bogle*[59] the Commonwealth and Commonwealth Hostels Ltd sued for the price of board and lodging supplied by the plaintiffs in a hostel built on land leased by the government and designed to house migrant families. Commonwealth Hostels had given notice of a general rent increase to the defendant, with whom it had an agreement for the provision of accommodation.[60] After making some payments at the new rent the defendant refused to meet the increment and relied upon a price order under the Prices Regulation Act of the state of Victoria as rendering the increase illegal. The plaintiffs, suing on the basis of an implied contract to pay at the increased rate, claimed immunity from this kind of statutory regulation. The majority of the High Court held the proper plaintiff to be Commonwealth Hostels, an entity which, it was concluded, could not claim to share in the enjoyment of crown immunity.[61] Therefore the state act and order applied according to their plain terms. But Fullagar J, expressing views concurred in by the majority, said that were the Commonwealth the proper plaintiff it would not be bound by the Victorian act. In so observing he generalized in these words; ' ... the State Parliament has no power over the Commonwealth.'[62] That remark echoes the sentiment of the *Gauthier* case in Canada and foreshadows the majority judgment in *Commonwealth* v *Cigamatic Pty*.[63] His Honour added, in language more neatly tailored to the case at hand, 'I should think it impossible to hold that the Parliament of Victoria could lawfully prescribe the uses which might be made by the Commonwealth of its own property,

---

59 (1953), 89 C.L.R. 229. This decision is also considered supra, at 37.
60 There were other defendants, in largely similar situations, in two companion cases which were disposed of together with and in a like fashion to *Bogle*.
61 The decision must be taken to have impliedly overruled *Marshall* v *Commonwealth Hostels Ltd*, [1953] V.L.R. 503, in so far as it held that Commonwealth Hostels was immune from the Victorian Prices Regulation Act.
62 (1953), 89 C.L.R. 229, at 259
63 (1962), 108 C.L.R. 372. This case is discussed supra, at 36, and infra, at 114–15.

the terms upon which the property might be let to tenants, or the terms upon which the Commonwealth might provide accommodation for immigrants introduced into Australia.'[64] Implicit in this statement is a possible basis for an exclusive power immunity. The Commonwealth Parliament has exclusive jurisdiction with respect to 'places acquired by the Commonwealth for public purposes' under section 52(i) of the constitution. In *Bogle* the land on which the hostel was built was held under lease by the government and, consequently, could be regarded as a place acquired by the Commonwealth. The application of the Victorian legislation would then be precluded as inconsistent with the exclusive nature of the federal power. But that point was not specifically taken and there has, to date, been no judicial recognition that the subsection of the constitution which has been cited extends to land obtained by the Commonwealth simply on a leasehold arrangement.[65]

By way of qualification to the general principle of immunity Fullagar J stated in *Bogle* that the Commonwealth may become 'affected by' state law.[66] He instanced a sale of goods act of a state as the appropriate source of 'the terms and effect' of a contract entered into by the Commonwealth in that state.[67] This qualification is a reflection of other, earlier *obiter* remarks of Dixon J,[68] the sense of which emerges again in *dicta* from the same source subsequent to *Bogle*.[69]

In Australia, as in Canada, there is a difficult problem of reconciliation which has exercised several commentators.[70] It arises in that jurisdiction from the statement in *Bogle* of a principle and of a qualification upon it, both of which have received some subsequent support in the leading case of *Commonwealth v Cigamatic Pty*.[71]

When faced with a nice question of distinction it is wise to return to basic principles. It has been suggested that the existence of a form of governmental immunity is often the underlying basis for recognizing an intergovernmental immunity since that is frequently the only prerogative which the federal crown is able

64 (1953), 89 C.L.R. 229, at 260
65 See Howard *Australian Federal Constitutional Law* (2d ed 1972), at 487.
66 (1953), 89 C.L.R. 229, at 260
67 Ibid
68 In *Federal Comm'r of Taxation v Official Liquidator of E.O. Farley Ltd* (1940), 63 C.L.R. 278, at 308, and *Re Richard Foreman & Sons Pty; Uther v Federal Comm'r of Taxation* (1947), 74 C.L.R. 508, at 528
69 In *Commonwealth v Cigamatic Pty* (1962), 108 C.L.R. 372, at 378
70 See Zines, 'Sir Owen Dixon's Theory of Federalism' (1965), 1 *F.L.R.* 221, at 236–41; Howard *Australian Federal Constitutional Law* (2d ed 1972), at 108–17; Evans, 'Rethinking Commonwealth Immunity' (1972), 8 *M.U.L.R.* 521, at 532–8; Fajgenbaum & Hanks *Australian Constitutional Law* (1972), at 555–60.
71 (1962), 108 C.L.R. 372, at 377–8

to rely on in the face of state or provincial statutes. The constitutional immunity of the federal crown is, as suggested earlier, to be limited preferably to protecting it in the exercise of its prerogatives.[72]

The theory of governmental immunity is that the crown should not be *prejudiced* in its *rights* by the application to it of legislation which does not specially include the sovereign.[73] It has been noted in a previous section of this chapter that crown servants are often subject to prohibitory statutes on the basis that the crown's rights are not prejudiced by the imposition of liability upon the servant. But it was also observed that a crown servant is free of any such statute which does not purport to bind the crown if he is acting pursuant to orders or a specific duty which can only be complied with effectively by violating the statute. In the latter situation the statute comes into direct conflict with the servant's mandate from the crown and to apply it would be to prejudice the crown. But otherwise the servant is personally accountable for offences committed in the course of his service. Though the statute would then be applied against an instrumentality of the crown, the crown's right to order the servant to act in breach of the statute remains unimpaired. It is only the latter right which is protected by the prerogative rule. These principles have been applied recently in an interjurisdictional context by the Ontario Court of Appeal, in *R* v *Stradiotto*,[74] in determining the applicability of a provincial statute to a federal crown servant.

By analogy, in the contract situation it can be argued that it is the federal executive's right to agree to contractual terms which contradict a state or provincial statute which should be protected by the immunity rule. If an express term of a government contract, like an explicit direction of the federal crown, cannot be reconciled with a state or provincial statute then, but only then, governmental immunity should result whenever the federal crown is not specially included by the local statute. Intergovernmental immunity would also pertain on the view we have taken as to the interrelationship between the prerogative and the constitutional principle.[75] This approach leaves considerable room for the application of the statutory contract law of a state or province, for the rights of the federal crown will not normally be prejudiced by it in the relevant sense.

Some support for this kind of distinction in the circumstances in which provincial laws can apply against the federal crown is to be found in *Spooner Oils Ltd* v *Turner Valley Gas Conservation Board*.[76] In deciding that a provincial gas conservation statute could not interfere with the rights, originating in federal

72 See supra, at 38–40.
73 See supra, chapter 1.
74 [1973] 2 O.R. 375 (C.A.)
75 See supra, at 34–40.
76 [1933] 4 D.L.R. 545 (S.C.C.)

regulations, of lessees of dominion public lands the Supreme Court said, *per* Duff CJ:

Where the regulations under which Dominion lands are leased, *or the stipulations of such leases*, contain provisions dealing with the very subject matter of the provincial legislation, then it is quite obvious that these latter must prevail in the case of conflict.[77] [emphasis added]

The implication is that, otherwise, provincial legislation would apply in relation to leasehold contracts with the federal crown.

There are, of course, limits to those matters which may be the subject of express agreement under the general law of contract. For example, the parties to an agreement could not give legal effect by any force of words to an arrangement under which no consideration passed or which was illegal. The rules about the effect of any such arrangement would apply to federal crown contracts as part of the common law of contract of the appropriate state or province. If these or other essential requirements of a valid contract took statutory form then the crown would probably be equally precluded from suing on an agreement which did not satisfy the conditions. The theory would be that the federal crown must take the cause of action as it finds it in the sense that a contract according to state or provincial law must first exist. But there may be other legal requirements to a successful claim in contract in a particular case which are not fundamental to the existence of a valid underlying agreement. If they could not, by their very nature, be varied by the express agreement of the parties then it may be that such requirements, if introduced by state or provincial statute, would not affect the federal crown. Thus a state or provincial Statute of Frauds[78] or Limitations Act,[79] dealing with the enforceability rather than the validity of agreements, might not apply against the federal crown in an action by it in contract. The crown, of course, has no opportunity in either of those situations of creating an 'immunity,' as circumstances might dictate, by contracting on terms inconsistent with, and hence as it were overriding, the statute.

Applying the above reasoning to the *Bogle* case, the state prices regulation

---

77 Ibid, at 560–1. The decision against the applicability of the provincial statute was also put on the basis of an exclusive power immunity, the lands subject to lease being dominion public property (see s 91(1A) of the BNA Act). And see also *Bank of N.S.* v *The Queen* (1961), 27 D.L.R. (2d) 120, at 151 (Exch.).

78 But cf *R* v *Hay*, [1924] V.L.R. 97, a decision which was based, however, on the 'statute for the public good' exception to the rule of Crown immunity from statute, which has since been discredited, see supra, at 4.

79 Consider *William Crosby & Co.* v *Commonwealth* (1963), 109 C.L.R. 490, at 494.

statute could be said to be incompetent to affect the contractual liability of the tenants of the Commonwealth to pay a given amount of rent, for that matter was the subject of an express stipulation by the Commonwealth. On the other hand, the proposition that state laws can affect the Commonwealth in matters of contract is supportable on the basis that the Commonwealth would not be prejudiced by such laws in the event that there were no inconsistency between the express terms of a contract and state legislation. At the same time the Commonwealth would be uninhibited in its right to contract on terms giving rise to a direct conflict with a different outcome.[80] The particular example offered of subjection to state statute law, that is in relation to the terms and effect of a sale of goods contract, fits this distinction admirably. The statutory provisions in that respect generally control the meaning and import of such a contract only in the absence of express agreement otherwise.[81] Thus they do not normally preclude effect being given to the express terms of a contract.

Turning to the Canadian cases, in *Dominion Building* the provincial legislation did not interfere with the right of the dominion to contract, in express terms, that time was of the essence of an agreement nor did it conflict with any provision to this effect in the agreement under review. Thus there was no impairment of the freedom of contract of the federal government[82] and the provincial legislation could be considered applicable on that basis.[83] The provincial statute in *Gauthier* also did not conflict with the express terms of the agreement to which the federal crown was a party in that case and one might be led to conclude that it too would bind the dominion. But the Supreme Court held to the contrary. However, the rule established by the statute under review was not one

---

80 A similar explanation of *Bogle* is proposed by Howard, see his *Australian Federal Constitutional Law* (2d ed 1972), at 115–16. He takes the view, however, that the provisions of the Judiciary Act control the application of state laws in the *Bogle* situation and the explanation of the *obiter* remarks in the latter case are given within the framework of the operation of that act.

81 Consider ss 13–31 of the Goods Act 1928, of Victoria, which was the specific statute referred to by Fullagar J in *Bogle* (1953), 89 C.L.R. 229, at 260.

82 This was also true of the application of the Quebec Civil Code against the federal crown in *Arthur Kofman & Associates* v *The Queen*, [1975] F.C. 557. In *Palmer* v *The King*, [1952] 1 D.L.R. 259 (Exch.), in which provincial statute law was held not to apply against the federal crown, there would have been an impairment of the crown's freedom of contract.

83 This analysis, however, does not appear to fit the case of *R* v *Board of Transport Comm'rs* (1967), 65 D.L.R. (2d) 425 (S.C.C.), which appl'd *Dominion Building*. But in the former case the court seems to have been of the view that the crown was subject to the legislation in question because it had taken advantage of it (see 430), which of course is a basis for avoiding the operation of governmental immunity altogether (see supra, at 10–14).

that could be the subject of express agreement according to the common law, for contracting parties could not make the authority of an arbitrator irrevocable.[84] *Gauthier* might then be explained as an instance in which the federal crown must be treated as immune from a provincial statute because the crown could have no opportunity to contract on terms inconsistent with the statutory restriction and so secure an *ad hoc* 'immunity' as it were.

Admittedly this rationalization of the Australian and Canadian jurisprudence has its shortcomings. And it has little to support it in the actual reasoning of the decisions under discussion though it fits the judicial conclusions reasonably well. But it is consistent with fundamental immunity principles as evidenced by analagous distinctions made in Canadian decisions dealing with the application of provincial penal statutes to the federal crown.

For the long term one method of resolving the existing uncertainty in this area of crown liability might be by federal legislation equating the position of the federal crown in proceedings in contract, which are brought by or against it, to that of a subject. The end would be to make any pertinent state or provincial as well as federal statutes applicable. At present it is not absolutely certain that section 64 of the Australian Judiciary Act has that effect.[85] And there is no general Canadian legislation which might be taken to apply provincial or federal statutes in this context, except possibly provincial statutes of a very early pre-confederation origin, in proceedings against the federal crown.

But the case that was made for this kind of approach in relation to tort liability questions[86] does not stand up when it comes to the matter of contractual liability. In the former context it made sense to recommend the application of state or provincial statutes through the vehicle of crown proceedings legislation. The rights of a claimant in tort are determinable after harm has been occasioned through litigation and, if not, at least against the backdrop of that possibility. But the law governing contractual arrangements, which are the product of planned activity, ought logically to speak at the time such arrangements are entered into. The law should presumably be in contemplation then rather than at the time there has been a breakdown in the agreement and litigation has ensued. Moreover in a breach of contract situation an action at law is not the only remedial avenue open to the aggrieved party. He may simply choose to treat a breach by the other party, if sufficiently substantial, as discharging the contract and relieving him of any further obligations thereunder.

It would be preferable, therefore, to assimilate the position of the crown to

84 See the *Gauthier* case (1918), 40 D.L.R. 353, at 364 (S.C.C.).
85 See supra, at 69–77.
86 See supra, at 77–9.

that of a subject for the purposes of contractual liability in some other manner than by crown proceedings legislation. The statutory abolition of governmental immunity would go some distance towards reducing the discrepancies between the position of the crown and the subject in this area of the law as well as in others. But if that step is not taken, or to the extent that it does not eliminate intergovernmental immunity, then the legislature ought to address the particular question of the necessity of the crown enjoying any special position as a party to an agreement with one of its subjects. It is easy to conceive of some peculiar requirements that might be insisted upon in relation to government contracts, for example a prerequisite of public competition or tendering or the adherence by a party contracting with the crown to certain minimum standards of commercial behaviour that might not otherwise apply of their own force. But any such requirements may be introduced by special legislation or indeed, given the powerful bargaining position of governmental authorities, simply through administrative practice. There is no consequent need for a general immunity of the crown from statute law affecting contractual rights and liabilities. Any such immunity is enjoyed at the expense of the interests of subjects of the crown and indeed falls unevenly on that class of persons.

5

The Effect of Statutes
upon the Crown as Creditor

By virtue of a royal prerogative the crown is entitled to be accorded priority in respect of its debts or claims in competition with the debts or claims of a subject when they are of equal degree.[1] This rule of preference relates to claims *in personam* and not *in rem*, with the result that it does not resolve the respective rights of secured creditors, one of which is the crown.[2] Neither does it determine which of two creditors, one being the crown, should be given first place if one claim is secured and the other is unsecured, for there is no true competition in this case, the secured property being withdrawn from the estate of the debtor which is available for the satisfaction of his general debts.[3] Legislation may, of course, govern the position of either or both of the classes of secured and unsecured creditors as to priority or otherwise. Its capacity thus to affect the crown is the central subject of this chapter.

STATUTES AFFECTING THE SECURITY OF CREDITORS

A statute may give security to, or enable the taking of security by, a creditor. This effectively gives a person holding such security a superior position, which he might not otherwise enjoy, over the crown where the latter is an unsecured creditor.[4] The rights of the crown may be said to be affected by this kind of legisla-

---

1 *Re Henley & Co.* (1878), 9 Ch.D. 469 (C.A.); *R* v *Bank of N.S.* (1885), 11 S.C.R. 1; *N.S.W. Taxation Comm'rs* v *Palmer*, [1907] A.C. 179 (P.C.); *A.G. of N.S.W.* v *Curator of Intestate Estates*, [1907] A.C. 519 (P.C.)
2 *Montreal Trust Co.* v *The King*, [1924] 1 D.L.R. 1030, at 1031 (B.C.C.A.). But see *A.G. of Can.* v *Canadian Imperial Bank of Commerce* (1973), 41 D.L.R. (3d) 749 (Alta S.C.).
3 See *Re United Pacific Transport Pty*, [1968] Qd R. 517, at 521.
4 Cf *Re Millingen's Ltd*, [1934] S.A.S.R. 72; *Re Blue Bird Gold Mines* (1942), 44 W.A.L.R. 85

tion but not sufficiently directly to bring into play the rule of governmental immunity. The crown need not be named in such a statute for the security holder to realize an advantage, to the extent of his security, over all the unsecured creditors, the crown not excepted. This conclusion finds support in *Re John Wiper Ltd*,[5] in which the South Australian Supreme Court held that a state statute is competent to create a lien in a subject so as to give priority over the Commonwealth as an unsecured creditor. The immunity enjoyed by the federal crown, of an intergovernmental variety in that case, was not thought to prevent the statutory security from operating to give the subject priority in the ordinary course over the crown.

The crown as a secured creditor is unaffected, however, by a statutory prescription of priorities as between securities, or as between securities and other competing interests, if the legislation does not purport to bind the crown expressly or by necessary implication.[6] It does not follow that the crown is entitled to have its security preferred over the competing interests of the subject. The situation is quite unlike that which prevails in the event that a statute ranking the claims of unsecured creditors does not bind the crown. In that case a crown prerogative subsists unimpaired, giving a preference to the crown over subjects with claims of equal degree. But, as has already been noticed, there is no comparable prerogative priority when it comes to secured claims. Consequently, the ranking of securities and other property interests, so far as the crown's rights are concerned, falls logically to be determined by ordinary common law principles.[7] That being the case, that interest which was created first in time takes priority. There is an exception to this rule if a *bona fide* purchaser for value acquires a legal estate without notice of a prior equitable interest. In that event the subsequent legal interest prevails.[8] The crown can be no better off than is warranted by this common law régime. Therefore the crown may well find itself in a subordinate position notwithstanding its freedom from statutory regulation. It can,

5 See *Re John Wiper Ltd* (1972), 5 S.A.S.R. 360, at 377–8 (F.C.). And cf *Bartlett* v *Osterhout*, [1931] 3 D.L.R. 609 (Ont. S.C.). But cf *Re Adams Shoe Co., ex p. Town of Penetanguishene*, [1923] 4 D.L.R. 927, at 930–1 (Ont. S.C.). In *Re General Fireproofing Co.*, [1937] 2 D.L.R. 30 (S.C.C.), the issue was avoided.

6 *R* v *Sanford*, [1939] 1 D.L.R. 374 (N.S.S.C. in banco). And cf *Pulkrabek* v *Russell* (1908), 8 W.L.R. 8 (Man. K.B.).

7 See *Montreal Trust Co.* v *The King*, [1924] 1 D.L.R. 1030 (B.C.C.A.). The result, though perhaps not the reasoning, in *Bartlett* v *Osterhout*, [1931] 3 D.L.R. 609 (Ont. S.C.), is consistent with the statement in the text. But see *A.G. of Can.* v *Canadian Imperial Bank of Commerce* (1973), 41 D.L.R. (3d) 749 (Alta S.C.).

8 For the detail of the common law rules, see Sykes *The Law of Securities* (2d ed 1973), at 314–37.

of course, always take the benefit of legislation[9] so that, by registering its security, it may obtain whatever advantage is accorded by statute as a consequence of that action.

If execution creditors are given security upon registration of their judgments and priority is granted to the first registered judgment, then the position of the crown, if unaffected by the statutory scheme, is quite different. The reason is that the crown possesses a prerogative right to have its executions preferred over those of a subject.[10] Thus, since the statute is incapable of providing the governing rule for the resolution of the competing claims of the crown and a subject, the crown is free to insist upon its prerogative so as to put it ahead of the subject.[11]

In some Australian jurisdictions, though not apparently in Canada,[12] the crown is given a special lien over its debtor's land. This has the effect of conferring a priority on the crown over others who might acquire an interest in the debtor's land subsequent to the crown lien or its registration, whichever is the crucial date for determining priorities under the crown lien legislation.[13] Of course, whenever the crown claims a form of security which is a creature of statute it must come squarely within the statute and cannot claim a greater interest or higher status than is actually conferred.[14] The crown will not normally be taken by resorting to such a statute, however, to have waived its right to later insist upon such prerogatives as it possesses independently of statute.[15]

Legislation may limit the rights of a security holder in various ways and, if applicable to the crown, restrict it in its position as creditor. But statutory requirements that a creditor value his security in the event of the bankruptcy of the debtor and that it redeem a prior encumbrancer have been held inapplicable

9 See the cases cited in note 29, chapter 1.
10 *R* v *Wells* (1807), 104 E.R. 1094; *A.G.* v *Leonard* (1888), 38 Ch.D. 622
11 *R* v *Hamilton* (1962), 37 D.L.R. (2d) 545 (Man. Q.B.). And see also *Emerson* v *Simpson* (1962), 32 D.L.R. (2d) 603 (B.C.S.C.). However, the crown's claim may have so crystallized that the crown cannot insist upon first execution, see *Tudor Holdings Ltd* v *Robertson* (1974), 43 D.L.R. (3d) 752 (B.C.S.C.).
12 See *Re Hardy*, [1929] 1 D.L.R. 300 (Ont. S.C., App. Div.), as to the position in the province of Ontario.
13 See Sykes, at 173–5, 368–9, for a description of the crown lien and how it operates in the Australian states. The crown can also make use of the extraordinary remedy provided by the writ of extent to seize its debtor's property, where that procedure has not been withdrawn by statute, see *R* v *Sansoucy*, [1948] 3 D.L.R. 821 (Exch.).
14 *Great West Life Assurance Co.* v *Baptiste*, [1924] 3 D.L.R. 1061 (Alta S.C., App. Div.). And cf *R* v *The Ship 'City of Windsor'* (1896), 5 Ex. C.R. 223, and *Bartlett* v *Osterhout*, [1931] 3 D.L.R. 609 (Ont. S.C.).
15 *Emerson* v *Simpson* (1962), 32 D.L.R. (2d) 603 (B.C.S.C.); *R* v *Hamilton* (1962), 37 D.L.R. (2d) 545 (Man. Q.B.). And cf *R* v *Bank of N.S.* (1885), 11 S.C.R. 1; *Re Oriental Holdings Pty*, [1931] V.L.R. 279. And see supra, at 12.

to the crown where it is not bound by the relevant statute expressly or by necessary implication.[16] And the federal crown has been held free of the requirements of a provincial act that insists upon registration of a security as a condition of its validity as against a *bona fide* purchaser for value without notice, the rule of governmental immunity from statute being cited in support.[17]

This result, or rather the possibility of such a result, is sometimes avoided by federal statute equating the rights, and inferentially the responsibilities, of the crown in the matter of taking security with those of private individuals. For instance, in *Re Mar-Lise Industries Ltd*[18] the Industrial Development Bank of Canada,[19] a federal crown agency, was held subject to the obligation to register chattel mortgages which it had taken in order to preserve their validity against third parties. That registration requirement, contained in a provincial statute, was applied against the federal agency notwithstanding that the statute expressly excluded the crown from its reach. The governing legislation of the IDB deemed it to be a subject for the purpose of taking security thus effecting, in essence, a submission to the relevant provincial law, being that applying between subject and subject and not that applying to the crown. There was no room, then, for the operation of either governmental or intergovernmental immunity.[20]

Parliament may also legislate under its public property power in the constitution (section 91(1A)) to effectively secure the opposite result. That is, it may exempt security which the federal crown or its agent holds from provincial registration statutes in the event that there might not already be an immunity independent of a federal exclusionary provision.[21]

The Canadian Farm Loan Act, reviewed in *Reid* v *Canadian Farm Loan Board*,[22] was far less explicit than the IDB Act in evidencing an intention to subject the entity, which it established, to provincial law relating to the validity or enforceability of securities. The Board simply had power to take securities, including mortgages as understood in the provinces of Canada, and authority to cease granting loans in a given province in the event of statutory restrictions be-

---

16 *Re Post* (1920), 20 S.R. (N.S.W.) 457; *Re Rowe & Man.*, [1942] 4 D.L.R. 754 (Man. K.B.) (but cf *Great West Life Assurance Co.* v *Baptiste*, [1924] 3 D.L.R. 1061, at 1065 (Alta S.C., App. Div.))
17 *R* v *Sanford*, [1939] 1 D.L.R. 374 (N.S.S.C. in banco). See also *R* v *Powers*, [1923] Ex. C.R. 131; *Re Buckingham*, [1922] N.Z.L.R. 771.
18 (1968), 5 D.L.R. (3d) 487 (Ont. C.A.)
19 This entity has been succeeded by the Federal Business Development Bank, see S.C. 1974–5, c 14.
20 See supra, at 53.
21 *R* v *Powers*, [1923] Ex. C.R. 131
22 [1937] 4 D.L.R. 248 (Man. K.B.). Compare the result in *Re Soldier Settlement Act*, [1939] 2 W.W.R. 199 (Sask. Dist Ct).

ing imposed therein to the prejudice of the security of Board loans. This was sufficient basis for the court to advance, as an alternative ground, a conclusion that the Board's constitutive statute subjected it to provincial mortgage law.[23] Thus, assuming the Board was a federal crown agent, it was subject nonetheless to a Manitoba debt adjustment statute requiring a commissioner's certificate before the sale or foreclosure of a mortgage on land when it took foreclosure proceedings in that province.

The *Reid* decision also turned on the fact that the crown, having taken advantage of the relevant legislation, was therefore subject to its burdens, a principle that arose as a qualification upon the operation of governmental immunity.[24] However, only one of the foreclosure proceedings in that case was strictly statutory, namely that in relation to a mortgage under the Torrens title system, while the other under the registry system was basically judicial. Therefore the second ground of decision could only apply to the Torrens mortgage unless the simple fact of taking a mortgage in statutory form and registering it pursuant to the provincial Registry Act also constituted acceptance of the benefits of provincial statute law.[25] If so, the statutory burden, on foreclosure, namely the consent requirement, seems too unrelated to be carried with those particular benefits.[26] In the case of the Torrens mortgage the statutory scheme for foreclosure necessitated such evidence being produced by the applicant as the registrar required. Accordingly the registrar insisted upon a certificate of the commissioner under the debt adjustment statute. The burdens of the latter enactment, therefore, had a fairly immediate relationship to the benefits of the statute on which the crown placed reliance.

In none of the cases involving a claim to immunity in an interjurisdictional context did the exclusive power of the Canadian parliament in relation to federal public property (section 91(1A) of the BNA Act),[27] feature as a serious consideration in support of immunity of the federal crown from provincial legislation deal-

23 And cf *Bank of Montreal* v *Bay Bus Terminal (North Bay) Ltd* (1971), 24 D.L.R. (3d) 13 (Ont. H.C.), aff'd at (1972), 30 D.L.R. (3d) 24, see esp. at 25 (Ont. C.A.).
24 See supra, at 10–14.
25 The fact that foreclosure proceedings were commenced in a provincial court, which was later to be described as the decisive factor in the case (see *Deeks McBride Ltd* v *Vancouver Associated Contractors Ltd*, [1954] 4 D.L.R. 844, at 847 (B.C.C.A.)), would at most subject the federal crown to the practice and procedure of that court and not the substantive statute law of the province, see supra, at 13.
26 See La Forest *Natural Resources and Public Property under the Canadian Constitution* (1969), at 191.
27 In Australia the comparable exclusive federal power is referable to 'places acquired by the Commonwealth for public purposes' (s 52(i) of the constitution), which is ostensibly much narrower than s 91(1A).

ing with secured debts.[28] Yet such an argument would seem to hold some promise of acceptance. The reasoning of decisions holding provincial land registration statutes incapable of defeating an unrecorded reservation of minerals in grants of federal crown land because of section 91(1A) of the BNA Act[29] might well extend to protect a federal property interest by way of security from the effects of provincial legislation. An immunity so based, that is one of an exclusive power variety, has this practical consequence that it cannot be surrendered by simple federal statute. On the other hand a governmental or intergovernmental immunity may be overcome by an appropriately worded statute of the provincial legislature or federal parliament, respectively.[30]

STATUTES AFFECTING THE CROWN'S PREROGATIVE OF PRIORITY

We turn now to the situation where the crown is an unsecured creditor with a claim in competition with that of a subject also unsupported by security. In these circumstances the prerogative rule of crown priority comes into play.[31] In fact this rule is simply an illustration of a far more general prerogative privilege, that is that whenever the rights or title of the crown and a subject concur and hence come into competition, the crown is to be preferred.[32] The House of Lords has intimated, however, that the crown may not be entitled to priority when its claim arises out of an ordinary commercial transaction.[33] That doubt has led the courts of the province of Alberta to deny the crown the benefit of the prerogative in

---

28 Such an argument was unsuccessful in *Reid* v *Canadian Farm Loan Bd*, [1937] 4 D.L.R. 248 (Man. K.B.).
29 *Prudential Trust Co.* v *The Registrar, Land Titles Office, Humbolt Land Reg'n Dist.* (1957), 9 D.L.R. (2d) 561, at 562–3 (S.C.C.); *A.G. of Can.* v *Toth* (1959), 17 D.L.R. (2d) 273, at 276 (Sask. Q.B.); *Re Director of Soldier Settlement* (1960), 25 D.L.R. (2d) 463 (Alta S.C.)
30 See supra, at 29–33, and infra, at 146–55.
31 See cases cited supra, in note 1.
32 *R* v *Wells* (1807), 104 E.R. 1094, at 1096, appr'd in *N.S.W. Taxation Comm'rs* v *Palmer*, [1907] A.C. 179, at 182 & 185 (P.C.), and foll'd in *Crowther* v *A.G. of Can.* (1959), 17 D.L.R. (2d) 437, at 443–4 *per* MacDonald J, Parker J concurring (N.S.S.C. in banco), and *Bank of Montreal* v *A.G. of Can.* (1970), 14 D.L.R. (3d) 619, at 623–4 (B.C.S.C.).
33 See *Food Controller* v *Cork*, [1923] A.C. 647, at 659–60 *per* Lord Atkinson & at 666–7 *per* Lord Shaw (H.L.)

respect of such a claim.[34] In Australia the issue is now decided against any exception to the rule of priority for business debts.[35]

There are two ways in which the prerogative rule of priority may be effectively displaced by statute. Legislation which equates creditors or provides a scale of priorities for creditors and is declared to be binding on the crown will leave the matter of the ranking of a claim advanced by the crown, in the circumstances governed by the statute, to be determined by reference solely to the statute.[36] The presumption that the crown is not bound by statute, leaving it free among other things to insist upon traditional prerogatives, is thus displaced by express mention of the crown. Secondly, legislation which does not bind the crown explicitly may give directions as to how some particular types of crown debts are to be dealt with as an incident to what purports to be a comprehensive scheme for the administration of the assets of a debtor. In these circumstances there is an inference that the crown is precluded from asserting a right of priority independent of the statute and a necessary implication that the crown is bound by the statute.[37] But the crown is not subject to winding up legislation which simply provides that debts are to be paid *pari passu* subject to priorities for some specific kinds of claims, none of which necessarily pertains to the crown.[38] No implication is properly drawn from these facts that the statutory scheme binds the crown and has replaced the prerogative. Nor is the prerogative deemed to have been waived if the crown has proved in a liquidation or bankruptcy and received dividends thereunder in respect of its claim.[39]

34 See *R* v *Workmen's Compensation Bd* (1962), 36 D.L.R. (2d) 166 (Alta S.C.), which was rev'd on appeal though appr'd on this point, see (1963), 40 D.L.R. (2d) 243, at 244 (Alta S.C., App. Div.), and *Alta Gov't Telephones* v *Selk*, [1974] 4 W.W.R. 205 (Alta Dist. Ct). In other cases the issue has been avoided, see *Re Cardston U.F.A. Co-operative Ass'n Ltd, ex p. The King*, [1925] 4 D.L.R. 897 (Alta S.C.), and *Straka* v *Straka* (1970), 11 D.L.R. (3d) 733 (Alta S.C.).

35 *Re K.L. Tractors Ltd* (1961), 106 C.L.R. 318, at 336. The question was left open by the New Zealand Supreme Court in *Tasman Fruit-packing Ass'n Ltd* v *The King*, [1927] N.Z.L.R. 518.

36 *Re Cardston U.F.A. Co-operative Ass'n Ltd, ex p. The King*, [1925] 4 D.L.R. 897 (Alta S.C.); *Re Standard Pharmacy Ltd*, [1926] 2 D.L.R. 300 (Alta S.C.); *Re Allen, ex p. Official Receiver* (1954), 16 A.B.C. 154 (Fed. Ct of Bkpcy). See also *Re Mutual Traders Ltd*, [1943] N.Z.L.R. 254

37 *Food Controller* v *Cork*, [1923] A.C. 647 (H.L.); *Re Denton Sub-divisions Pty* (1968), 89 W.N. (Pt 1) (N.S.W.) 231. As to the general principles which are, in effect, applied in this kind of case see supra, at 19–21.

38 *Re Ockerby & Co.* (1922), 25 W.A.L.R. 25 (F.C.); *Re Oriental Holdings Pty*, [1931] V.L.R. 279; *Re K.L. Tractors Ltd* (1961), 106 C.L.R. 318, at 336

39 *R* v *Bank of N.S.* (1885), 11 S.C.R. 1; *N.S.W. Taxation Comm'rs* v *Palmer*, [1907] A.C. 179 (P.C.); *Re Oriental Holdings Pty*, [1931] V.L.R. 279. This proposition is equally

It seems to be accepted that a federal statute passed pursuant to a bankruptcy and insolvency power in the constitution is capable of binding the crown in the right of a state or province so as to preclude it from asserting priority as a creditor in bankruptcy or insolvency proceedings.[40] The intergovernmental immunity of the states and provinces from federal legislation apparently is not extensive enough to preclude this kind of regulation.[41]

But state or provincial legislation cannot bind the federal crown so as to interfere with its prerogative right of priority over the claims of subjects. As far as Australia is concerned this matter was settled by the High Court in *Commonwealth v Cigamatic Pty*[42] which overruled, in this respect, an earlier contrary decision in *Re Richard Foreman & Sons Pty; Uther v Federal Commissioner of Taxation*[43] (*Uther's* case). Cigamatic was an insolvent corporation in process of winding up under the Companies Act of New South Wales. The Commonwealth having lodged two claims with the liquidator, for sales tax and for telephone charges, sued for declaratory and injunctive relief establishing its right to payment in priority to the other unsecured creditors. The Companies Act prescribed a scheme of priorities purporting to bind the Commonwealth which, if applicable, would effectively deny the privilege which the federal authority had asserted. The majority in the High Court sustained the Commonwealth's claim to preference in the face of the state statute. Dixon CJ, who had written a dissent in *Uther's* case,[44] attached particular importance to the fact that the Commonwealth was relying upon a crown prerogative though in contemporary terms he would describe it, more accurately, as a fiscal right of government. With this the state

true if it is a case of the federal crown proving in a liquidation under state or provincial law, see *Re Richard Foreman & Sons Pty; Uther v Federal Comm'r of Taxation* (1947), 74 C.L.R. 508, at 515–16 *per* Latham CJ; *Commonwealth v Cigamatic Pty* (1962), 108 C.L.R. 372, at 378–9 *per* Dixon CJ. And cf *Crowther v A.G. of Can.* (1959), 17 D.L.R. (2d) 437, at 441–2 (N.S.S.C. in banco).

40 *Re Cardston U.F.A. Co-operative Ass'n Ltd, ex p. The King*, [1925] 4 D.L.R. 897 (Alta S.C.); *Re Standard Pharmacy Ltd*, [1926] 2 D.L.R. 300 (Alta S.C.); *Re Hardy*, [1928] 3 D.L.R. 255 (Ont. S.C.), aff'd on other grounds at [1929] 1 D.L.R. 300 (Ont. S.C., App. Div.); *R v Trustee of Leach* (1929), 11 C.B.R. 214 (N.B.S.C.); *Federal Comm'r of Taxation v Official Liquidator of E.O. Farley Ltd* (1940), 63 C.L.R. 278, at 313–14 *per* Dixon J & at 323 *per* Evatt J; *Re Richard Foreman & Sons Pty; Uther v Federal Comm'r of Taxation* (1947), 74 C.L.R. 508, at 529 *per* Dixon J, dissenting

41 It was suggested earlier that there may be some room for argument on this point, see supra, at 42.

42 (1962), 108 C.L.R. 372

43 (1947), 74 C.L.R. 508

44 For a trenchant criticism of this dissenting judgment see Sawer, 'State Statutes and the Commonwealth' (1962), 1 *U. of Tasmania L. Rev.* 580.

could not interfere.[45] Yet he also suggested, in this judgment and in dissent in *Uther's* case, that there is a broader principle underlying the Commonwealth's immunity from this kind of state legislation, that is that the state has no power to control legal rights and duties pertaining between the Commonwealth and its subjects.[46] The views of the Chief Justice secured substantial support from the other majority judges in *Cigamatic*.[47] Of the possible versions of immunity which are offered, the first and narrower one has more to commend it. A detailed argument to this effect has been put in an earlier chapter.[48]

A number of Canadian cases, none of which proceeded as far as the Supreme Court of Canada or the Privy Council, have come to a result similar to that in *Cigamatic*.[49] The privilege of the federal crown as a creditor to stand outside an administration of assets pursuant to provincial statute, so far as priority questions are concerned, has been cast as a consequence of the inability of a provincial legislature to affect a prerogative of the crown in right of the dominion.[50] *Gauthier* v *The King*[51] and cases which have followed it have been relied upon as sufficient authority in this respect. Some of the decisions were put on the basis of the absence of any provision in the relevant provincial statute to the effect that the crown was bound, that is that governmental immunity pertained, as well as on the basis of the intergovernmental immunity given recognition in *Gauthier*.[52]

---

45 See also, to similar effect, the judgment of Dixon J in *Federal Comm'r of Taxation* v *Official Liquidator of E.O. Farley Ltd* (1940), 63 C.L.R. 278, at 307–8.
46 See *Cigamatic* (1962), 108 C.L.R. 372, at 377–8, and *Uther's* case (1947), 74 C.L.R. 508, at 528 & 530.
47 The effect of the other majority judgments is described supra, at 36.
48 See supra, at 38–40.
49 *Toronto & Toronto Electric Comm'rs* v *Wade*, [1931] 4 D.L.R. 928 (Ont. S.C.), aff'd on other grounds at [1932] 3 D.L.R. 509 (Ont. C.A.); *Re Sternschein* (1965), 50 D.L.R. (2d) 762 (Man. Q.B.); *Re Mendelsohn* (1959), 22 D.L.R. (2d) 748 (Ont. S.C., Master), rev'd on consent at (1960), 25 D.L.R. (2d) 778 (Ont. H.C.). See also *R* v *Star Kosher Sausage Mfg Co.*, [1940] 4 D.L.R. 365 (Man. K.B.) (prerogative of first execution); *Crowther* v *A.G. of Can.* (1959), 17 D.L.R. (2d) 437 (N.S.S.C. in banco) (prerogative of priority when rights of the crown and a subject concur); *Emerson* v *Simpson* (1962), 32 D.L.R. (2d) 603 (B.C.S.C.) (prerogative of first execution); *R* v *Hamilton* (1962), 37 D.L.R. (2d) 545 (Man. Q.B.) (prerogative right to have execution preferred over that of a subject).
50 In one case, *R* v *Lithwick* (1921), 57 D.L.R. 1 (Exch.), the crown had a statutory claim to priority but the statute was regarded as simply recognizing and preserving the prerogative priority; see ibid, at 4. See also *Re Adams Shoe Co., ex p. Town of Penetanguishene*, [1923] 4 D.L.R. 927, esp. at 931 (Ont. S.C.).
51 (1918), 40 D.L.R. 353 (S.C.C.)
52 *R* v *Star Kosher Sausage Mfg Co.*, [1940] 4 D.L.R. 365 (Man. K.B.). See also *Crowther* v *A.G. of Can.* (1959), 17 D.L.R. (2d) 437 (N.S.S.C. in banco); *R* v *Hamilton* (1962), 37 D.L.R. (2d) 545 (Man. Q.B.).

There is, however, an early Privy Council decision which does not fall in readily with this otherwise consistent line of Canadian authority.[53] The case is *Exchange Bank* v *The Queen*.[54] It concerned a claim by the crown in right of Canada and in right of the province of Quebec to be paid its debts in priority to the other ordinary creditors in a liquidation under a dominion statute. The Judicial Committee found that under French law, which was applied in Quebec before confederation in matters of property, and under the Civil Code and Civil Procedure Code of Quebec, the king could not claim priority for his debts except in the limited case of monies owed by officers of the king collected on his account. This law was held applicable and, accordingly, the claim of the crown was rejected. No distinction was made between the debts owed to the province[55] and those owed to the dominion,[56] which governments were not represented separately. This looks like a case, then, in which the federal crown was effectively controlled in the exercise of the prerogative of priority by provincial statute.

Three possible explanations for the decision may be advanced. Firstly, it may be argued that the court was really applying the codes as part of the preconfederation statute law of the province which is kept alive by section 129 of the BNA Act.[57] That section continues in force the laws in effect before the union, except as otherwise provided in the act, subject to alteration by the appropriate legislatures, federal or provincial, in accordance with the distribution of authority under the constitution. The argument meets the difficulty that the dominion was not in existence when the codes were adopted so that it cannot be said that the provincial law, which is thought to have been preserved, ever extended or indeed could have been extended to the crown in its federal right.[58] But before 1867 the

53 Laskin has suggested that the decision in question may well be wrong, see his *Canadian Constitutional Law* (3d rev ed 1969), at 554–5 (this suggestion is retained in Abel (ed) *Laskin's Canadian Constitutional Law* (4th ed rev. 1975), at 527–8).

54 (1885), 11 App. Cas. 157 (P.C.)

55 As to the application of the Quebec Civil Code to such debts see *Re St Lawrence Investment & Trust Co.* (1937), 63 B.R. 546.

56 In explaining the *Exchange Bank* decision in *Liquidators of the Maritime Bank* v *Receiver General of N.B.*, [1892] A.C. 437 (P.C.), the Privy Council referred specifically to dominion debts as having been denied a preference on the basis that 'the law of the province of Quebec' governed the prerogative, see 441.

57 See La Forest *Natural Resources and Public Property under the Canadian Constitution* (1969), and *R* v *Murray*, [1965] 2 Ex. C.R. 663, at 667, note 6 (decision aff'd at (1967), 60 D.L.R. (2d) 647 (S.C.C.)).

58 See *Re D. Moore Co.*, [1928] 1 D.L.R. 383, at 395–6 *per* Middleton JA (Ont. C.A.) (but Masten JA expressed the contrary view, at 396–9, and the three other members of the court did not consider this question), and *Re Mendelsohn* (1959), 22 D.L.R. (2d) 748, at 753 (Ont. S.C., Master), rev'd on consent at (1960), 25 D.L.R. (2d) 778 (Ont. H.C.).

crown, without differentiation as to the capacities in which it might act, would have been subject to the Quebec codes so far as they dealt with its privilege as a creditor. The very subject matter of the relevant provisions was a right peculiar to the sovereign, and the crown would have been bound by necessary implication at the time of their enactment.[59] The notion of the unity and indivisibility of the crown,[60] though not always faithfully adhered to, would seem to be particularly appropriate here as justification for treating the codes as binding upon the crown even in its new aspect after the event of confederation.[61] Any suggestion that there may be a federal crown immunity from unaltered colonial statutes, which derives in some way from the Canadian constitutional scheme, seems to be precluded by section 129. That section preserves such statutes 'as if the Union had not been made.' That language may be taken to secure not only their general validity but their operation in particular circumstances in which comparable provincial statutes, though valid, could not now operate in light of the confederation arrangement.[62] This has been the effect attributed to a similar provision of the Australian constitution.[63]

Secondly, the case may be viewed as doing no more than applying the inherited French law, which was bestowed on the colony of Quebec, in a comparable manner to that in which the court would apply the common law to the federal crown in any other province to which it was directed by the appropriate choice of law rule.[64] The civil law which limited the priority of the crown as a creditor may therefore be considered as part of the general law to which the crown in any capacity is subject in the province of Quebec, at least in relation to its general rights and minor prerogatives which are not essential to the supremacy of the crown.[65] The extensive treatment given by the Privy Council to the Que-

---

59 For the relevant rule of governmental immunity see art. 9 of the Quebec Civil Code of 1866. Under that article the crown is subject to such statutes as specially include its rights and prerogatives, a form of expression which should be taken to allow for inclusion of the crown by necessary implication just as a reference to the inclusion of the crown by express mention ought to be so taken, see supra, at 17–19.
60 See supra, at 23–4.
61 But cf *Municipal Council of Sydney* v *Commonwealth* (1904), 1 C.L.R. 208, at 231 *per* Griffith CJ.
62 But see *Holmstead* v *Minister of Customs & Excise*, [1927] Ex. C.R. 68, at 74.
63 Viz. s 108. See *R* v *Bamford* (1901), 1 S.R. (N.S.W.) 337, ref'd to with apparent approval in relation to the matter under consideration in *Worthing* v *Rowell & Muston Pty* (1970), 123 C.L.R. 89, see esp. at 94 *per* Barwick CJ, at 116 & 120 *per* Menzies J & at 129 *per* Windeyer J, and in *R* v *Phillips* (1970), 125 C.L.R. 93, at 99 *per* Barwick CJ.
64 See La Forest, at 10–11 & 146, and Gibson, 'Interjurisdictional Immunities in Canadian Federalism' (1969), 47 *Can. Bar Rev.* 40, at 44.
65 For this limitation see *Monk* v *Ouimet* (1874), 19 L.C.J. 71, at 73–4 *per* Dorion CJ (Q.B.).

bec codes may be understood as simply to confirm that the applicable French law had not been changed so as to provide a special facility to the crown, comparable to the common law prerogative of priority, which the dominion could take advantage of as it could any other provincial statutory provision.

Thirdly, the position may be taken that while there is indeed a 'common law' to which the federal crown is generally subject in its activities in Quebec, that law is to be found in the codes themselves rather than in the pre-code French law.[66] Therefore the federal crown could claim no higher position as a creditor than the codes permitted, just as a judicially developed limitation on the prerogative in any other province would inhibit the crown in making a claim within that jurisdiction. There is authority, however, which seriously detracts from this argument in its indication that the Civil Code does not apply of its own force against the federal crown.[67] The first two explanations of the *Exchange Bank* decision are, therefore, to be preferred. The first seems more in accord with what the Privy Council actually said in its opinion. In particular their Lordships stated: 'the Crown is bound by the Codes, but ... the subject of priorities is exhaustively dealt with by them, so that the Crown can claim no priority except what is allowed by them.'[68] While no specific mention was made of section 129 of the BNA Act, the effect of the codes upon the federal crown is explained most convincingly on the basis of their pre-confederation origins.

A state or provincial statute may not purport to remove the prerogative of priority as enjoyed by the federal crown in any direct way but may simply classify a variety of unsecured debts so that they are then of a higher degree than certain debts which may be owed to the federal government. If fully effective the statute would then eliminate the possibility of the federal crown relying upon its prerogative of priority to give its debts a higher ranking than those which would have been of the same degree but for the statutory classification. It is unlikely that governmental immunity would restrict the operation of this kind of statute, for it is directed generally to the status of a given category of debts. It only affects the prerogative of priority indirectly so far as it may remove the element of equality in the degree of debts, owed to a subject and to the crown, that would otherwise have come into competition.[69] It is equally true that the federal crown would not be affected sufficiently directly by such a debt classification statute,

66 See Garant, 'Contribution à l'Etude du Statut Juridique de l'Administration Gouvernmentale' (1972), 50 *Can. Bar Rev.* 50, at 63–6.
67 See *Palmer* v *The King*, [1952] 1 D.L.R. 259 (Exch.), and *R* v *Nord-Deutsche Versicherungs-Gessellschaft* (1971), 20 D.L.R. (2d) 444 (S.C.C.), considered supra, at 63–4.
68 (1885), 11 App. Cas. 157, at 164 (P.C.)
69 Compare *A.G. of B.C.* v *Royal Bank & Island Amusement Co.*, [1937] 3 D.L.R. 393 (S.C.C.). For a discussion of the general principle involved see supra, at 7–8.

passed by a state or province, for intergovernmental immunity to operate.[70] Though if the state or provincial enactment were revealed as simply a colourable attempt to postpone debts owed to the federal crown then it may be expected that a court would decline to sustain the legislation in its effect upon the federal crown as creditor.[71]

STATUTES AFFECTING THE RIGHT OF EQUALITY AS BETWEEN CROWN CLAIMS

Sometimes a competition may arise not between the crown and a subject, but between the crown in one right and the crown in another right. Throughout the British Empire no distinction was made between one government and another in the exercise of the crown prerogative of priority of debts.[72] It may be assumed from this general principle of equality that in the event of a deficiency of assets to satisfy the claims of competing governments the claims would have to be paid *pari passu*. The federal constitutions of Australia and Canada as enacted by the imperial parliament did not purport to limit access to the prerogative of priority. It could therefore be claimed by the dominions, as representing the crown in entirely new rights, or by the state or provincial governments, in the exercise of their respective functions.[73] And as at common law priority could be asserted without territorial limitation to the jurisdiction in right of which the crown claimed or in which the claim arose.[74] Neither constitution gave or implied an overriding primacy to the prerogative as it might be exercised by the central authority. Therefore in a competition between debts of the federal government and of a state or province, equal treatment had to be accorded and a distribution made *pari passu*. The same rule was applied when the competing governments asserted not prerogative rights of first payment but statutory rights of first pay-

---

70 Cf *Re John Wiper Ltd* (1972), 5 S.A.S.R. 360, at 377–8 (F.C.).
71 Consider, for example, *Minister of Finance for B.C.* v *First National Bank* (1973), 40 D.L.R. (3d) 739 (S.C.C.).
72 *Re Oriental Bank Corp, ex p. The Crown* (1884), 28 Ch. D. 643
73 See *R* v *Bank of N.S.* (1885), 11 S.C.R. 1; *Liquidators of the Maritime Bank* v *Receiver General of N.B.*, [1892] A.C. 437 (P.C.); *Federal Comm'r of Taxation* v *Official Liquidator of E.O. Farley Ltd* (1940), 63 C.L.R. 278, at 303–4 *per* Dixon J & at 321–2 *per* Evatt J. And cf *A.G. of N.S.W.* v *Butterworth & Co. (Australia)* (1938), 38 S.R. (N.S.W.) 195.
74 *Re Commonwealth Agricultural Service Eng'rs Ltd* [1928] S.A.S.R. 342 (F.C.).

ment. The leading cases are *Federal Commissioner of Taxation* v *Official Liquidator of E.O. Farley Ltd*[75] (*Farley's* case) and *Re Silver Brothers Ltd.*[76]

There is, in fact, no conflict between the priority of the federal crown and that of the state or provincial crown in these situations since the preference is one over the claims of subjects only and not over the claims of the crown in another right. Where there are insufficient assets there is naturally a competition for full satisfaction but no inconsistency in the nature of the governmental claims advanced. Only if both authorities claimed a single object which, unlike a fund, is incapable of rateable distribution would it be necessary to rank the claimants, in which case it has been suggested that priority would be given to the federal authority.[77]

It may be that the debts or claims of the two governments are not of equal degree. For example, a state government may have proceeded to judgment on its debt so that it has become, as a matter of common law, a debt of record which is superior to either a specialty or a simple contract debt, which may be the highest the Commonwealth can pitch its claim. Dixon J has said, *obiter*, that the state would be entitled to have its claim satisfied in full, ahead of the Commonwealth, in these circumstances.[78] The effect would be to treat the rule of equality as limited in the same way as the rule of priority, that is as operative only when the competing debts or claims are of equal degree. It might appear that the competing claims in *Silver Brothers* were not of the same degree for the dominion debt was constituted a first charge on the assets of the taxpayer while the provincial debt was not. But for the purposes of Canadian bankruptcy legislation that fact does not make the crown a secured creditor.[79] Therefore in that case the dominion was only able to claim in a bankruptcy as an unsecured creditor in respect of a debt which was of the same degree as that on the basis of which the province claimed. *Silver Brothers* was consequently a case of competing crown debts of equal degree advanced by the two levels of government, which was also the basis on which *Farley's* case was argued. And, as has been said, in both cases the debts were treated on a parity.

A state or provincial statute may purport to confer a priority over subjects

75 (1940), 63 C.L.R. 278. And see *Re Union Theatres Ltd* (1933), 35 W.A.L.R. 89; *Re Navilla Ice Cream Co.*, [1934] 4 D.L.R. 741 (Ont. S.C.); *Re Walter's Trucking Service Ltd* (1965), 50 D.L.R. (2d) 711 (Alta S.C., App. Div.).
76 [1932] A.C. 514 (P.C.). See also *Stroud & Dakota Enterprises Ltd* v *Imperial Oil Ltd* (1961), 28 D.L.R. (2d) 366 (Sask. C.A.).
77 See *Re Walter's Trucking Service Ltd* (1965), 50 D.L.R. (2d) 711, at 719 (Alta S.C., App. Div.).
78 *Farley's* case (1940), 63 C.L.R. 278, at 317–18. Starke J apparently disagreed, see 298–9.
79 See *Moore* v *The Queen* (1957), 15 D.L.R. (2d) 681 (N.B.S.C., App. Div.).

upon a particular kind of claim of a state or province. Such a priority may, like other priorities under local legislation, be overridden by federal statute when asserted in an administration of assets under federal jurisdiction, for example in a bankruptcy.[80] Where the situation is unaffected by federal enactment there is no discernible basis for disturbing the equal ranking rule and giving the state or province preference over the federal government simply because it has a statutory priority while the federal crown may only enjoy a prerogative priority. Indeed, to give the state or provincial statute such an effect would violate the principle of intergovernmental immunity, which has prevented local statutes from effectively postponing federal crown claims in favour not of the state or provincial crown but of its subjects.[81]

Nor does there seem to be any reason for preferring the federal crown when it has a statutory priority over subjects and the state or province relies upon the prerogative as giving it a like first position. Indeed, even though the federal statute might conceivably be taken as intended to confer a privileged position on federal crown debts ahead of the governmental claims of a state or province, as well as ahead of subjects, it is liable to be interpreted narrowly so far as possible so that the rule of equality is not disturbed. Again the *Farley*[82] and *Silver Brothers*[83] decisions supply the authority.

In the latter case the Privy Council construed a provision in a dominion taxing statute which created a priority for federal tax claims as not affecting the rights of the provincial crown as a creditor, absent express mention of the crown. It was thought that the federal Interpretation Act's statement of governmental immunity from statute required as much.[84] But what were the 'rights' of the provincial crown – to have its debt fully satisfied or to have its debt ranked on an equal footing with that of the federal crown? This the case does not answer, for the province was content to claim no more than equality. In the absence of authority it seems that the proper conclusion must be that the provincial crown has, at best, a right to equal treatment, for it was no part of the prerogative to give priority over competing governments. A provincial statute which might be thought to create such a priority over the federal government would no doubt be construed, if possible, so as not to affect the right of the federal crown to equality in the same way that the federal statute was so read in *Silver Brothers*.

80 *Re F.E. West & Co.* (1921), 62 D.L.R. 207 (Ont. S.C.); *Re Polycoating & Films Ltd* (1965), 51 D.L.R. (2d) 673 (Ont. C.A.)
81 See, for example, *Commonwealth v Cigamatic Pty* (1962), 108 C.L.R. 372.
82 (1940), 63 C.L.R. 278
83 [1932] A.C. 514 (P.C.)
84 See supra, at 24–5 for a fuller discussion of the case in relation to this aspect of its holding.

The principle is, therefore, that a statute giving priority to certain federal crown debts, but not expressed as binding the crown, is not to operate so as to diminish the right of the provincial government to have its claim ranked equally with that of the federal government. By a parity of reasoning other debts due to the federal crown of a kind not given a priority by such a statute should also be paid *pari passu*.[85] A competition involving agencies or departments of a single government is not, of course, unheard of, despite the existence of a consolidated revenue fund. But if the federal statute in question is one providing for the administration of assets it may, in its comprehensiveness and particular conferral of priority on some crown debts, oust the prerogative of priority over subjects.[86] The crown, in any right, could not then assert a privilege to have its debts ranked equally with those crown debts given a statutory priority. The right to equality presupposes that the competing governmental claim, for which equal treatment is claimed, takes priority over the claims of subjects. And any argument to that effect cannot, in these circumstances, survive the statute because it in fact eliminates the prerogative of priority.

In *Farley's* case[87] the High Court had to consider the effect upon state tax claims of Commonwealth legislation which required a liquidator to set aside sufficient funds to meet federal income tax. Evatt J, relying on the *Silver Brothers* decision, applied the rule of construction that Commonwealth legislation ought 'not to be treated as cutting down prerogatives of the state except where there are express words or a 'very strong, perhaps necessary or irresistible implication' to this effect.[88] Rich J thought that a general section in a federal act ought not to be taken, without clear and explicit language, to override the state's right to rank equally with the Commonwealth and to priority over the subject. He felt that the nature of those rights, belonging as they do to the Treasury and being of the same nature as the competing rights of the Commonwealth, was such as to raise 'considerations of governmental comity and constitutional practice.'[89] Dixon J took the view[90] that it was not incidental to the taxation power, which was the only possible basis for the federal priority provision, to defer a state's claim for a tax debt to that of the Commonwealth given the governmental and fiscal nature of the respective claims.[91] Accordingly, construing the federal statute within

---

85 See *Commonwealth* v *Cigamatic Pty* (1962), 108 C.L.R. 372, at 379 *per* Dixon CJ (but contrast the view of Taylor J, dissenting, at 387–8).
86 See cases cited supra, note 37, and the accompanying text.
87 (1940), 63 C.L.R. 278
88 Ibid, at 326
89 Ibid, at 292
90 A view not shared by Evatt J, see ibid, at 324–6.
91 Ibid, at 314–17

power, he held that it did not alter the rule of equal ranking between Commonwealth and state debts. The three other members of the court[92] were able to reach the conclusion that the rule of equality was not disturbed without reference to any restrictive rule of statutory interpretation.

But if federal legislation asserts, in clear terms, an absolute priority over the crown as represented by a state or province, then the federal claim must be given priority.[93] The conflict which is required to be resolved in this way is not, as has sometimes been suggested,[94] between the federal priority provision and the state or provincial rule of priority. There is no such conflict because this latter rule of priority, even where it has statutory expression,[95] does not normally indicate any preference over federal claims. Rather the conflict or inconsistency is one between the federal statutory rule and the judicial rule of equality.

Under the bankruptcy and insolvency power[96] the central parliament is capable of legislating to postpone any claim by a state or province to that of the federal crown just as it can favour certain claims of its subjects over those of a state or province.[97] But its capacity to do the same thing under its taxation power is not so clear, as is evidenced by the opinion of Dixon J, referred to above, in *Farley's* case. The Privy Council had suggested earlier, in *Silver Brothers*, that the taxing power of the Canadian parliament would support the conferral of priority upon a tax debt of the dominion over that of a province.[98] The case was followed in this respect in *South Australia* v *Commonwealth*,[99] upholding a provision in a Commonwealth income tax act which was part of a uniform taxation scheme. The section of the act which was sustained was to the effect that a taxpayer should not pay any state tax on income for any year in which he was subject to federal income tax until he had first met the federal levy. The effective result of this direction was to give Commonwealth income tax debts a preferred position,

---

92 Latham CJ, Starke & McTiernan JJ
93 *Re Silver Brothers Ltd*, [1932] A.C. 514, at 521 (P.C.); *Farley's* case (1940), 63 C.L.R. 278, at 313–14, & 323–4; *Industrial Development Bank* v *Valley Dairy Ltd*, [1953] 1 D.L.R. 788 (Ont. H.C.)
94 *Re Silver Brothers Ltd*, [1932] A.C. 514, at 521 (P.C.)
95 Unless each statute asserted a priority over the crown in the other right, in which case the state or provincial statute would have to be read down to bring it within constitutional power, or be held unconstitutional, and either course would remove the conflict in the legislation.
96 In s 91(21) of the BNA Act and s 51(xvii) of the Australian constitution.
97 *Re Silver Brothers Ltd*, [1932] A.C. 514, at 521 (P.C.); *Farley's* case (1940), 63 C.L.R. 278, at 313–14 *per* Dixon J. See also *Vict.* v *Commonwealth* (1957), 99 C.L.R. 575, at 611–12, 624, 630, 658, & 659.
98 [1932] A.C. 514, at 521 (P.C.)
99 (1942), 65 C.L.R. 373

as to collection, over any state income tax debts whether the taxpayer was solvent or not, by obliging the taxpayer, under threat of sanction, to pay federal tax first.

However, in a second uniform tax case, *Victoria v Commonwealth*,[100] the High Court, by a 4-3 majority, declined to follow its earlier decision on this point and found the same federal provision upheld in the *South Australian* case to be unconstitutional. Dixon CJ, in a judgment concurred in by Kitto J, considered that the section under attack was not incidental to the power of taxation, having in mind the purpose of the section. The context in which it appeared revealed that it was designed to make it more difficult for states to impose an income tax pursuant to their concurrent and independent taxing powers.[101] McTiernan J characterized the federal provision as in substance a law in respect of state rather than federal income tax in that it purported to alter the time for the payment of state tax which the state might fix.[102] But both Dixon CJ and McTiernan J would also have held invalid any attempt to postpone the payment of civil debts owed to subjects of the crown until tax obligations to the Commonwealth were satisfied.[103] This suggests a much more general limitation on the federal taxing power. The judgment of Taylor J emphasizes that the law was not one to secure the full benefit of the federal tax, for it was not referable exclusively to a situation where there might be insufficient assets to satisfy all creditors.[104] The three dissenters[105] preferred to stand by the decision, on this particular point, in the first uniform tax case. It is clear, then, that this was not a case in which the state enjoyed any inherent intergovernmental immunity from federal law nor, even more clearly, a prerogative immunity in the manner of *Silver Brothers*. Rather the Commonwealth provision simply failed to find support under the only appropriate federal head of power, a result that might have been unchanged even if it were not state debts but ordinary commercial debts the collection of which was postponed in favour of the federal authority.

CONCLUSION

It has been seen that the crown as a creditor enjoys a number of advantages over other creditors, except where that position has been altered by statute. This is the result both of immunity of a governmental and intergovernmental order and

100 (1957), 99 C.L.R. 575
101 Ibid, at 613–15
102 Ibid, at 625–6
103 See ibid, at 615 & 625–6.
104 Ibid, at 660
105 Williams, Webb & Fullagar JJ

of prerogatives which the crown enjoys in the role of creditor. Where there are insufficient assets of a debtor to satisfy all claimants, the special position of the crown operates to the obvious prejudice of subjects. It is particularly difficult to justify that result when the crown's claim arises out of an activity which has obvious commercial features and is closely akin to activities which are pursued in the private sector. The government acts in such a manner, for example, when it serves through its agencies as a general source of borrowing or credit. In this kind of situation legislation is appropriate to equate the position of the crown with that of a subject. In fact legislatures have acted from time to time to produce this result.

A common form of monetary claim by governments is on account of unpaid taxes. In this case it is arguable that the state should be entitled to a preferred position since its interest is in securing the receipt of funds to support those essential services on which all subjects have come to rely. A tax debt can be distinguished from other debts because of this general public purpose underlying taxation schemes. Therefore the government in pursuing tax claims may quite properly be accorded certain advantages. But even so the precision of a statutory statement of the position of the crown as tax creditor, in response to the particular needs of government, is to be preferred to the absolute and blanket privileges that pertain under the common law.

Contemporary statutes dealing generally with the rights of creditors often make provision for crown debts, fitting them in for example to a comprehensive scheme of priorities. However, as has been indicated, state or provincial statutes of that nature cannot always affect the federal crown because of intergovernmental immunity. Therefore the central parliament must take action if the federal authority is to be brought under the general scheme of regulation.

Competition can arise between the interests as creditors of the two levels of government in a federal system. The foregoing review of the cases has revealed that the courts have tended to equate the position of the two orders of authority, in the absence of legislation explicitly conferring an absolute priority on the federal crown over the crown in right of a state or province. This would seem a sensible resolution of the issue, recognizing the co-ordinate nature of executive authority in a federal system. At the same time it assumes that the needs of the national political entity will ultimately prevail if the central parliament deems federal priority to be necessary and legislates accordingly.

6

The Crown as Taxpayer

GOVERNMENTAL IMMUNITY

The imposition of taxes must necessarily have a statutory basis. The Bill of Rights of 1688 requires as much.[1] The crown like its subjects is, therefore, taxable only if it is rendered liable by statute. And a taxing statute has no different operation upon the crown than any other kind of statute in that it must contain express words or a necessary implication that the crown is bound before it will be recognized as effecting that result.[2] There is the occasional suggestion that crown immunity from tax depends upon a separate prerogative entitling the crown to stand outside a taxing statute which prejudices it.[3] This theory offers a degree of flexibility to the crown in that it has the opportunity of waiving its immunity as the occasion may require.[4] It could not take that action if non-liability to tax followed from the fact that the taxing act did not reach the crown. What is effectively the same facility exists, however, if the taxing statute is simply inapplic-

---

1 1 Will. & Mar. sess. 2, c 2. And see *A.G.* v *Wilts United Dairies* (1922), 91 L.J.K.B. 897 (H.L.); *Commonwealth* v *Colonial Combing, Spinning & Weaving Co.* (1922), 31 C.L.R. 421.

2 *Mersey Docks* v *Cameron* (1865), 11 E.R. 1405, at 1413 (H.L.); *Greig* v *University of Edinburgh* (1868), L.R. 1 Sc. & Div. 348, at 350; *Hornsey U.D.C.* v *Hennell*, [1902] 2 K.B. 73, at 80

3 See *Madras Electric Supply Corp.* v *Boarland*, [1955] A.C. 667 (H.L.), especially the judgment of Lord Keith, but compare the judgments of Lord MacDermott and Lord Reid, at 684–5 and 686–9 respectively.

4 But the notion that the crown must positively assert the prerogative before immunity is properly accorded to it is clearly contrary to authority (see *Madras Electric Supply Corp.* v *Boarland*, [1955] A.C. 667, at 689 *per* Lord Reid (H.L.)), and conducive to considerable uncertainty (see *Inland Revenue Comm'rs* v *Whitworth Park Coal Co.*, [1958] Ch. 792, at 824 (C.A.), decision aff'd at [1961] A.C. 31 (H.L.)).

able to the crown, which seems to be the predominant view. In that event if the crown is willing to assume the burden of a tax it may pay an amount equivalent to the tax as if the act in fact were to bind it.[5]

Since the crown enjoys governmental immunity from taxation it is free, so long as the immunity persists, from the obligation of contributing to the general cost of public services even though it may take advantage of them. It does not follow that it is necessarily relieved of responsibility for paying for those services of which it has taken a direct and quantifiable benefit.[6] Compensation for a utility such as water[7] which is supplied by a local government body to crown property has been recovered through successful claims in restitution or quasi-contract.[8] A local authority in making such a claim against the crown need not rely on the statute or by-law imposing the appropriate levy or rate on property owners or occupiers generally. Such enactments are apt not to bind the crown by reason of its governmental immunity. But the prescribed rate may serve as a guide to determining the amount which is a fair and reasonable sum to be paid by the crown for the service provided for it.[9]

In the event of a claim of immunity from tax two questions may be put, which reflect the primary considerations that pertain to a finding of governmental immunity from other kinds of statutes.[10] Firstly, does the person who has asserted the privilege fall into one of the classes of persons entitled to its advantage? Secondly, would the tax, if exacted, prejudicially affect a governmental interest

5 *Madras Electric Supply Corp.* v *Boarland*, [1955] A.C. 667, at 689 *per* Lord Reid (H.L.). And see also *Municipal Council of Sydney* v *Commonwealth* (1904), 1 C.L.R. 208, at 232 *per* Griffith CJ.
6 In *Essendon Corp.* v *Criterion Theatres Ltd* (1947), 74 C.L.R. 1, in which it was held that municipal rates were inapplicable to the Commonwealth as the occupier of property, Dixon J made the point, at 17, that the rates were taxes and not charges for services, suggesting that different considerations might apply if that were not so. And cf *Reference re Tax on Foreign Legations*, [1943] 2 D.L.R. 481 (S.C.C.), and *St John* v *Fraser-Brace Overseas Corp.* (1958), 13 D.L.R. (2d) 177 (S.C.C.), in which it was said that the immunity enjoyed by foreign governments, in accordance with the principles of international law, does not free such governments from any obligation to pay for municipal services, such as water or electricity, though it does exempt them from tax (see esp. at 492 in the *Foreign Legations* reference and at 183 in the *Fraser-Brace* case). .
7 But apparently compensation for a water connection cannot be recovered on the same basis, see *Hutt Golf Course Estate Co.* v *Hutt City Corp.*, [1945] N.Z.L.R. 56 (C.A.).
8 In *Minister of Justice for Can.* v *City of Levis*, [1919] A.C. 505 (P.C.), and *Auckland* v *The King* (1924), 26 G.L.R. 415, which were distinguished in *Auckland City* v *Auckland Metropolitan Fire Bd*, [1967] N.Z.L.R. 615
9 See *Minister of Justice for Can.* v *City of Levis*, [1919] A.C. 505, at 514 (P.C.). And see also *A.G. of Can.* v *City of Toronto* (1893), 23 S.C.R. 514.
10 See supra, at 14–15 and 8–10.

or purpose? It is often only the first question which gives rise to any controversy. Positive answers to both questions will clearly support the conferral of immunity. Though, as will be noted, immunity may result in some situations in which an affirmative answer cannot apparently be given to the first question.

The sovereign is personally entitled to immunity from tax and so are its servants irrespective of their rank within the civil service hierarchy.[11] Corporate entities or composite groups of individuals such as boards or commissions[12] may be subject to such a degree of governmental control as to make them crown agents or agencies, in which case they share in the immunity.[13] If a body falls within this last category it will normally be the case that a tax upon it will amount to the taxation of a crown interest so as to satisfy the second condition of immunity. But an individual servant may be subject to tax in his personal or non-official capacity and in that case the crown will not usually be prejudiced.[14]

There is also a class of persons, often local authorities, which early English decisions recognize as being *in consimili casu* with servants of the crown, for they exercise essentially governmental functions, for example the operation of a court house or a police station. In that role they have been held free of taxes – of a

---

11 *Bank voor Handel en Scheepvaart* v *Administrator of Hungarian Property*, [1954] A.C. 584, see esp. at 612–15 *per* Lord Reid (H.L.). Lessees of the crown are not in any sense its instrumentalities and therefore are not entitled, as a class, to governmental immunity on that basis: *A.G. of Qd* v *A.G. of the Commonwealth* (1915), 20 C.L.R. 148, at 170 *per* Isaacs J & at 179 *per* Higgins J.

12 The principles for determining crown agency status are discussed in Hogg *Liability of the Crown* (1971), c 8, and McNairn, 'The Ontario Crown Agency Act' (1973), 6 *Ottawa L. Rev.* 1, at 2–9. A comparison of the Australian and Canadian cases that have had to decide whether a particular entity is a crown agent or not indicates that, generally speaking, there is a greater readiness on the part of the Canadian courts to find in favour of crown status (but cf *C.L.R.B.* v *C.N.R.* (1974), 45 D.L.R. (3d) 1 (S.C.C.)).

13 Entities were held to be crown agents and not subject to tax in *R* v *McCann* (1868), L.R. 3 Q.B. 141, aff'd ibid, at 677; *Halifax* v *Halifax Harbour Comm'rs*, [1935] 1 D.L.R. 657 (S.C.C.); *Re C.B.C. Assessment*, [1938] 4 D.L.R. 764 (Ont. C.A.); *Recorders Ct* v *C.B.C.*, [1941] 2 D.L.R. 551 (Que. K.B., App. Side); *Re Sask. Gov't Ins. Office & City of Saskatoon*, [1948] 2 D.L.R. 30 (Sask. C.A.); *Montreal* v *Montreal Locomotive Works Ltd*, [1947] 1 D.L.R. 161 (P.C.).

Entities were held not to be crown agents and subject to tax in *Grieg* v *University of Edinburgh* (1868), L.R. 1 Sc. & Div. 348; *Re N.S. Power Comm'n & Bank of N.S.*, [1935] 3 D.L.R. 494, judgment of Graham J (N.S.S.C. in banco); *Northern Sask. Flying Training School* v *Buckland*, [1944] 1 D.L.R. 285 (Sask. C.A.); *Grain Elevators Bd (Vict.)* v *Dunmunkle Corp.* (1946), 73 C.L.R. 70; *Launceston Corp.* v *The Hydro Electric Comm'n* (1959), 100 C.L.R. 654; *Gladstone Town Council* v *Gladstone Harbour Bd*, [1964] Qd. R. 505 (F.C.).

14 See infra, note 31.

property variety in practice.[15] Though frequently referred to, these decisions have not been controlling in any case of recent vintage.[16]

Governmental immunity does, however, afford some immediate benefits to persons who are not within the above categories when a provision of a taxing statute has the potential for prejudicing crown property, a prospect which the immunity rule seeks to prevent. For example, a tax upon a trustee in respect of property to which the crown alone is beneficially entitled is in essence a tax on crown property. It is, as such, objectionable if the legislation imposing the levy does not bind the sovereign expressly or by necessary implication.[17] In that event, the trustee will be free of tax. And a statutory authority to seize property in order to realize a tax cannot, absent the special inclusion of Her Majesty, be invoked against crown property even if that property is in the hands of a subject who is not an instrumentality of the crown.[18] But when a personal as opposed to a property tax is imposed upon a person who is not a servant or agent of the crown the primary obligation, that is to pay the tax, will be enforceable in that it is capable of satisfaction without any necessary reference or resort to crown property or assets.[19]

If a taxpayer happens to be in a contractual relationship with the crown, for example as the supplier of goods or services,[20] as a lessee,[21] or as a purchaser under an agreement for sale of real property,[22] then a tax upon him in relation to a

15 See *Mersey Docks* v *Cameron* (1865), 11 E.R. 1405 (H.L.); *Coomber* v *Justices of the Co'y of Berks* (1883), 9 App. Cas. 61 (H.L.).
16 See Hogg, at 213.
17 *R* v *McCann* (1868), L.R. 3 Q.B. 141, at 146, decision aff'd ibid, at 677; *Perry* v *Eames*, [1891] 1 Ch. 658, at 668-9; *Hornsey U.D.C.* v *Hennell*, [1902] 2 K.B. 73, at 80. And cf *Grain Elevators Bd (Vict.)* v *Dunmunkle Corp.* (1946), 73 C.L.R. 70, at 83-4; *Launceston Corp.* v *The Hydro-Electric Comm'n* (1959), 100 C.L.R. 654, at 658. The limited scope of the principle is evident from *Mersey Docks* v *Cameron* (1865), 11 E.R. 1405 (H.L.).
18 Cf *Robertson* v *Hopper* (1909), 12 W.L.R. 5, at 8 (Sask. S.C.); *Montreal* v *A.G. of Can.*, [1923] A.C. 136, at 144 (P.C.); *Vancouver* v *A.G. of Can.*, [1944] 1 D.L.R. 497, at 502 (S.C.C.).
19 *Re Rush & Tompkins Constr. Ltd* (1961), 28 D.L.R. (2d) 441 (B.C.S.C.). In *Bennett & White (Calgary) Ltd* v *Municipal District of Sugar City No. 5*, [1951] A.C. 786 (P.C.), a municipal taxing provision was viewed, as a matter of construction, as not applicable to a person in possession of federal crown property.
20 Cf *R* v *Bell Telephone Co.* (1935), 59 B.R. 205 (App. Side), and *Northern Sask. Flying Training School* v *Buckland*, [1944] 1 D.L.R. 285 (Sask. C.A.).
21 Cf *A.G. of Qd* v *A.G. of the Commonwealth* (1915), 20 C.L.R. 148; *Smith* v *Vermillion Hills Rural Council*, [1916] 2 A.C. 569 (P.C.); *Montreal* v *A.G. of Can.*, [1923] A.C. 136 (P.C.).
22 Cf *Osborne* v *Commonwealth* (1911), 12 C.L.R. 321, at 340-1, 348, & 368-9; *Southern Alta Land Co.* v *Rural Municipality of McLean* (1916), 29 D.L.R. 403 (S.C.C.).

subject matter of the contract is not objectionable though he may be able to pass on some or all of the burden of the tax to the crown.[23] The effect upon crown property or interests, in this situation, is not sufficiently direct to justify an extension of the right to assert governmental immunity to those contracting with the crown. If it is truly an interest of the subject, in the transaction or arrangement, which has been singled out for tax, there can be no objection to the tax on governmental immunity grounds. This is so even if the calculation of the amount of the tax is not limited by reference to the value of that private interest.[24]

In *Bank voor Handel en Scheepvaart* v *Administrator of Hungarian Property*[25] the contentious issue was whether there was any prejudice to a crown interest or purpose in the imposition of tax in the peculiar circumstances that gave rise to that litigation. In particular, the House of Lords had to decide whether the Custodian of Enemy Property in whom gold, held for the appellant bank in England, had been vested was justified in paying income tax on the profits realized from the investment of the proceeds of the sale of the gold. If so the bank, on the recognition of its claim to the funds at the conclusion of hostilities, was only entitled to recover the proceeds and the 'fruits' thereof less tax paid. But the bank argued that the custodian was a crown servant and the profits in his hands constituted crown income and, as such, were exempt from tax. Therefore, in its contention, no deduction on account of tax was proper. It was held, firstly, that the custodian was a crown servant and, secondly, by a bare majority, that the crown had a sufficient interest in the income to warrant it being treated as immune from taxation.

While under the control of the custodian the interest of the former owner of 'enemy property' was clearly extinguished but the crown was not, in the interim, entitled to the beneficial interest. Consequently, neither the assets nor the revenue derived therefrom could be freely diverted to the central fisc. But it was enough in the majority's view that the government could, without the aid of a further act of parliament, give directions as to the disposal of enemy property when peace was achieved. That was implicit in its power under the Trading with the Enemy Act to make 'arrangements' for such disposition, a sufficiently flexible expression to allow distribution of the property to other than its former owners as particular circumstances might dictate. The crown, therefore, had such an interest in the property that to tax its servant, the custodian, on that property would be to prejudice the crown. A different conclusion would be called for if

23 See *A.G. of Can.* v *City of Montreal* (1885), 13 S.C.R. 352, at 363–5 *per* Strong J, dissenting.
24 Cf *Re Cochrane & Cowan* (1921), 64 D.L.R. 209, at 212–13 (Ont. S.C., App. Div.); *Vancouver* v *A.G. of Can.*, [1944] 1 D.L.R. 497, esp. at 513 (S.C.C.).
25 [1954] A.C. 584 (H.L.)

the custodian simply received income which he was obliged without any discretion on the crown's part to turn over ultimately to some private person.[26] The income would then be taxable in the absence of any prejudicial effect upon a crown interest or purpose. It is evident from this case that a crown interest need not be very substantial for immunity to exist.[27]

Immunity from tax legislation is often asserted in relation to real property taxes. The immunity extends not to property owned by the crown but to property occupied by or for the sovereign.[28] Hence it is the character of the occupation rather than the title to the land which is crucial. Because of this fact lessees of private land for the crown may claim immunity.[29] It is not material that the land itself is not owned by the crown. On the other hand lessees of crown land, even if they are servants or agents of the crown, are not necessarily free of property tax.[30] They will be immune only if their occupation is essential for the performance of their duties and is not for their own benefit, so that to tax them would be an interference with a crown purpose.[31]

Nowadays the matter of crown liability to tax is not normally left to be governed by the ordinary principles of governmental immunity from statute. Rather the crown, its representatives, or property interests are likely to be declared, in specific terms, to be either subject to or exempt from tax. Real property assessment acts, for instance, will often provide an exemption for the lands of Her Majesty, for those who occupy such lands, or for both. To the extent that the exemption mirrors that immunity that would otherwise exist, cases concerning its ambit are relevant in determining the scope of the immunity and vice versa. If the exemption is a limited one and does not correspond to the full reach of governmental immunity its specification will usually be taken as introduced *ex abundante cautela* and not as intended to displace the larger immunity.[32]

In jurisdictions in which exemption from rating is accorded to crown lands rather than the occupation of such lands liability to tax turns simply on whether

26 *Per* Lord Reid, at 621
27 At least where the benefit of immunity falls upon the sovereign or one of its servants or agents, see ibid, at 614–15, 618–19, & 629.
28 *Mersey Docks* v *Cameron* (1865), 11 E.R. 1405, esp. at 1413 & 1427 (H.L.); *R* v *McCann* (1868), L.R. 3 Q.B. 141, aff'd ibid, at 677; *Halifax* v *Halifax Harbour Comm'rs*, [1935] 1 D.L.R. 657 (S.C.C.); *Criterion Theatres Ltd* v *Melbourne & Metropolitan Bd of Works*, [1945] V.L.R. 267
29 *Mersey Docks* v *Cameron* (1865), 11 E.R. 1405, at 1413 (H.L.)
30 Ibid
31 *Gambier* v *Overseers of Lydford* (1854), 118 E.R. 1171; *Martin* v *Assessment Comm. of West Derby* (1883), 11 Q.B.D. 145 (C.A.); *Showers* v *Assessment Comm. of Chelmsford Union*, [1891] 1 Q.B. 339 (C.A.)
32 See *Smithett* v *Blythe* (1830), 109 E.R. 876; *Weymouth* v *Nugent* (1865), 122 E.R. 1106, at 1111; *Hornsey U.D.C.* v *Hennell*, [1902] 2 K.B. 73, at 81.

it is crown property which is the subject of the attempt to tax. It is really a matter of indifference whether or not the person in occupation is there for the benefit of the crown.[33] The essential requirement for exemption is to show that a governmental interest is prejudiced in the limited sense that the tax is sought to be applied to the lands of Her Majesty.

A state commission could not satisfy that condition in *State Electricity Commission of Victoria* v *City of South Melbourne*[34] and, accordingly, was denied exemption from municipal rates levied against lands held in its own name, whether or not it was an agent of the crown, a point which the High Court left open. The commission's constitutive statute provided specifically for the acquisition of lands in fee simple by the commission from the crown, though it also contemplated that the commission might simply be given permission to use and occupy crown lands. So far as title to land was taken by the commission it was held that it could not secure the benefit of the exemption from tax in favour of 'property of Her Majesty.' Thus the court rejected any suggestion that the exemption also protected lands occupied on behalf of the crown by its agent.

INTERGOVERNMENTAL IMMUNITY

Taxation of Government Instrumentalities

In the early years of the federal experience in both Australia and Canada uncritical acceptance was given to the proposition that the application of a local taxing act to emoluments of a federal crown servant constituted an impermissible interference with a federal instrumentality.[35] In both countries the American doctrine of immunity of instrumentalities,[36] which had a very respectable genesis in the judgment of Chief Justice Marshall in *McCulloch* v *Maryland*,[37] was adopted. The

33 *Essendon Corp.* v *Blackwood* (1877), 2 App. Cas. 574, at 587 (P.C.); *Grain Elevators Bd (Vict.)* v *Dunmunkle Corp.* (1946), 73 C.L.R. 70, at 83–4 *per* Dixon J
34 (1968), 118 C.L.R. 504, foll'd in *Perth* v *Metropolitan Region Planning Authority*, [1969] W.A.R. 137
35 See *D'Emden* v *Pedder* (1904), 1 C.L.R. 91; *Deakin* v *Webb* (1904), 1 C.L.R. 585, over-ruling *Re Income Tax Acts (No. 4), Wollaston's Case* (1902), 28 V.L.R. 357 (F.C.). The leading Canadian case was *Leprohon* v *City of Ottawa* (1878), 2 O.A.R. 522, but see also *Ex p. Owen* (1881), 20 N.B.R. 487 (F.C.); *Ackman* v *Town of Moncton* (1884), 24 N.B.R. 103 (F.C.); *Coates* v *Town of Moncton* (1886), 25 N.B.R. 605 (F.C.); *Ex p. Burke* (1896), 34 N.B.R. 200; *R* v *Bowell* (1896), 4 B.C.R. 498. And cf *Ex p. Killam* (1898), 34 N.B.R. 530 (F.C.).
36 See Sackville, 'The Doctrine of Immunity of Instrumentalities in the United States and Australia: A Comparative Analysis' (1969), 7 *M.U.L.R.* 16, at 19–35.
37 (1819), 17 U.S. 316

theory behind the protection thus afforded was that to tax federal officers would be to diminish the compensation agreed upon by the national government as an adequate return for their services. If the states or provinces were allowed this liberty they might even take it to excess so that the ability to retain crown servants or to transfer them freely, between jurisdictions of differing tax rates, would be threatened. There was some textual justification in the constitutions for limiting the powers of the states and provinces to tax, so as to avoid these dangers, in the exclusive federal power concerning the public service.[38] In Canada, particularly, reliance was placed on this authority. The Canadian provision, unlike its Australian counterpart, deals specifically with the remuneration aspect of government employment. It enables Parliament to pass laws 'fixing ... and providing for the Salaries and Allowances of Civil and other Officers of the Government of Canada.'[39] To allow provincial taxation of such salaries was considered to be incompatible with this power. In Australia the immunity came to be regarded as depending principally upon general implications from the constitution which necessitated that state power be read narrowly as not encompassing authority to tax federal instrumentalities.

The Privy Council, in a direct appeal from a state court in *Webb* v *Outtrim*,[40] disapproved of the doctrine of implied immunity as it had been propounded by the High Court and held the salary of a Commonwealth officer subject to state income tax. But the High Court, in a demonstration of its independence in the resolution of constitutional questions, declined to follow the Privy Council in the next comparable case to come before it, *Baxter* v *Commissioner of Taxation (New South Wales)*.[41] The court was not unanimous, however, as it had been on previous occasions. Isaacs J, who dissented along with Higgins J, could find no interference with the Commonwealth in non-discriminatory state taxation of the income of federal officers for it did not touch their functions as Commonwealth officials.[42]

In Canada by contrast, *Webb* v *Outtrim*, though an Australian appeal, did herald in a very proximate way the beginning of the end of the immunity of federal officers from general provincial taxation. The New Brunswick Supreme Court in *Abbott* v *City of St John*,[43] on the compulsion of *Webb* v *Outtrim*, reversed the previous line of provincial court authority according immunity. The

38 Viz. s 52(ii) of the Australian constitution and s 91(8) of the BNA Act
39 BNA Act, s 91(8)
40 [1907] A.C. 81 (P.C.)
41 (1907), 4 C.L.R. 1087. And see also *Flint* v *Webb* (1907), 4 C.L.R. 1178.
42 (1907), 4 C.L.R. 1087, at 1165
43 (1908), 38 N.B.R. 421 (F.C.). In the New Brunswick court the case was styled *R* v *City of St John, ex p. Abbott*.

Supreme Court of Canada, in its first confrontation with this issue, affirmed, though with only limited reliance upon the Privy Council opinion, which had been rendered just two years previously.[44] The court rejected the argument that there was any implied limitation on the express provincial taxing power and that a tax upon the income of dominion officers would conflict with the authority of parliament to fix their salaries. Any potential for abuse of the provincial taxing authority was deemed an inadequate ground for limiting its scope.[45]

The principle of the *Abbott* case was soon to be applied to support the inclusion of the salaries of federally appointed judges, which the British North America Act entrusts parliament to fix and provide, within a general provincial income tax scheme.[46] The independence of the judiciary, which is assured constitutionally in the case of superior courts to the extent of granting tenure to judges and placing judicial salaries outside provincial authority,[47] could not be said to be called in question by such taxation.[48]

By the time *Amalgamated Society of Engineers* v *Adelaide Steamship Co.*[49] (the *Engineers* case) came to be decided in 1920 the doctrine of implied immunities of instrumentalities had been held in Australia to afford protection to government instrumentalities not only from taxation of benefits from employment but from any regulation by the other level of political authority in the federal division.[50] In fact the instances of this latter protection were rather more plausible, for the effect was to insulate the servants and agents of government from control in their performance of functions which were clearly on behalf of the crown and possessed no element of personal benefit. But by this time the claims of the doctrine were far too exaggerated to survive much longer given its earlier manifestations and its now reciprocal operation. The High Court had come to accord a privileged status to state instrumentalities in the face of Commonwealth legislation[51] as well as to Commonwealth instrumentalities in relation to state

44 (1908), 40 S.C.R. 597
45 *Bank of Toronto* v *Lambe* (1887), 12 App. Cas. 575 (P.C.), was applied in this respect.
46 *Toronto* v *Morson* (1917), 38 D.L.R. 224 (Ont. S.C., App. Div.). See also *Judges* v *A.G. of Sask.*, [1937] 2 D.L.R. 209 (P.C.). And cf *Cooper* v *Commissioner of Income Tax for Qd* (1907), 4 C.L.R. 1304.
47 BNA Act, ss 99 & 100
48 See *Judges* v *A.G. of Sask.*, [1937] 2 D.L.R. 209 (P.C.).
49 (1920), 28 C.L.R. 129
50 See *Federated Amalgamated Gov't Ry & Tramway Service Ass'n* v *N.S.W. Ry Traffic Employees Ass'n* (1906), 4 C.L.R. 488 (*Railway Servants* case); *Australian Workers' Union* v *Adelaide Milling Co.* (1919), 26 C.L.R. 460 (*Wheat Lumpers* case). And see, as to a further tax immunity, *Commonwealth* v *N.S.W.* (1906), 3 C.L.R. 807.
51 See the *Railway Servants* case (1906), 4 C.L.R. 488, and the *Wheat Lumpers* case (1919), 26 C.L.R. 460.

legislation. The *Engineers* case, which presented a claim by certain state trading concerns to immunity from Commonwealth legislative control in relation to industrial disputes,[52] proved to be the occasion for laying to rest the immunity doctrine. In refusing to except the state from Commonwealth regulation the High Court disavowed the doctrine of implied immunities of instrumentalities. But it evinced a rather cautious approach to previous authority, offering a tentative explanation of the cases which had held Commonwealth servants immune from state tax. It considered those decisions to be supportable on the basis of an inconsistency between a Commonwealth statute, fixing the servant's salary or requiring a receipt for salary, and the state taxing statute held inapplicable, which made the salary or the issuing of a receipt the subject of tax.[53] That inconsistency, of course, had to be resolved in favour of the federal statute by virtue of the paramountcy provision of the constitution (section 109).

A few years later the Privy Council in a Canadian appeal, *Caron v The King*,[54] held that a provincial government minister was liable to federal income tax on the salary and indemnity which he received for his service in the cabinet and the legislature. The reasoning of the majority in *Abbott v City of St John*[55] was specifically approved. Finally, in *Forbes v Attorney General of Manitoba*[56] the Judicial Committee was faced for the first time in a Canadian case with the very situation that *Abbott* had presented, that is a provincial attempt to tax a dominion civil servant on his income. It was held that the tax did no violence to the authority of parliament to fix the salaries of civil servants and that the possibility of the power to tax crown servants being used *in terrorem* was by the way. The *Abbott* case was again given the imprimatur of the highest appellate tribunal.[57]

In *West v Commissioner of Taxation (New South Wales)*[58] a state treated a pension received by a former member of the Commonwealth civil service as subject to tax under its general income tax legislation. The pension had been paid pursuant to the terms of the Commonwealth's Superannuation Act. That act was silent on the question of the taxability of benefits provided but other legislation, the Financial Emergency Acts, authorized regulations prescribing the maximum liability of salaries and pensions to income tax, including that of a state. Regula-

---

52 Under the constitution the Commonwealth has authority to pass laws with respect to 'Conciliation and arbitration for the prevention and settlement of industrial disputes' extending beyond the limits of any one State' (s 51(xxxv)).
53 The cases so explained were *D'Emden v Pedder* (1904), 1 C.L.R. 91; *Deakin v Webb* (1904), 1 C.L.R. 585; *Baxter v Commissioner of Taxation (N.S.W.)* (1907), 4 C.L.R. 1087.
54 [1924] A.C. 999 (P.C.)
55 (1908), 40 S.C.R. 597
56 [1937] A.C. 260 (P.C.)
57 And see *Judges v A.G. of Sask.*, [1937] 2 D.L.R. 209 (P.C.), for a further approval.
58 (1937), 56 C.L.R. 657

tions had in fact been made establishing limits upon the taxation of salaries but not upon the taxation of pensions.

The High Court was unanimous in holding the pension liable to tax. Four members of the six-man bench took the position that there was no inconsistency between a law providing for a pension and a general state act taxing income, including superannuation benefits.[59] Various references were made to the Canadian cases of *Abbott*, *Caron*, and *Forbes* as sources of support for this proposition. This conclusion appears to be inconsistent with the explanation in the *Engineers* case of the earlier cases involving state taxation of the income of Commonwealth servants as turning on an inconsistency between a Commonwealth law and the state taxing act. But only Latham CJ was prepared to say that those pre-*Engineers* cases were no longer good law.[60] Dixon and McTiernan JJ distinguished the earlier cases on the basis that they did not involve a situation in which the Commonwealth had given a clear indication that the remuneration paid its servants was to be subject to tax.[61] It had given such an indication in the case at hand as the result of legislation enabling protection by regulation and the government declining to afford it in the case of pensions.[62] But despite this ingenious attempt to provide a distinction, the decision as a whole indicates that the slender reed of authority left to the earlier decisions by the *Engineers* case must now be regarded as severely impaired.

A federal crown servant may be entitled to benefits from employment that are not of a monetary character. And the receipt or the utilization of these 'fringe benefits' may also be the occasion for the imposition of a local tax. For example, the occupation of premises provided by the federal government for its employees may be subject to assessment. This is perfectly proper if the occupation is a beneficial one and not required for the performance of the servant's duties. This latter criterion evolved in response to claims to the enjoyment of governmental immunity from tax.[63] And it has been the basis, in addition to section 125 of the BNA Act, which is discussed in the next section, for the resolution of interjurisdictional immunity claims by Canadian government servants occupying crown land.[64] The result is similar to that reached on the question of immunity from

59 Latham CJ, ibid, at 667–70, Starke J, at 677, Dixon J, at 678–81 & Evatt J, at 710
60 Ibid, at 667 & 670
61 Ibid, at 683 *per* Dixon J & at 714 *per* McTiernan J
62 See the judgment of McTiernan J, ibid, at 714. And see also the judgment of Rich J, at 675–6.
63 See supra, note 31.
64 See *Re Cochrane & Cowan* (1921), 64 D.L.R. 209 (Ont. S.C., App. Div.), and *Watters* v *Watrous*, [1950] 2 D.L.R. 574 (Sask. C.A.). And cf *Stinson* v *Middleton Township*, [1949] 2 D.L.R. 328 (Ont. C.A.). See also *Phillips & Taylor* v *Sault Ste Marie*, [1954] 3 D.L.R. 81 (S.C.C.), which turned exclusively on s 125.

137 The crown as taxpayer

local taxes on income and pensions received by a federal crown servant. That is, no protection exists to the extent that there is no interference with a crown function and the tax relates merely to a benefit accruing to the taxpayer in his personal capacity.

Immunity from Taxes on Property

Both the Canadian and Australian constitutions make specific provision for immunity from property taxes.[65] Section 125 of the British North America Act is in these terms:

No Lands or Property belonging to Canada or any Province shall be liable to taxation.

And section 114 of the Australian constitution reads, in the relevant part, as follows:

A State shall not, without the consent of the Parliament of the Commonwealth ... impose any tax on property of any kind belonging to the Commonwealth, nor shall the Commonwealth impose any tax on property of any kind belonging to a State.

The similarities in the two sections are not coincidental, for the former undoubtedly provided part of the inspiration for the latter.[66] The divergences which exist have not produced any significant differences in the impact of the two sections. In fact neither provision presents as great an inhibition, as might be expected, upon the exercise of taxing powers.

The immunity in Canada appears, on the face of it, not to be confined to one of an interjurisdictional character as it clearly is under the Australian constitution. But the Canadian provision has been interpreted as limited to proscribing taxes by a province on the dominion, and vice versa.[67] Another literal difference

---

65 The Indian constitution also makes such provision, but with a number of qualifications that do not appear in the Canadian and Australian constitutions, see arts. 285 & 289 of the Constitution of India Act, 1950.

66 *A.G. of N.S.W.* v *Collector of Customs for N.S.W.* (1908), 5 C.L.R. 818, at 853 & 855 *per* Higgins J

67 See *B.C. Power Comm'n* v *Victoria*, [1951] 2 D.L.R. 480, at 481 (B.C.C.A.), and *Re Taxation of University of Manitoba Lands*, [1940] 1 D.L.R. 579, at 587 *per* Trueman JA, dissenting in part (Man. C.A.). It has also been suggested that s 125 protects the property of one province from taxation by another province, see Abel (ed) *Laskin's Canadian Constitutional Law* (4th ed rev. 1975), at 744.

that has so far proved inconsequential is that the Canadian constitution describes the kinds of levies that are prohibited as taxes on 'lands and property' whereas the Australian constitution refers to taxes on 'property of any kind.'[68] A final textual variation that may be noted is the inclusion in the Australian section of a permitted technique for the federal authority to decline the benefit of immunity, that is by consent of the Commonwealth parliament,[69] which has no Canadian counterpart. But even absent a similar qualification upon the immunity conferred by section 125 of the BNA Act, the Supreme Court has indicated in *R* v *Breton*[70] that the immunity of federal crown property from tax may be avoided by a federal statute which expressly or by necessary implication subjects that property to the otherwise prohibited levy.[71] The immunity which was recognized in that case was put on the basis of section 125, as an alternate ground, and the only 'waiver' legislation referred to, the federal Crown Liability Act, was not of a kind falling within the above description. Therefore the immunity conferred by section 125 persisted.

Though the prohibition against the imposition of state property taxes upon the Commonwealth is capable of variation by the consent of parliament, the reciprocal immunity of the states from Commonwealth property taxes is, in terms, absolute. This absence of symmetry may have been the accident of drafting, for the clause granting an immunity in favour of state property was tacked on as an amendment to the provision for Commonwealth immunity during the course of one of the constitutional conventions.[72] But even though a state may be unable to surrender its immunity from Commonwealth property taxes there is no great inconvenience to the working of a co-operative federal system. Grants could, nonetheless, be made by the states to the Commonwealth in lieu of taxes on their property, to make up for lost revenue, without doing violence to section 114.[73] Though if that were to happen it would appear somewhat anomalous in that, on

---

68 *A.G. of N.S.W.* v *Collector of Customs for N.S.W.* (1908), 5 C.L.R. 818, at 853 *per* Higgins J

69 The consent must take the form of a legislative act; *Municipal Council of Sydney* v *Commonwealth* (1904), 1 C.L.R. 208, at 232 *per* Griffith CJ; *Carter* v *Egg & Egg Pulp Marketing Bd (Vict.)* (1942), 66 C.L.R. 557, at 595 *per* Williams J

70 (1967), 65 D.L.R. (2d) 76 (S.C.C.)

71 Ibid, at 81

72 See Quick & Garran *The Annotated Constitution of Australia* (1901), at 948. The 'consent of Parliament' clause was apparently modelled on s x of art. 1 of the constitution of the United States. That provision, like s 114 as it was originally proposed, purports only to confer an immunity on the central government and not on the states.

73 Cf *Municipal Council of Sydney* v *Commonwealth* (1904), 1 C.L.R. 208, at 232 *per* Griffith CJ

the broader scale, the revenue imbalance is on the side of the federal authority. Therefore redress by the transfer of funds has generally been in the other direction, that is from the Commonwealth to the states.[74]

In Canada there seems no reason why a provincial legislature could not effect a surrender of a section 125 immunity just as it has been suggested that parliament might surrender the immunity which favours federal property under that section.[75] In any case the device of grants in place of taxes, by either level of authority, is also available under the Canadian federal system, section 125 presenting no impediment in that regard.[76]

The property tax prohibition has been considered in both Australia and Canada against the background of a claim by a state or province to immunity from federal customs duties on goods imported from abroad.[77] In *Attorney General of New South Wales* v *Collector of Customs for New South Wales*[78] (the *Steel Rails* case) a state claimed duty free status for steel rails which it imported from England for the construction of state railways. The High Court rejected the claim, concluding that section 114 did not prevent this form of levy against a state. A distinction was taken by reference to general usage, statutes, and the constitution itself between duties of customs and taxes on property, the former focussing on the act of importation rather than property as such. There was at least, then, a plausible meaning of section 114 which would exclude duties as an alternative to a wider meaning that might include them. Any ambiguity, however, had to be resolved by construing section 114 subject to the constitution as a whole. In that case the result must be that, to give proper scope to the powers of the Commonwealth to impose customs duties and to regulate commerce (sections 88, 90, & 51(i) of the constitution), the narrower meaning ought to be preferred. It was not doubted, however, that the authority to lay duties of import on goods came, in part at least, under the federal power of 'taxation' (section 51(ii)).

The Privy Council reached a similar conclusion, but in a more cryptic fashion as was its practice, about the effect of section 125 of the BNA Act upon the power of the Canadian parliament to impose customs duties on the provinces. In *At-*

---

74 Pursuant to the grants power under s 96 of the Australian constitution
75 See *R* v *Breton* (1967), 65 D.L.R. (2d) 76 (S.C.C.).
76 Grants are in fact made pursuant to the Municipal Grants Act, R.S.C. 1970, c M-15, directly to municipalities in lieu of taxes on federal crown lands. *Ottawa Public School Bd* v *Ottawa*, [1953] 1 D.L.R. 692 (Ont. C.A.), involved an issue of the proper disposition of such grant money once received by a municipality.
77 A like prohibition in the Indian constitution, in art. 289(1), has also been considered in the same context with the same result that was arrived at in Australia and Canada, see *Re Sea Customs Act, S. 20(2)*, A.I.R. (50) 1963 S.C. 1760.
78 (1908), 5 C.L.R. 818

torney General of British Columbia v *Attorney General of Canada*[79] *(Liquor Import* case), the Judicial Committee said that section 125 must be read in light of the scheme of the constitution. In fact it appears in part of the BNA Act dealing with the allocation and control of property, the bulk of which falls to the provinces. It was said that the section, so placed, should not be interpreted as excluding the operation of laws made in exercise of federal legislative powers under another part of the constitution. In particular it ought not to limit statutes passed pursuant to the power of parliament to regulate trade and commerce throughout the dominion (section 91(2) of the BNA Act), which exhibits no partiality in its operation. Earlier in the judgment the Board had found the source of dominion power to levy customs duties[80] in both the trade and commerce power (section 91(2)) and the taxation power (section 91(3)).

Given the paucity of reasoned argument to support the result which the Privy Council reached, we are forced to speculate as to the true grounds of the decision. Did reasoning similar to that in the Australian *Steel Rails* case, which was given no more than passing reference, in fact appeal to the Judicial Committee as it did to the Supreme Court[81] in an earlier stage of the case? Before venturing an answer to this question two other possible bases for the decision should be considered. Section 125 might conceivably be taken as protecting only that property which is the subject of other provisions in part VIII of the constitution, in which it occurs, a view espoused by Idington J in the Supreme Court. While this would no doubt exclude the liquor acquired by British Columbia from the operation of section 125, it would also exclude all provincial or federal property acquired since confederation, which would seem to narrow the section excessively. Secondly, it is arguable that the reason section 125 was not offended by the imposition of customs duty in the *Liquor Import* case was because that section is subordinate, either generally or in relation to the trade and commerce power, to section 91 if not also to section 92. Those sections confer legislative authority on the Canadian parliament and the provincial legislatures respectively. But this view, particularly in its broader forms, also tends to rob section 125 of any significant scope. The most defensible position is that which was articulated in the

79 [1924] A.C. 222 (P.C.)
80 According to the Privy Council opinion the case also concerned sales and excise tax. But there is no evidence of this element in the report of the Supreme Court's disposition of the case. In the absence of any discussion in this aspect on the part of either court the case should not be taken as justifying the application of federal sales and excise taxes to the goods of a province. This represents a change in the position which I have previously taken, see McNairn, 'The Ontario Crown Agency Act' (1973), 6 *Ottawa L. Rev.* 1, at 15–16.
81 See [1923] 1 D.L.R. 223 (S.C.C.).

Steel Rails case. That is a prohibition upon property taxes could be meant either to include or exclude customs duties but the simultaneous conferral of powers on the central authority sufficient to enable the regulation of import trade indicates that the more restrictive meaning is appropriate. Because the relevant federal authority, unlike that which supports the raising of most federal taxes, flows in part from the trade and commerce power this approach may give the impression that that power overrides section 125. But this is only the apparent result of construing section 125 in light of the constitution as a whole.

Some financial impositions may be excluded from the protection of section 125 or section 114 because they are not truly taxes but charges for services.[82] And levies that are undoubtedly taxes may be outside the reach of either provision because they do not relate to property. Examples of the latter are a pay-roll tax,[83] a stamp duty on the giving of a receipt,[84] a tax on occupation,[85] and a tax on a transaction.[86] Of course it will often be extremely difficult in practice to distinguish between a tax on property and a tax on a person in respect of property or between a tax on property and a tax on an activity or transaction involving property. The cases from which the above examples were drawn suggest, however, that these are indeed legitimate distinctions in determining whether a particular tax runs afoul of section 125 or section 114 in its application to the other level of government in the federation.

It will be remembered that the immunity of the crown from real property taxes at common law was a consequence not of crown ownership of the land assessed but of an occupation of land by or on behalf of the crown. Some statutory exemptions from tax in the Australian states have been taken to substitute the reverse principle. It may also be important in a particular case to decide whether section 114 of the Australian constitution or section 125 of the BNA Act does the same thing.

82 See *A.G. of Can.* v *Registrar of Titles*, [1934] 4 D.L.R. 764 (B.C.C.A.). But compare *R* v *Breton* (1967), 65 D.L.R. (2d) 76 (S.C.C.), in which it was held that s 125 would be violated if the federal crown were subject to a tax, which reflected the cost of municipal sidewalk repairs, imposed by provincial statute on proprietors who failed to fulfill their duty to keep adjoining sidewalks in repair. For a more extended discussion of the distinction between taxes and charges for services, and its significance for s 125 purposes, see LaForest *The Allocation of Taxing Power under the Canadian Constitution* (1967), at 154–6.
83 See *Vict.* v *Commonwealth* (1971), 122 C.L.R. 353.
84 See *D'Emden* v *Pedder* (1904), 1 C.L.R. 91.
85 See *Phillips & Taylor* v *Sault Ste Marie*, [1954] 3 D.L.R. 81 (S.C.C.). Compare *Stinson* v *Middleton Township*, [1949] 2 D.L.R. 328 (Ont. C.A.). See also *Sammartino* v *A.G. of B.C.* (1971), 22 D.L.R. (3d) 194 (B.C.C.A.).
86 See *A.G. of N.S.W.* v *Collector of Customs for N.S.W.* (1908), 5 C.L.R. 818, at 845 *per* Isaacs J & at 854 *per* Higgins J.

Dixon J apparently thought that section 114 might change the emphasis in the same way that some taxing statutes have done. In declining an invitation to hold invalid the imposition of a municipal rate upon the Commonwealth as inconsistent with section 114, he said in *Essendon Corporation* v *Criterion Theatres Ltd*[87] that:

It has been thought that perhaps the purpose in the Constitution of so much of s. 114 as gives to Commonwealth property immunity from State taxation and of so much as creates the reciprocal immunity for State property is to ensure that mere ownership by State or Commonwealth of property is enough to give the property protection from the taxes of the other government. That is to say mere ownership by Commonwealth or state is made enough, in order that immunity should not depend upon the nature or purpose of the use, if any, to which the property might be put ... [88]

Latham CJ in the same case felt constrained to find that the Commonwealth acquired some kind of property interest in the assessed land, which it had taken possession of under national security regulations, for section 114 to operate as a barrier to the imposition of the tax.[89] At common law immunity would have resulted simply from the fact that the land was occupied by the crown. The other members of the court decided the case without reference to section 114 except to indicate that it was unnecessary to pass on the argument so based.

The Full Court has never in fact had to decide whether the possible function of section 114, about which Dixon J speculated, represents the correct view. It may be recalled, however, that in *State Electricity Commission of Victoria* v *City of South Melbourne*,[90] the High Court held that lands acquired by the Commission were outside a statutory exemption for 'land the property of Her Majesty.' This was so even though the Commission may have been a crown agent occupying for the crown, a matter that it was thought unnecessary to decide. It seems proper, therefore, to treat section 114 as similarly introducing, as the criterion of immunity from a land tax, the existence of a crown property interest as the subject of tax. Whether section 125 of the BNA Act plays a similar role has not been the subject of specific judicial comment. However, the fact that the Supreme Court has sustained the application of a provincial tenant's tax, despite section 125, to a federal crown servant required by his employment to occupy a govern-

---

87 (1947), 74 C.L.R. 1
88 Ibid, at 18
89 Ibid, at 13
90 (1968), 118 C.L.R. 504, considered supra, at 132.

ment residence[91] suggests that immunity is to be delimited in the same way under section 125. Apart from the constitution, the tenant's occupation might well have been regarded as one for the crown and hence as qualifying for immunity from tax,[92] the fact that the tax was not imposed upon crown lands as such being inconsequential. But under section 125 the absence of any burden upon crown lands was clearly telling against immunity.

General Immunity from Tax

Apart from the immunity expressly provided by the two constitutions does a further and larger intergovernmental tax immunity exist? It has already been pointed out that a tax by one political unit upon a servant of the other level of government, in his non-official capacity, is unobjectionable. But let it now be supposed as a starting point for further discussion that a state or provincial tax, not concerned with property, is levied upon the federal crown or one of its instrumentalities in relation to an exercise of official functions. Subsequently attention will be directed to the permissible impact of a similar federal tax upon the crown in right of a state or province.

State or Provincial Taxation of the Federal Government

General Principles: In *Essendon Corporation v Criterion Theatres Ltd* [93] the High Court held that the Commonwealth was not liable to tax under a municipal rating statute. But only Dixon J rested the decision on a general lack of competence on the part of the state to levy a tax directly on the Commonwealth in respect of the exercise of its functions – in this case the central government was acting in its defence role. This incapacity, he explained, followed from 'the system of government established by the Constitution.' The features of that system which he listed include not only those that would suggest a general Commonwealth immunity from state statute law, but also some that tend to support an immunity specifically from tax laws. In particular, Dixon J mentioned the independence of the federal fiscal system and the elaboration of financial relations between the central and state governments in the constitution.[94] He went on to argue that his conclusion was not inconsistent with the overruling of the immunity of instrumentalities doctrine in the *Engineers* case.[95] That earlier doctrine, he maintained,

91 In *Phillips & Taylor* v *Sault Ste Marie*, [1954] 3 D.L.R. 81 (S.C.C.)
92 See the cases cited supra in notes 31 and 64.
93 (1947), 74 C.L.R. 1
94 Ibid, at 22
95 (1920), 28 C.L.R. 129

would have been inapposite here and the latter case, in any event, did not rule out any implications whatsoever from the constitution. Indeed it contained a specific reservation concerning taxation powers. The Chief Justice, Sir John Latham, put his decision on the basis that the general words of the rating legislation could not embrace the Commonwealth in light of section 114 of the constitution. But he added, rather tentatively, that it was his view that it was fundamental to a federal constitutional arrangement that the states or provinces cannot tax the Commonwealth or the dominion and that a reciprocal, but more limited, immunity also exists.[96] The three other members of the court expressed no opinion on the alleged general immunity of the Commonwealth from state tax.

In *Australian Coastal Shipping Commission* v *O'Reilly*,[97] counsel for the state of Victoria attacked the validity of a Commonwealth act conferring an immunity from state tax upon the Commission equivalent to that enjoyed by the Commonwealth itself. But in this case, coming some fifteen years after the *Essendon* decision, it was conceded, for the purposes of argument, that a state could not in fact tax the Commonwealth.[98] And no fact situation presenting an issue of Commonwealth immunity from state tax has since given rise to reported litigation.

For those who would put the case against such an immunity there is a threshold argument that section 114 of the constitution is exhaustive of the reach of Commonwealth immunity from state taxes. But, as has been observed earlier, the specification in a statute of immunity in a limited respect has been viewed as motivated by an abundance of caution and not as intended to substitute an impoverished version of a larger immunity.[99] No doubt the same view could be taken of the inclusion of a restricted immunity in the written portion of a constitution. Moreover section 114, if exhaustive of Commonwealth immunity from state tax, must surely be exhaustive of state immunity from Commonwealth tax. The latter proposition, however, cannot be sustained unimpaired after the recent decision in *Victoria* v *Commonwealth*.[100] Indeed, the state was held liable to the payment of Commonwealth pay-roll tax in that case, but no member of the High Court opted for the short answer that since the tax was outside section 114 no immunity could exist. And Menzies J formally expressed the view that section 114 'is not an exhaustive statement of the protection of the Commonwealth or of a state from the taxation laws of the other.'[101]

96 (1947), 74 C.L.R. 1, at 14. See also *Municipal Council of Sydney* v *Commonwealth* (1904), 1 C.L.R. 208, at 236 *per* Barton J.
97 (1962), 107 C.L.R. 46
98 See ibid, at 70.
99 See text accompanying note 32, supra.
100 (1971), 122 C.L.R. 353
101 Ibid, at 393

The opinions of Dixon J and Latham CJ in the *Essendon* case receive additional support from the later cases of *Commonwealth* v *Bogle*[102] and *Commonwealth* v *Cigamatic Pty*,[103] which recognized an intergovernmental immunity of the Commonwealth from regulatory, rather than taxing, legislation of a state. The intergovernmental tax immunity of the Commonwealth, apart from that under section 114 of the constitution, seems to be simply an instance of the general immunity referred to in those two decisions. This appears to be so despite the intimations of Dixon J in the earlier *Essendon* case that tax immunity may be a special case with its own unique justification.

It will be recalled that the position was taken in a previous chapter that the general intergovernmental immunity of the Commonwealth ought to be limited to protecting the Commonwealth from the reach of state legislation in so far as it might prejudice the federal crown in the exercise of its prerogatives.[104] Those prerogatives include governmental immunity from statute so that the Commonwealth would be free of state taxes on this approach if the state taxing legislation did not bind the Commonwealth expressly or by necessary implication. But it would not otherwise be immune,[105] for no other prerogatives seem to be available to the federal crown in the face of this kind of state legislation, namely that imposing a tax. Should immunity from state taxing statutes purporting to bind the Commonwealth be deemed necessary then the central parliament could always legislate to effectively create such an immunity.[106]

In Canada the position is probably the same as in Australia, that is, the federal government enjoys an immunity, arguably within the limits just referred to, from provincial taxes other than those from which there is specific constitutional protection. But there is very little authoritative comment on the matter. In repudiating the old doctrine of immunity of instrumentalities it was said in a Canadian case,[107] as it had been said in an Australian case,[108] that the inclusion of an express exemption for property tax in the constitution constitutes a denial of any other implied limitation on local taxing powers in favour of the federal authority. But that was long before the recognition of a rather different form of intergovernmental immunity in *Gauthier* v *The King*.[109] The rationale of that de-

102 (1953), 89 C.L.R. 229, discussed at length at 37 and 100–1
103 (1962), 108 C.L.R. 372, discussed at length at 36 and 114–15
104 See supra, at 38–40.
105 Except, of course, when s 114 of the constitution was applicable
106 See infra, at 155–8.
107 *Abbott* v *City of St John* (1908), 40 S.C.R. 597, at 608–9 *per* Davies J, disappr'd on
    this point in *R* v *Anderson*, [1930] 2 W.W.R. 595, at 597 *per* Trueman JA (Man. C.A.)
108 *Webb* v *Outtrim*, [1907] A.C. 81, at 91 (P.C.)
109 (1918), 40 D.L.R. 353 (S.C.C.)

cision, recognizing an immunity of the federal authority from a provincial arbitration provision, would seem to support a comparable immunity from provincial taxing legislation. And three subsequent decisions have in fact adverted to the possibility of a general immunity of the federal government from provincial taxation.[110]

There are a number of cases in which a claimant of immunity failed in an attempt to come under the umbrella of section 125 and was, therefore, denied exception from provincial taxes or charges. But the circumstances were such that there appears to have been no basis for according the party relying on section 125 the benefit of an implied intergovernmental immunity, though generally there is no discussion of that possibility. In one case[111] the federal crown would undoubtedly have been liable to the payment of provincial land registration charges because it took advantage voluntarily of the registration legislation.[112] In another,[113] a crown servant occupying crown land in the course of his employment would have been liable to a provincial tax on occupation since the relevant taxing provision purported expressly to bind the crown in right of Canada or any province. In other cases the claimant was either unable to establish that it was an instrumentality of the federal government[114] or that the tax would prejudice the crown,[115] in which events it is unlikely that any general intergovernmental immunity would pertain. The section 125 cases do not, therefore, by their silence on the question, preclude the argument that the federal government can take advantage of its general intergovernmental immunity when faced with the kind of provincial levies that do not fall within section 125. That was simply an argument that, while it might have been made, was liable to fail in the situations that have come before the courts.

Surrender of Immunity: The intergovernmental immunity of the federal authority, on the preferred view as to its scope, will not persist in the face of state or provincial taxing statutes which expressly or by necessary implication bind the federal crown.[116] But in fact the initiative to avoid immunity has often been taken at the central level rather than leaving it to the states or provinces, individually, to extend their taxing legislation to the crown in its national right. The federal ac-

110 *R* v *Anderson*, [1930] 2 W.W.R. 595, at 597 *per* Trueman JA (Man. C.A.); *Halifax* v *Halifax Harbour Comm'rs*, [1935] 1 D.L.R. 657, at 668 (S.C.C.); *R* v *Breton* (1967), 65 D.L.R. (2d) 76, at 81 (S.C.C.)
111 *A.G. of Can.* v *Registrar of Titles*, [1934] 4 D.L.R. 764 (B.C.C.A.)
112 See the cases cited supra in note 81 of chapter 2.
113 *Phillips & Taylor* v *Sault Ste Marie*, [1954] 3 D.L.R. 81 (S.C.C.)
114 *Northern Sask. Flying Training School* v *Buckland*, [1944] 1 D.L.R. 285 (Sask. C.A.)
115 See, for example, *Smith* v *Vermillion Hills Rural Council*, [1916] 2 A.C. 569 (P.C.).
116 See supra, at 38.

tion has taken the form of statutes which purport to effect a surrender of inter-governmental tax immunity.[117] Two major difficulties are encountered in this event. Firstly, if the federal surrender is sustainable constitutionally under an exclusive federal power, can the state or provincial taxing statute apply in the circumstances in which immunity is surrendered? It would appear on first impression that if the local taxing legislation were extended to the federal crown it would be in relation to a matter or a class of subject, as the case may be, within the exclusive authority of the central parliament.[118] Secondly, even if the relevant federal power does not itself preclude the application of the local statute, is a statutory surrender of immunity capable of overcoming a legislative incapacity on the part of a state which is based on the permanent features of the federal constitution?[119] These concerns will be examined in turn after brief reference to the Australian cases, which appear to support the effectiveness of a statutory surrender of immunity.

At the time when the salaries of Commonwealth government employees were thought to be generally immune from state income tax, such salaries were held in *Chaplin* v *Commissioner of Taxes for South Australia*[120] to be taxable. This was because of Commonwealth legislation which purported to negate any suggestion of interference with Commonwealth powers in the application of a general state tax law to such salaries. With the retrenchment in the *Engineers* case[121] the result in *Chaplin* was described in terms of an application of state tax law, quite valid in itself, which was not inconsistent with a provision of federal legislation.[122] In *Australian Coastal Shipping Commission* v *O'Reilly*[123] McTiernan J reiterated the proposition that parliament has power to 'waive' the Commonwealth's constitutional immunity from tax but elaborated only to the extent of saying that such a waiver may be effected by a law in relation to the persons intended to be subjected to tax.[124]

The particular head of power that seems to justify federal legislation surrendering that immunity which is now understood to belong to the Commonwealth, and those who may be said to act for it in the relevant sense, is the 'incidental

---

117 See, for a contemporary example, the Crown Corporations (Provincial Taxes and Fees) Act, R.S.C. 1970, c C-37.

118 See Howard *Australian Federal Constitutional Law* (2d ed 1972), at 124–32.

119 See *Flint* v *Webb* (1907), 4 C.L.R. 1178, at 1194 *per* Higgins J, and *West* v *Commissioner of Taxation (N.S.W.)* (1937), 56 C.L.R. 657, at 700 *per* Evatt J.

120 (1911), 12 C.L.R. 375

121 (1920), 28 C.L.R. 129

122 Ibid, at 157

123 (1962), 107 C.L.R. 46

124 Ibid, at 59

power' of section 51 (xxxix) of the constitution. This power, unlike its Canadian equivalent, which is not express but the product of judicial craftsmanship, is not limited to enabling legislation on matters ancillary to the (other) enumerated federal legislative powers. It also authorizes enactments on matters incidental to the execution of any power vested by the constitution in the government of the Commonwealth, which includes the executive power of the Commonwealth by virtue of chapter II of the constitution. The surrender of intergovernmental immunity is, doubtless, incidental to the execution of that executive power. If the immunity surrendered is enjoyed in relation to activities, matters, or persons that are the subject of specific grants of federal authority under the constitution then other heads of power will also be appropriate.[125] For example, the Commonwealth parliament could legislate to surrender the immunity enjoyed by a crown employee in the postal service under section 51(v), supported if necessary by the incidental power. Under the BNA Act, similarly, specific federal powers such as that over the postal service (section 91(5)) are available. And should enumerated federal powers under the Canadian constitution prove inadequate, the general power to enact laws for the peace, order, and good government of Canada, in the opening paragraph of section 91, is capable of supplying the necessary authority given the intimate relationship of the activities of those acting on behalf of the federal crown to the national government.[126] But nearly all of the federal powers under the Canadian constitution that hold potential for application are exclusive as must be, inferentially, the incidental power of the Commonwealth when called in aid to support legislation concerning the federal executive power.[127]

The tradition of Canadian constitutional interpretation is not to disallow a particular application of provincial legislation simply because the national parliament is competent, under some exclusive federal power, to deal with the very subject matter of the provincial statute in its questioned application.[128] Rather the court engages in a process of characterization of the provincial statute to determine whether it may have an 'aspect' referrable to a provincial power, such power consisting of enumerated classes of subjects for legislative action. While deference is paid to the mutual exclusiveness of the two lists of powers, federal and provincial, it is recognized that similar legislation may in some circumstances

---

125 Howard demonstrates convincingly why the federal public service power is inappropriate, see Australian Federal Constitutional Law (2d ed 1972), at 130, and Evans demonstrates convincingly why the federal taxation power is inappropriate, see 'Rethinking Commonwealth Immunity' (1972), 8 *M.U.L.R.* 521, at 541–2.
126 See *Jones* v *A.G. of Can.* (1974), 45 D.L.R. (3d) 583, at 588–9 (S.C.C.).
127 See Howard, at 126–7.
128 See generally Lederman, 'The Concurrent Operation of Federal and Provincial Laws in Canada' (1963), 9 *McGill L.J.* 185.

emerge from both central and local legislatures in the proper exercise of their respective constitutional functions.[129] This phenomenon has been explained in terms of the notion that a particular form of legislation may possess a 'double aspect,' federal and provincial.

For the purpose of determining the validity of a particular application of a provincial statute it is considered important to look at the statute as a whole, in its generality, as well as in that operation of it which is challenged. There is always the possibility of a finding that the statute is *intra vires* but cannot constitutionally apply in a given situation. But there is a tendency to avoid that conclusion if at all possible and to dispose of a given case on the basis of a general determination of validity or invalidity.

The results of the characterization process are somewhat uneven in the sense that the provincial legislatures are conceded differing degrees of latitude in passing laws which confront the claims of different federal heads of power. This does not mean that some federal powers are more exclusive than others. Rather the explanation is that because of the nature and wording of any given federal power it is more or less likely to leave room for the operation of provincial statutory provisions in areas that could be covered by comparable statutory provisions passed pursuant to the federal power.

Should both the Canadian parliament and a provincial legislature pass laws, each possessing an aspect sufficient to sustain its initial validity, in a so-called 'overlapping field' then the further question must be asked; do the two laws conflict? If they do the federal statute has paramountcy and the provincial statute is, to the extent of the conflict, in abeyance or temporarily inapplicable in the circumstances covered by the federal statute. This is the result not of any specific provision in the constitution but of a doctrine derived by the courts from the nature of the general scheme of the confederation instrument.[130]

It follows from these principles that the federal parliament could surrender an immunity by legislative action which, if upheld, would not necessarily lead to the conclusion that a provincial act could not validly impose an otherwise impermissible liability on the federal crown. In most cases it may be supposed that the notion of double aspect would come to the rescue of the provincial statute or a questioned application of it.

In Australia it is not customary for a court to characterize a state law in the process of deciding upon its constitutionality.[131] As a general practice this is not

---

129 *Hodge* v *The Queen* (1883), 9 App. Cas. 117, at 130 (P.C.)
130 See *A.G. of Ont.* v *A.G. of Can.*, [1896] A.C. 348, at 366 (P.C.).
131 But cf *West* v *Commissioner of Taxation (N.S.W.)* (1937), 56 C.L.R. 657, at 668–9 *per* Latham CJ.

unexpected since most federal powers are concurrent with state power, the latter consisting of an undifferentiated residue of authority. Thus a state law is generally sustainable so long as there is no objectionable conflict with a Commonwealth law.[132] But if it is alleged that a state law is with respect to an exclusive subject matter for federal legislation, then it is appropriate not only to make some determination of the scope of the federal power but to characterize the state law so that it falls within or without the range of that power.[133] It is not a case, as in Canada, of tying the state act in to some specific power. Rather it is simply a matter of deciding whether it has an aspect other than that which would support a similar federal enactment.

It is true that the very existence of some exclusive federal powers, such as that in relation to Commonwealth places (section 52 (i)), are invariably taken to preclude important applications of general state statutes. But, if the Canadian experience is any guide, this does not mean that the existence of every exclusive federal power need have just as inhibiting an effect upon the operation of state statutes. There may indeed be room for the recognition of a state aspect to the questioned application of a state enactment even if the Commonwealth parliament could validly cover the same ground under one of its exclusive powers. Thus a general state tax law could conceivably apply to the Commonwealth crown though the surrender of immunity from tax, removing the impediment to such application, was a matter falling within the exclusive authority of the Commonwealth under section 51(xxxix) of the constitution.[134] This position might obtain consistently with the notion that general state laws on just about any subject cannot apply in federal places, within section 52(i), the spatial focus of that exclusive power precluding all such extensions of state law.[135]

Though we might conclude that a tax statute, or some other kind of statute for that matter, passed by a state or a province can apply to the federal government without running afoul of an exclusive power immunity, there remains the question of whether the implied immunity of the federal government can be surrendered simply by a federal statute assenting to an assumption of the burden of the local statute. The other side of the immunity coin appears to be a legislative incapacity of a state or province to reach the federal government. And it seems, at first blush, that this would be beyond alteration by federal statute though the

---

132 See *Worthing* v *Rowell & Muston Pty* (1970), 123 C.L.R. 89, at 93–4 *per* Barwick CJ.
133 Cf the judgment of Williams J, Rich J concurring, in *Carter* v *Egg & Egg Pulp Marketing Bd (Vict.)* (1942), 66 C.L.R. 557.
134 Accord Evans, 'Rethinking Commonwealth Immunity' (1972), 8 *M.U.L.R.* 521, at 543–5
135 See *Worthing* v *Rowell & Muston Pty* (1970), 123 C.L.R. 89, and *R* v *Phillips* (1970), 125 C.L.R. 93.

latter might restrict the opportunities for the operation of immunity principles by the device of a submission to state or provincial laws.[136]

But the reason that a state or province cannot tax the federal government is not that its grant of legislative power under the constitution does not authorize such a tax. Indeed in Australia the *Engineers* case[137] firmly rejected the notion that there is any implied limitation on the scope of legislative powers granted by the constitution in favour of the state or Commonwealth governments.[138] Thus a state is acting within power if it purports to extend a law to the Commonwealth, so long as it does not exceed any express constitutional limitations.[139] Rather the inability of a state and, we may assume, of a province to tax the federal government is not lack of power but a limitation, derived from the constitutional arrangement, on the way in which an admitted power may be exercised. It depends, then, on notions of abuse of power. The latter is a familiar ground for judicial review of administrative action. And in that context there could conceivably be some difference in terms of reviewability if action is taken in abuse of power as opposed to excess of power.[140] So also there may be a difference in the constitutional context, for while a surrender of intergovernmental immunity by federal act could not remedy a lack of power on the part of a state or province to tax the federal government, it could logically be treated as removing an objection that such a tax would be an abuse of power. This accords with the proposition that seems to have been accepted in Australia, but has been poorly explained, that the federal parliament can legislate to surrender its tax immunity with the effective result that it is, thereafter, taxable by a state.

In the *Engineers* case the High Court disclaimed any concern with arguments about the possibility of abuse of power as a ground for confining a constitutional grant of authority.[141] Reference was made to the Privy Council opinion in the

136 As to the use of this device to avoid an intergovernmental immunity see supra, at 53. The device of incorporation by reference of state or provincial statutes, which is considered at 52–3, is singularly inapt for subjecting the federal government or its servants or agents to state or provincial tax. Local tax legislation so incorporated would become federal by adoption and the tax which it imposed part of federal rather than state or provincial revenues.

137 *Amalgamated Soc'y of Eng'rs* v *Adelaide Steamship Co.* (1920), 28 C.L.R. 129

138 See especially the explanation of the result of the *Engineers* case by Latham CJ in *West* v *Commissioner of Taxation (N.S.W.)* (1937), 56 C.L.R. 657, at 664–5.

139 The reservations expressed in the *Engineers* case about laws affecting the prerogative or imposing taxes have proved to have been unwarranted, at least in the terms in which they were stated, see Howard *Australian Federal Constitutional Law* (2d ed 1972), at 74–7 & 87–8.

140 Consider *Smith* v *East Elloe R.D.C.*, [1956] A.C. 736, at 754–6, 763–4 & 772, but see also at 768 (H.L.).

141 (1920), 28 C.L.R. 129, at 151

Canadian appeal of *Bank of Toronto* v *Lambe*[142] in support of this undoubtedly sound principle. But the High Court seems to have gone so far as to suggest that should such an abuse in fact materialize it would be a matter not for the courts but for the electorate.[143] Subsequent Canadian experience indicates, however, that the judiciary need not always be incapable of playing a corrective role in these circumstances. In the *Lambe* case admittedly the Privy Council refused to limit the provincial taxing power in favour of banks, being a subject of exclusive federal jurisdiction. But in a later reference, *Attorney General of Alberta* v *Attorney General of Canada*[144] (the *Alberta* reference), the same tribunal considered a provincial tax on banks which was clearly revealed, by the context of the taxing legislation and the effective level of the imposition, as designed to put banks in the province out of business and hence as invalid. Here indeed was an actual abuse of power, readily discernible, and therefore reviewable. Indeed some of the justifications of a more general character for holding legislation unconstitutional, namely colourability and discrimination, reflect a particular form of abuse of power recognized in administrative law. A colourable act is, and a discriminatory act may be, evidence of an exercise of a power for an improper purpose, which is an accepted basis for judicial review of administrative action.

It is true, of course, that in constitutional cases the courts usually talk simply in terms of whether a statute is *intra* or *ultra vires*, giving no distinctive description to their inquiry in situations such as that in the *Alberta* reference, which could be analyzed in terms of abuse of power. This is not unexpected, for most of the time abuse of power may just as well be regarded as a form of excess of power. In either case the consequence is invalidity. But it does seem legitimate and purposeful to make the distinction in considering the ability of the federal parliament to act so as to effectively subject the national government to tax or other liability at the hands of the states or provinces.

A legislature cannot, of course, alter the express terms of the constitution such as those effecting a division of legislative powers except as may be provided by the constitution itself. But the need for a similar restriction is not as apparent when an implied constitutional provision like that of general intergovernmental immunity is in question. Furthermore the abuse of power which prompts the recognition of that immunity flows from an adverse effect on governmental functions. There is no fixed content or scope to the latter under the constitution such as there is in the case of legislative functions, the distribution of which may only be changed by constitutional amendment.

142 (1887), 12 App. Cas. 575 (P.C.)
143 But see *Melbourne Corp.* v *Commonwealth* (1947), 74 C.L.R. 31, at 82 *per* Dixon J.
144 [1939] A.C. 117 (P.C.)

There is some support in the Australian cases for the notion that the inter-governmental immunity, which was recognized subsequent to the *Engineers* case,[145] is in fact a response to circumstances of abuse of power and that this is to be distinguished from excess of power. The cases which help to sustain this analysis are *Melbourne Corporation* v *Commonwealth*[146] (the *State Banking* case) and *Victoria* v *Commonwealth*[147] (the *Pay-roll Tax* case). There is a certain un-evenness in the results of application of the abuse of power limitation against the states, on the one hand, and against the Commonwealth, on the other. In general, federal enactments have been given more latitude in reaching state governments than have state enactments in reaching the Commonwealth. This situation may be explained as the result of an assumption derived from the constitution, that is that what is an improper purpose for a state statute purporting to control the other level of government need not be an improper purpose for a similar Commonwealth statute.

In the *State Banking* case the High Court held invalid a provision of a Commonwealth act which had the effect of requiring a state to bank with the central bank or, much less conveniently, establish its own state corporation to conduct its banking activities. Latham CJ clearly rejected the argument that the questioned provision was not a law relating to banking (section 51(xiii) of the constitution),[148] but nonetheless held it unconstitutional as a law dealing with an essential state governmental function, which law the Commonwealth had no power to make.[149] Rich J took the view that the provision came *prima facie* under the banking power but was invalid as involving an impairment of an essential function of state government.[150] It is not clear whether the other members of the court who were in the majority accepted or rejected the argument that the requirement that the states bank with a governmental institution was a law with respect to banking. They did rely in part, though, on the element of discrimination against the states that was involved, a circumstance relevant to a finding of abuse of power.[151] Windeyer J in the subsequent *Pay-roll Tax* case interpreted

145 (1920), 28 C.L.R. 129
146 (1947), 74 C.L.R. 31. This case is also considered supra, at 43.
147 (1971), 122 C.L.R. 353
148 (1947), 74 C.L.R. 31, at 50 & 52
149 Ibid, at 54 & 61
150 Ibid, at 65 & 69
151 Sir Owen Dixon always regarded the *Engineers* case as leaving open the question of wheth-er a constitutional grant of power would support a law discriminating against the other level of government, see for example his judgment in this case, ibid, at 79. This assumption about what the *Engineers* case decided, or rather didn't decide, serves to remove any in-consistency between that decision and the *State Banking* case, to the extent that the latter turns on an objectionable discrimination against the states, but not otherwise.

the judgments, as a whole, as deciding that the law was one with respect to banking though subject to condemnation because directed towards the states.[152] He went on to say that the subject matter of Commonwealth constitutional powers is not to be limited by implication but that:

implications arising from the existence of the States as part of the Commonwealth and as constituents of the federation may restrict the manner in which Parliament can lawfully exercise its powers to make laws with respect to a particular subject matter. These implications ... relate to the use of a power not to the inherent nature of the subject matter of the law.[153]

He would associate an improper use of constitutional power, which the *State Banking* case exemplified, with the limitation upon the permitted purpose of Commonwealth laws in the opening paragraph of section 51 of the constitution, that is that such laws are to be 'for the peace order and good government of the Commonwealth.'[154] Likewise the usual description of the law-making power in the colonial constitutions, preserved by the Australian constitution, as an authority to pass laws for the peace, order (or welfare), and good government of the colony[155] may be taken to similarly limit the purposes for which state laws may be passed[156] if any textual justification is needed for this understanding of intergovernmental immunity in its reciprocal form.

These isolated judgments are suggestive, though hardly decisive, of the existence of a distinctive abuse of power rationale for the recognition of an implied intergovernmental immunity. And this basis best accommodates the assumed authority of the Commonwealth parliament to surrender immunity so that state laws effectively apply thereafter in an otherwise constitutionally proscribed fashion. It also goes some way, incidentally, to explain why the post-*Engineers* decisions recognizing a form of intergovernmental immunity are not inconsistent with the *Engineers* decision itself. It will be remembered that that case discounted the possibility of any implied limitations on the constitutional powers of one level of political authority in the federation in favour of the executive of the other. But it did not, notably, preclude the argument that an exercise of constitutional authority is objectionable on abuse of power grounds. The contemporary

152 (1971), 122 C.L.R. 353, at 402. Gibbs J agreed, see at 422. And see the judgment of Walsh J, at 406. But compare the judgments of Menzies J, at 387, and of Barwick CJ, Owen J concurring, at 372.
153 Ibid, at 403
154 Ibid
155 See Lumb *The Constitutions of the Australian States* (3d ed 1972), at 81.
156 *West v Commissioner of Taxation (N.S.W.)* (1937), 56 C.L.R. 657, at 669 *per* Latham CJ

form of intergovernmental immunity, given recognition for instance in *Commonwealth* v *Cigamatic Pty*,[157] may be justified as the result of an improper exercise of state powers rather than the state having exceeded any implicit limitation upon the scope of its powers.

The authority of the Canadian parliament to give up the implied immunity from provincial statutes which is enjoyed by the federal government has received but limited judicial attention. No doubt the reasoning applied in relation to the Australian situation is appropriate to the Canadian context. However, there is another way of putting the proposition that the national parliament is free to surrender an immunity from local legislation, so far as the Canadian situation is concerned. It will be recalled that in *Gauthier* v *The King*,[158] which fathered the notion of intergovernmental immunity under the Canadian constitution, Mr Justice Anglin put the special position of the federal crown in relation to provincial legislation this way: 'Provincial legislation cannot *proprio vigore* take away or abridge any privilege of the Crown in right of the Dominion.'[159] This description of the relevant immunity leaves room for provincial statutes applying against the federal crown where there is something in addition to the force of the provincial statute to assist in accomplishing that result. A provincial act cannot be taken of its own force to bind the federal crown but such an act could, conceivably, so operate in the presence of a federal statute surrendering the immunity enjoyed by the crown. This conclusion finds support in *R* v *Breton*,[160] referred to earlier in this chapter in relation to section 125 of the BNA Act. Fauteux J, giving the judgment of the Supreme Court in that case, envisaged the possibility of federal legislation overcoming not only the particular immunity of section 125 but also the general immunity resulting from the principle that provincial legislation cannot of its own force bind the crown in right of Canada.[161]

Extension of immunity: An attempted extension of tax immunity by the federal parliament presents problems that are at once similar and different from those raised by a contraction of immunity. In the first place some constitutional basis needs to be found for the federal act enlarging immunity. If the appropriate federal power is exclusive there may be some doubt about the ability of the state or province to have extended its tax thus far in any event.[162] But here that sort of

157 (1962), 108 C.L.R. 372, considered supra, at 36 and at 114–15
158 (1919), 40 D.L.R. 353 (S.C.C.), considered supra, at 34–6 and at 95–8
159 Ibid, at 365, Anglin J concurring. Fitzpatrick CJ, however, put the immunity this way: that the provinces do not have executive, legislative, or judicial power to bind the federal government, ibid, at 356.
160 (1967), 65 D.L.R. (2d) 76 (S.C.C.)
161 Ibid, at 81
162 See supra.

concern is of academic interest only, for the state or provincial tax could not apply in any event in the circumstances in which parliament has created an immunity. The reason is that there is an objectionable conflict between the federal act conferring immunity and the particular application of the local taxing statute which must be resolved in favour of the former.

It might be objected that the federal supremacy provision under the Australian constitution, section 109, has no role to play where one of the competing laws was passed under an exclusive power since both laws could not be initially valid, which section 109 has sometimes been said to presuppose.[163] But in fact that section has often been regarded as applicable when a Commonwealth law in competition with a state law was passed under an exclusive power.[164] And in Australia, as in Canada, there is some judicial practice of finessing constitutional power questions and disposing of a case, if possible, by resort simply to inconsistency considerations.[165] This being the case it would seem to be perfectly proper for a court simply to determine the validity of a Commonwealth statute conferring immunity and to proceed directly to conclude that a given state law could not apply in the face of the federal statute. That result might be reached on the grounds that section 109 prevented any such application without consideration being given to the initial validity of the state law in its questioned application.

The authority of the Commonwealth to create an immunity from state tax law has been affirmed in several circumstances. In *West v Commissioner of Taxation (New South Wales)*[166] both Latham CJ and Starke J said *obiter* that the Commonwealth could competently act to protect the income of its servants from state tax but without mention of any specific federal power.[167] Evatt J disagreed, pointing out particularly the inadequacy of the federal taxation power (section 51(ii) of the constitution) as a source of authority in this regard.[168] In an earlier case, *Commonwealth v Queensland*,[169] the High Court had upheld a federal provision making Commonwealth government bonds free of income tax, federal or

163 *Carter v Egg & Egg Pulp Marketing Bd (Vict.)* (1942), 66 C.L.R. 557, at 573 *per* Latham CJ
164 *R v Brisbane Licensing Ct; Ex p. Daniell* (1920), 28 C.L.R. 23, at 29 & 32; *Engineers* case (1920), 28 C.L.R. 129, at 155; *Colvin v Bradley Brothers Pty* (1943), 68 C.L.R. 151, at 158 *per* Latham CJ
165 See *Johnston v Krakowski* (1965), 113 C.L.R. 552; *Reference re s. 92(4) of the Vehicles Act (Sask.)* (1958), 15 D.L.R. (2d) 225, at 231 *per* Cartwright J, dissenting (S.C.C.); *A.G. of Ont. v Barfried Enterprises Ltd* (1963), 42 D.L.R. (2d) 137, at 141 *per* Martland J, Ritchie J concurring, dissenting (S.C.C.).
166 (1937), 56 C.L.R. 657
167 Ibid, at 670–2 & 677
168 Ibid, at 685
169 (1920), 29 C.L.R. 1

state, in reliance on the federal borrowing power (section 51(iv)). That power must, by its very nature, be assumed to be an exclusive power. It is not really necessary to speculate on whether the federal provision was redundant but, for reasons given earlier, it is arguable that there is no exclusive power immunity in these circumstances. Therefore in the absence as well of any implied immunity, the bonds being in private rather than government hands, a federal enactment was necessary to assure the tax free character of the bonds.

Most recently, in *Australian Coastal Shipping Commission v O'Reilly*,[170] the High Court upheld a provision in a Commonwealth statute establishing the Commission which purported to exclude that body from liability under any state tax law. The particular state tax sought to be imposed upon the Commission in that case was a stamp duty, which every person giving a receipt was required to pay. The Commission refused to pay the tax in relation to a receipt given in the course of its trading activities. The immunity provision was upheld principally on the basis of the trade and commerce power (section 51(i) of the constitution),[171] the Commission being established to engage in the interstate, overseas, and territorial shipping trade. The case had been argued on the assumption that the Commission would not be entitled to immunity as an agent of the Commonwealth independent of the tax exempt status conferred by its constitutive statute. Nevertheless Dixon CJ, whose judgment was concurred in by three other members of the court,[172] seems to treat the Commission as an instrumentality of the Commonwealth.[173] In any event he would confine his decision sustaining immunity to the statutory conferral of immunity upon entities engaged in some activity on behalf of the Commonwealth, though perhaps not crown agents in the strict sense.[174]

For one reason or another the Commonwealth might wish to confer an immunity from state tax upon persons bearing no relationship to the national government but engaged in activities subject to federal jurisdiction. It may be doubtful, as indicated, whether the principle of the *O'Reilly* case would be directly in point. And if the principle were so extendable without careful limitation the power of the state to tax could be seriously eroded. Menzies J, who disposed of the *O'Reilly* case on the explicit understanding that the Commonwealth had no

---

170 (1962), 107 C.L.R. 46
171 Mention was also made, in the various judgments, of these additional bases; the incidental power (s 51(xxxix)), the navigation and shipping power (s 98), and the territorial power (s 122). McTiernan J rested the validity of the challenged provision exclusively upon the incidental power, disclaiming any reliance on the trade and commerce power as misplaced.
172 Kitto, Taylor & Owen JJ
173 And see also the judgment of McTiernan J (1962), 107 C.L.R. 46, at 59–60.
174 But contrast in this respect the judgments of Windeyer J and Menzies J.

more extensive power to immunize the Commission from state tax than any purely commercial trader carrying on a similar business, was sensitive to this particular danger. His response, however, was not to strike down the immunity provision but simply to read it down. The result was that, in the case of stamp duties,
it was treated as providing protection from tax only in the case of receipts given
in the course of carrying on the authorized trade of the Commission. This left
the immunity applicable, however, in the circumstances of the case at hand.[175]

It may be expected that the Full Court would construe a power of the Commonwealth such as that over trade and commerce so as not to authorize a provision generally isolating a commercial undertaking which was totally independent
of government from the reach of an exercise of the constitutional power of the
state to tax, after the manner of *Victoria* v *Commonwealth*.[176] There, it may be
recalled, the High Court held that it was not incidental to the federal power of taxation to postpone the payment of state income tax in favour of federal income tax.

Under the Canadian constitution the argument for reading a federal power
restrictively so as to allow latitude for the provincial taxing authority is even
more compelling. In the Canadian context the latter authority is specified in an
enumeration of provincial powers and a principle of constitutional interpretation
is that the heads of power in the two primary lists of subjects for legislative action, federal and provincial, in the BNA Act must be read subject to a principle of
mutual modification. On that basis the powers of parliament should properly be
limited to allow scope for the provinces to exercise their taxing powers in respect
of entities independent of the federal crown.

The only Canadian decision affirming the jurisdiction of parliament to legislate to provide an immunity from provincial law is that of the Exchequer Court
in *R* v *Powers*.[177] Personal property security legislation was excluded as a potential embarrassment to a federal crown agency and the federal property power
(section 91(1A) of the BNA Act) was found to embody sufficient authority to
support the conferral by parliament of an immunity of that character though an
implied immunity was found to exist in any event.

Federal Taxation of a State or Province

The federal parliament seems to have been accorded considerably more latitude
in subjecting the other level of government to tax. In the early days of the Aus-

175 See (1962), 107 C.L.R. 46, at 67–9.
176 (1957), 99 C.L.R. 575, discussed supra, at 124.
177 [1923] Ex. C.R. 131. The provinces, on the other hand, cannot legislate so as to make
   their servants immune from federal legislation, see *Holmstead* v *Minister of Customs &*
   Excise, [1927] Ex. C.R. 68.

tralian federation the High Court was called upon in two cases to consider the Commonwealth's power to bring the states within its customs control. In *R* v *Sutton*[178] it held that Commonwealth customs legislation providing for the detention of imported goods, pending customs clearance, was applicable to goods brought in to Australia by one of the states. The prerogative rule that the crown is not bound by statute except by express words or necessary implication was said not to operate in favour of the state crown vis-à-vis Commonwealth legislation.[179] Isaacs J tackled the contention that the Commonwealth was without constitutional power to bring the states within the net of customs regulation by pointing to the opportunity of the states, which would be consequent upon the acceptance of such an argument, to set at naught federal regulation under various enumerated powers in the constitution. The doctrine of immunity of instrumentalities, he said, only protected the states from interference with governmental functions carried on within the territory of the state. He considered the doctrine inapplicable, therefore, in the case of a state attempt to bring in property from abroad in disregard of a Commonwealth law declared supreme in the matter by the constitution.[180]

This latter distinction was picked up and applied in *Attorney General of New South Wales* v *Collector of Customs for New South Wales*[181] (the *Steel Rails* case) which was decided at the same time. The court in this second case also considered that the effective exercise of the customs and commerce powers necessitated the inclusion of the states as subjects of regulation, which also took the matter outside the implied immunity of instrumentalities doctrine.[182] In this further proceeding the authority of parliament to levy a customs duty on the importation of goods by a state was directly in issue. It was not unexpected that a major objection to this exercise of Commonwealth power should be section 114 of the constitution. As has been indicated previously that objection was unsuccessful.[183] The result was that the state was required to pay customs duty.

The Canadian counterpart of the *Steel Rails* case is the *Liquor Import* case,[184] which similarly involved an attempt by a province to import goods without payment of duty but in circumstances much more likely to capture the public imagination. The result was the same but no other limitation upon dominion power

---

178 (1908), 5 C.L.R. 789, considered supra, at 26
179 The weight of opinion is now against this view, see supra, at 26–9.
180 (1908), 5 C.L.R. 789, at 811
181 (1908), 5 C.L.R. 818, see at 833, 836, & 853
182 Ibid, at 823–33, 834, & 842–3
183 See supra, at 139.
184 *A.G. of B.C.* v *A.G. of Can.*, [1924] A.C. 222 (P.C.), considered supra, at 139–41

than that contained in section 125 of the BNA Act seems to have been raised in argument.[185]

Commonwealth pay-roll tax legislation was challenged in its application to a state as an employer in *Victoria v Commonwealth*[186] (the *Pay-roll Tax* case), decided in 1971. The federal statute under review there did not concern customs or trade and was supportable in its general operation only under the taxing power (section 51(ii) of the constitution), which happens not to be an exclusive power. Arguably this left the situation untouched by the authority of the *Steel Rails* case. And by this time the result of *Melbourne Corporation v Commonwealth*[187] (the *State Banking* case) had demonstrated that there are constitutional limits to the regulation of the activities of the states by the Commonwealth. Nonetheless in the *Pay-roll Tax* case the Victorian government was held liable to the tax on the wages which it paid. Unlike the Commonwealth banking statute in the *State Banking* case this federal legislation was found not to interfere with the essential or governmental functions of the state or to threaten its separate existence[188] nor, in terms of the other ground which secured support in the *State Banking* case, to single out the states and place special burdens upon them. The fact that the payment of the tax would diminish the state's financial capacity to meet its commitments was not material.[189]

Two limitations upon Commonwealth taxation of the states may be culled from the various judgments. The qualification which received most support is that a Commonwealth tax may not discriminate against a state in the sense of imposing a special burden upon it.[190] And, secondly, a reservation was expressed by McTiernan J about a tax upon the appropriation of revenue to pay for services,[191] which is no doubt a particular instance of a law impairing the state in the exercise of its functions or threatening its independent existence. Federal taxes imposed directly upon provincial or state revenues are probably precluded[192] by the

185 It was not possible to argue that the crown in right of the province enjoyed a governmental immunity from federal customs legislation since the latter bound the provinces expressly, see chapter 2, note 15.
186 (1971), 122 C.L.R. 353
187 (1947), 74 C.L.R. 31
188 The conclusion was put in various forms by the different judges, see ibid, at 374, 386, 392, 398, 410–11, & 424.
189 Ibid, at 374 & 392
190 See ibid, at 403–4, 413, & 424.
191 Ibid, at 385–6
192 If this is so then provincial or state taxes upon federal revenues are no doubt precluded for similar, if not for other, reasons since the national parliaments also exercise an appropriation role which is constitutionally provided for, see ss 102–6 of the BNA Act and ss 81–3 of the Australian constitution.

specific conferral, by constitutional provision, upon the provincial legislatures[193] and upon some state parliaments[194] of the power to make appropriations from the provincial or state consolidated revenue fund.

There is a further, but related, impediment to the effective inclusion of the states or provinces within a federal taxation scheme. To the extent that the taxing authority may find it necessary to obtain judgment for the recovery of the amount of tax outstanding against a recalcitrant state or province, the latter will usually find itself in the position of being able to successfully resist the tax at the stage of enforcement of the judgment. This is because of the constitutional principle that it is for the states or provinces to appropriate the necessary funds for the satisfaction of obligations imposed upon them and therefore that such obligations are, in that respect, conditional at best. The Commonwealth would be obliged to sue a state in the High Court[195] and any judgment obtained would have to be satisfied by the state Treasurer according to section 66 of the Judiciary Act but only 'out of moneys legally available,' which presupposes appropriation.[196] The act does not itself effect a permanent appropriation. Indeed the cases referred to hereafter indicate that it could not do so consistent with the federal and state constitutions.

In *Australian Railways Union* v *Victorian Railways Commissioners*[197] awards made by the Commonwealth Court of Conciliation and Arbitration were held to be binding upon the state railway commissioners in line with the *Engineers* case.[198] Isaacs CJ and Starke J, in the course of their judgments, observed that the relevant state constitutions, preserved by the federal constitution but subject to it (per section 106 of the Australian constitution), prohibit any appropriation of money

193 The BNA Act contains such a provision in s 126 which is not, however, as explicit as it might be in indicating that it is the legislatures which are to exercise the appropriation function, though parliamentary custom would indicate as much. See LaForest *The Allocation of Taxing Power under the Canadian Constitution* (1967), at 153, discussing an argument of immunity based on s 126 that was advanced in *R* v *Bell Telephone Co.* (1935), 59 B.R. 205 (App. Side).

194 New South Wales, Queensland, Victoria, and Western Australia have such a provision in their constitutions, see Lumb *The Constitutions of the Australian States* (3d ed 1972), at 68–9. Perhaps Tasmania should also be included in this list (see the *A.R.U.* case (1930), 44 C.L.R. 319, at 389 *per* Starke J (discussed infra)) for its constitution Act is incomplete and must be read with the Australian Constitutions Act, 1850, 13 & 14 Vict., c 59 (Imp.) (see Lumb, at 34–5), which in s 14 makes appropriation of revenue a matter for the legislature but subject to provisos that have no post-federation relevance.

195 Judiciary Act 1903, s 38(c)

196 *N.S.W.* v *Bardolph* (1934), 52 C.L.R. 455

197 (1930), 44 C.L.R. 319

198 (1920), 29 C.L.R. 129

from the consolidated revenue fund except by the state parliament.[199] Nothing in the federal constitution was discovered that interfered with this state requirement. But its preservation did not detract from the full operation of an industrial award upon a state, which was what was questioned before the court.

The opinion expressed by Isaacs CJ and Starke J in this case was adopted in *New South Wales* v *Commonwealth*[200] (the *Garnishee* case), in which the Commonwealth's competence to reach state revenues was directly in issue. Under the Financial Agreements Enforcement Act the Commonwealth could, as an aid to realizing on the agreements that were the subject of the act, obtain a judicial declaration against a state. Such a declaration had the effect, *inter alia*, of creating a charge on state revenues enabling the Commonwealth thereafter to garnishee any money owing to the state. It was accepted that this kind of provision would not normally be supportable under the judicial power (pursuant to section 51 (xxxix) of the Australian constitution)[201] in the face of a state constitutional requirement of parliamentary appropriation. But a recent constitutional amendment (section 105A) remedied the deficiency of power in relation to the enforcement of Commonwealth-state financial agreements by making such agreements binding notwithstanding anything contained in state or federal constitutions and by enabling the central parliament to make laws for carrying out such agreements. A separate provision providing for garnishment before judgment was also upheld with particular reference to the same amendment to the federal constitution.

In a Canadian reference[202] to determine the liability of a province to pay to the federal government the costs of calling out the militia in a local emergency Duff J was moved to remark upon the possible contention, not in fact advanced, that the dominion could impose a duty to pay the expenses on the province *in invitum* and apart from contract. He said that this would be a plain violation of a fundamental principle of the BNA Act, the provincial legislatures having the exclusive right of appropriation of provincial revenues.[203]

While none of these cases concerned tax liability they do indicate that the central taxing authority cannot, constitutionally, be given all the enforcement tools that it might possess against a subject to use against a state or province as taxpayer. The power of the local legislature to appropriate revenues cannot be interfered with, absent specific authority to do so in the federal constitution.

---

199 (1930), 44 C.L.R. 319, at 352–4 & 389–90. See also the judgment of Dixon J, Rich J concurring, at 391–3.
200 (1932), 46 C.L.R. 155
201 See also s 75(iii), 76, & 78 of the constitution.
202 *A. G. of Can.* v *A. G. of N.S.*, [1930] 4 D.L.R. 82 (S.C.C.)
203 Ibid, at 84 *per* Anglin CJ, Rinfret, Lamont, & Smith JJ, concurring

CONCLUSION

As has been seen, the crown's liability to tax is similar to its accountability under regulatory statutes. Thus the two forms of immunity, governmental and intergovernmental, afford some relief to the crown from general levies imposed under statute. Instrumentalities of the crown share in that special position when there is an attempt to tax them in the performance of official functions.

The crown and its agents often take advantage of public services, however, though they are under no compulsion to contribute on the same basis as others to the cost of those services which happen to be met through general tax revenues. A 'free ride' situation such as this of course forces a heavier burden onto those who are obliged to pay tax. And at the same time the true costs of carrying out that governmental activity, which is allowed to proceed without the usual tax burdens, is masked.

The distortions arising from this immunity are accentuated in an interjurisdictional setting. In that situation it is not a matter of a government having simply foregone the dubious benefit of a tax upon itself. Rather it is another level of governmental authority, which depends upon a distinct group of taxpayers, which must do without some of its potential revenues. This hardship may be alleviated somewhat by appropriate transfer payments between governments to make up for the inability of the receiving government to exploit all the sources of revenue within its jurisdiction.

The case for subjecting the crown to the burden of a particular tax is perhaps strongest when it is engaged in a commercial type of undertaking in competition with entities in the private sector. We might expect a public enterprise of this kind to survive in the market place without the benefit of hidden subsidies such as those afforded by a tax holiday. That is not to suggest, however, that there would be any general consensus that a particular crown enterprise operating in this environment should be subject to any and every form of taxation. The public purpose behind the undertaking might suggest, for instance, that it ought not to be treated as generating profits subject to reduction through income tax though there might be agreement that it should be subject to other forms of tax.

It would seem to be clear that any extension of taxes to the crown must be rather finely tuned. Whether it is appropriate for the crown to assume the burden of a tax will depend, for example, on the nature of the tax, the crown entities or enterprises which may incur liability thereto and whether in the event of immunity one level of government would in effect be required to subsidize another level of government without any offsetting benefit.

The discussion in this chapter has indicated that there are various opportunities for bringing the crown or particular crown instrumentalities within a taxation scheme. Governmental immunity from tax, of course, will be eliminated if the taxing statute includes the crown expressly or by necessary implication. And the intergovernmental tax immunity of the central authority in the Australian and Canadian federations may be surrendered in particular circumstances by the national parliament with the result that a state or provincial taxing statute will apply thereafter to the central government. This is so even in the case of property taxes, from which there is a specific immunity under each of the two federal constitutions. Moreover it is arguable that a state or provincial taxing statute will extend to the federal crown if it clearly so provides.

The states and provinces may have somewhat less protection from federal taxes, except those of a property variety. But, as in the case of state or provincial taxation of the federal government, financial impositions may not be levied on that level of government which would stultify its very existence or would interfere with the legislative function of appropriating revenues. Short of that there is considerable room for general federal levies, such as customs duties, to apply by specific inclusion to the states or provinces.

The federal parliament is competent to confer a statutory immunity from a state or provincial tax upon those crown agents which it constitutes. This exercise of legislative power by parliament will prevent any possible application of the local taxing statute to those crown agents on paramountcy grounds. It is unlikely, however, that such an immunity could be validly created in favour of an entity totally independent of the federal crown. If this were possible it would enable the central parliament to impair seriously state or provincial taxation schemes simply by giving entities or activities subject to federal jurisdiction a preferred position with respect to those taxes that would normally be applicable.

Appendix

**Selected Provisions of the Australian Constitution, being
s 9 of the Commonwealth of Australia Constitution Act,
63 & 64 Vict., c 12 (Imp.), as amended to date**

CHAPTER I   THE PARLIAMENT

Part I - General

1   The legislative power of the Commonwealth shall be vested in a Federal Parliament, which shall consist of the Queen, a Senate, and a House of Representatives, and which is herein-after called 'The Parliament,' or 'The Parliament of the Commonwealth.'

Part V - Powers of the Parliament

51   The Parliament shall, subject to this Constitution, have power to make laws for the peace, order, and good government of the Commonwealth with respect to:
    i   Trade and commerce with other countries, and among the States:
    ii   Taxation; but so as not to discriminate between States or parts of States:
    iii Bounties on the production or export of goods, but so that such bounties shall be uniform throughout the Commonwealth:
    iv   Borrowing money on the public credit of the Commonwealth:
    v   Postal, telegraphic, telephonic, and other like services:
    vi   The naval and military defence of the Commonwealth and of the several States, and the control of the forces to execute and maintain the laws of the Commonwealth:
    vii Lighthouses, lightships, beacons and buoys:

   viii Astronomical and meteorological observations:

    ix Quarantine:

     x Fisheries in Australian waters beyond territorial limits:

    xi Census and statistics:

   xii Currency, coinage, and legal tender:

  xiii Banking, other than State banking; also State banking extending beyond the limits of the State concerned, the incorporation of banks, and the issue of paper money:

  xiv Insurance, other than State insurance; also State insurance extending beyond the limits of the State concerned:

   xv Weights and measures:

  xvi Bills of exchange and promissory notes:

 xvii Bankruptcy and insolvency:

xviii Copyrights, patents of inventions and designs, and trade marks:

  xix Naturalization and aliens:

   xx Foreign corporations, and trading or financial corporations formed within the limits of the Commonwealth:

  xxi Marriage:

 xxii Divorce and matrimonial causes; and in relation thereto, parental rights, and the custody and guardianship of infants:

xxiii Invalid and old-age pensions:

xxiiiA The provision of maternity allowances, widows' pensions, child endowment, unemployment, pharmaceutical, sickness and hospital benefits, medical and dental services (but not so as to authorize any form of civil conscription), benefits to students and family allowances:

 xxiv The service and execution throughout the Commonwealth of the civil and criminal process and the judgments of the courts of the States:

  xxv The recognition throughout the Commonwealth of the laws, the public Acts and records, and the judicial proceedings of the States:

 xxvi The people of any race for whom it is deemed necessary to make special laws:

 xxvii Immigration and emigration:

xxviii The influx of criminals:

 xxix External affairs:

  xxx The relations of the Commonwealth with the islands of the Pacific:

 xxxi The acquisition of property on just terms from any State or person for any purpose in respect of which the Parliament has power to make laws:

xxxii The control of railways with respect to transport for the naval and military purposes of the Commonwealth:

xxxiii The acquisition, with the consent of a State, of any railways of the State on terms arranged between the Commonwealth and the State:

xxxiv Railway construction and extension in any State with the consent of that State:

xxxv Conciliation and arbitration for the prevention and settlement of industrial disputes extending beyond the limits of any one State:

xxxvi Matters in respect of which this Constitution makes provision until the Parliament otherwise provides:

xxxvii Matters referred to the Parliament of the Commonwealth by the Parliament or Parliaments of any State or States, but so that the law shall extend only to States by whose Parliaments the matter is referred, or which afterwards adopt the law:

xxxviii The exercise within the Commonwealth, at the request or with the concurrence of the Parliaments of all the States directly concerned, of any power which can at the establishment of this Constitution be exercised only by the Parliament of the United Kingdom or by the Federal Council of Australasia:

xxxix Matters incidental to the execution of any power vested by this Constitution in the Parliament or in either House thereof, or in the Government of the Commonwealth, or in the Federal Judicature, or in any department or officer of the Commonwealth.

52 The Parliament shall, subject to this Constitution, have exclusive power to make laws for the peace, order, and good government of the Commonwealth with respect to:

i The seat of government of the Commonwealth, and all places acquired by the Commonwealth for public purposes:

ii Matters relating to any department of the public service the control of which is by this Constitution transferred to the Executive Government of the Commonwealth:

iii Other matters declared by this Constitution to be within the exclusive power of the Parliament.

CHAPTER II THE EXECUTIVE GOVERNMENT

61 The executive power of the Commonwealth is vested in the Queen and is exerciseable by the Governor-General as the Queen's representative, and extends to the execution and maintenance of this Constitution, and of the laws of the Commonwealth.

62 There shall be a Federal Executive Council to advise the Governor-General in the government of the Commonwealth, and the members of the Council shall be

chosen and summoned by the Governor-General and sworn as Executive Councillors, and shall hold office during his pleasure.

63 The provisions of this Constitution referring to the Governor-General in Council shall be construed as referring to the Governor-General acting with the advice of the Federal Executive Council.

64 The Governor-General may appoint officers to administer such departments of State of the Commonwealth as the Governor-General in Council may establish.

Such officers shall hold office during the pleasure of the Governor-General. They shall be members of the Federal Executive Council, and shall be the Queen's Ministers of State for the Commonwealth.

After the first general election no Minister of State shall hold office for a longer period than three months unless he is or becomes a senator or a member of the House of Representatives.

65 Until the Parliament otherwise provides, the Ministers of State shall not exceed seven in number, and shall hold such offices as the Parliament prescribes, or, in the absence of provision, as the Governor-General directs.

66 There shall be payable to the Queen, out of the Consolidated Revenue Fund of the Commonwealth, for the salaries of the Ministers of State, an annual sum which, until the Parliament otherwise provides, shall not exceed twelve thousand pounds a year.

67 Until the Parliament otherwise provides, the appointment and removal of all other officers of the Executive Government of the Commonwealth shall be vested in the Governor-General in Council, unless the appointment is delegated by the Governor-General in Council or by a law of the Commonwealth to some other authority.

68 The command in chief of the naval and military forces of the Commonwealth is vested in the Governor-General as the Queen's representative.

69 On a date or dates to be proclaimed by the Governor-General after the establishment of the Commonwealth the following departments of the public service in each State shall become transferred to the Commonwealth:

Posts, telegraphs, and telephones:
Naval and military defence:
Lighthouses, lightships, beacons, and buoys:
Quarantine.

But the departments of customs and of excise in each State shall become transferred to the Commonwealth on its establishment.

70   In respect of matters which, under this Constitution, pass to the Executive Government of the Commonwealth, all powers and functions which at the establishment of the Commonwealth are vested in the Governor of a Colony, or in the Governor of a Colony with the advice of his Executive Council, or in any authority of a Colony, shall vest in the Governor-General, or in the Governor-General in Council, or in the authority exercising similar powers under the Commonwealth, as the case requires.

CHAPTER III   THE JUDICATURE

71   The judicial power of the Commonwealth shall be vested in a Federal Supreme Court, to be called the High Court of Australia, and in such other federal courts as the Parliament creates, and in such other courts as it invests with federal jurisdiction. The High Court shall consist of a Chief Justice, and so many other Justices, not less than two, as the Parliament prescribes.

75   In all matters –
   i   Arising under any treaty:
   ii   Affecting consuls or other representatives of other countries:
   iii   In which the Commonwealth, or a person suing or being sued on behalf of the Commonwealth, is a party:
   iv   Between States, or between residents of different States, or between a State and a resident of another State:
   v   In which a writ of Mandamus or prohibition or an injunction is sought against an officer of the Commonwealth:
   the High Court shall have original jurisdiction.

76   The Parliament may make laws conferring original jurisdiction on the High Court in any matter –
   i   Arising under this Constitution, or involving its interpretation:
   ii   Arising under any laws made by the Parliament:
   iii   Of Admiralty and maritime jurisdiction:
   iv   Relating to the same subject-matter claimed under the laws of different States.

77   With respect to any of the matters mentioned in the last two sections the Parliament may make laws –
   i   Defining the jurisdiction of any federal court other than the High Court:
   ii   Defining the extent to which the jurisdiction of any federal court shall be exclusive of that which belongs to or is invested in the courts of the States:
   iii   Investing any court of a State with federal jurisdiction.

78   The Parliament may make laws conferring rights to proceed against the

Commonwealth or a State in respect of matters within the limits of the judicial power.

CHAPTER IV FINANCE AND TRADE

81 All revenues or moneys raised or received by the Executive Government of the Commonwealth shall form one Consolidated Revenue Fund, to be appropriated for the purposes of the Commonwealth in the manner and subject to the charges and liabilities imposed by this Constitution.

82 The costs, charges, and expenses incident to the collection, management, and receipt of the Consolidated Revenue Fund shall form the first charge thereon; and the revenue of the Commonwealth shall in the first instance be applied to the payment of the expenditure of the Commonwealth.

83 No money shall be drawn from the Treasury of the Commonwealth except under appropriation made by law.

But until the expiration of one month after the first meeting of the Parliament the Governor-General in Council may draw from the Treasury and expend such moneys as may be necessary for the maintenance of any department transferred to the Commonwealth and for the holding of the first elections for the Parliament.

86 On the establishment of the Commonwealth, the collection and control of duties of customs and of excise, and the control of the payment of bounties, shall pass to the Executive Government of the Commonwealth.

88 Uniform duties of customs shall be imposed within two years after the establishment of the Commonwealth.

90 On the imposition of uniform duties of customs the power of the Parliament to impose duties of customs and of excise, and to grant bounties on the production or export of goods, shall become exclusive.

On the imposition of uniform duties of customs all laws of the several States imposing duties of customs or of excise, or offering bounties on the production or export of goods, shall cease to have effect, but any grant of or agreement for any such bounty lawfully made by or under the authority of the Government of any State shall be taken to be good if made before the thirtieth day of June, one thousand eight hundred and ninety-eight, and not otherwise.

96 During a period of ten years after the establishment of the Commonwealth and thereafter until the Parliament otherwise provides, the Parliament may grant financial assistance to any State on such terms and conditions as the Parliament thinks fit.

98 The power of the Parliament to make laws with respect to trade and commerce extends to navigation and shipping, and to railways the property of any State.

105A 1 The Commonwealth may make agreements with the States with respect to the public debts of the States, including –
   a the taking over of such debts by the Commonwealth;
   b the management of such debts;
   c the payment of interest and the provision and management of sinking funds in respect of such debts;
   d the consolidation, renewal, conversion, and redemption of such debts;
   e the indemnification of the Commonwealth by the States in respect of debts taken over by the Commonwealth; and
   f the borrowing of money by the States or by the Commonwealth, or by the Commonwealth for the States.
   2 The Parliament may make laws for validating any such agreement made before the commencement of this section.
   3 The Parliament may make laws for the carrying out by the parties thereto of any such agreement.
   4 Any such agreement may be varied or rescinded by the parties thereto.
   5 Every such agreement and any such variation thereof shall be binding upon the Commonwealth and the States parties thereto notwithstanding anything contained in this Constitution or the Constitution of the several States or in any law of the Parliament of the Commonwealth or of any State.
   6 The powers conferred by this section shall not be construed as being limited in any way by the provisions of section one hundred and five of this Constitution.

CHAPTER V   THE STATES

106 The Constitution of each State of the Commonwealth shall, subject to this Constitution, continue as at the establishment of the Commonwealth, or as at the admission or establishment of the State, as the case may be, until altered in accordance with the Constitution of the State.

107 Every power of the Parliament of a Colony which has become or becomes a State, shall, unless it is by this Constitution exclusively vested in the Parliament of the Commonwealth or withdrawn from the Parliament of the State, continue as at the establishment of the Commonwealth, or as at the admission or establishment of the State, as the case may be.

108 Every law in force in a Colony which has become or becomes a State, and

relating to any matter within the powers of the Parliament of the Commonwealth, shall, subject to this Constitution, continue in force in the State; and,
until provision is made in that behalf by the Parliament of the Commonwealth,
the Parliament of the State shall have such powers of alteration and of repeal
in respect of any such law as the Parliament of the Colony had until the Colony
became a State.

109 When a law of a State is inconsistent with a law of the Commonwealth, the latter
shall prevail, and the former shall, to the extent of the inconsistency, be invalid.

114 A State shall not, without the consent of the Parliament of the Commonwealth,
raise or maintain any naval or military force, or impose any tax on property of
any kind belonging to the Commonwealth, nor shall the Commonwealth impose
any tax on property of any kind belonging to a State.

**Selected Provisions of the British North America Act,
30 & 31 Vict., c 3 (Imp.), as amended to date**

III EXECUTIVE POWER

9 The Executive Government and Authority of and over Canada is hereby declared
to continue and be vested in the Queen.

10 The Provisions of this Act referring to the Governor General extend and apply to
the Governor General for the Time being of Canada, or other the Chief Executive Officer or Administrator for the Time being carrying on the Government of
Canada on behalf and in the Name of the Queen, by whatever Title he is
designated.

IV LEGISLATIVE POWER

17 There shall be One Parliament for Canada, consisting of the Queen, an Upper
House styled the Senate, and the House of Commons.

VI DISTRIBUTION OF LEGISLATIVE POWERS

Powers of the Parliament

91 It shall be lawful for the Queen, by and with the Advice and Consent of the
Senate and House of Commons, to make Laws for the Peace, Order, and good

Government of Canada, in relation to all Matters not coming within the Classes of Subjects by this Act assigned exclusively to the Legislatures of the Provinces; and for greater Certainty, but not so as to restrict the Generality of the foregoing Terms of this Section, it is hereby declared that (notwithstanding anything in this Act) the exclusive Legislative Authority of the Parliament of Canada extends to all Matters coming within the Classes of Subjects next herein-after enumerated; that is to say,

1   The amendment from time to time of the Constitution of Canada, except as regards matters coming within the classes of subjects by this Act assigned exclusively to the Legislatures of the Provinces, or as regards rights or privileges by this or any other Constitutional Act granted or secured to the Legislature or the Government of a province, or to any class of persons with respect to schools or as regards the use of the English or the French language or as regards the requirements that there shall be a session of the Parliament of Canada at least once each year, and that no House of Commons shall continue for more than five years from the day of the return of the Writs for choosing the House: provided, however, that a House of Commons may in time of real or apprehended war, invasion or insurrection be continued by the Parliament of Canada if such continuation is not opposed by the votes of more than one-third of the members of such House.

1A   The Public Debt and Property.

2   The Regulation of Trade and Commerce.

2A   Unemployment insurance.

3   The raising of Money by any Mode or System of Taxation.

4   The borrowing of Money on the Public Credit.

5   Postal Service.

6   The Census and Statistics.

7   Militia, Military and Naval Service, and Defence.

8   The fixing of and providing for the Salaries and Allowances of Civil and other Officers of the Government of Canada.

9   Beacons, Buoys, Lighthouses, and Sable Island.

10   Navigation and Shipping.

11   Quarantine and the Establishment and Maintenance of Marine Hospitals.

12   Sea Coast and Inland Fisheries.

13   Ferries between a Province and any British or Foreign Country or between Two Provinces.

14   Currency and Coinage.

15   Banking, Incorporation of Banks, and the Issue of Paper Money.

16   Savings Banks.

17   Weights and Measures.

18   Bills of Exchange and Promissory Notes.
19   Interest.
20   Legal Tender.
21   Bankruptcy and Insolvency.
22   Patents of Invention and Discovery.
23   Copyrights.
24   Indians, and Lands reserved for the Indians.
25   Naturalization and Aliens.
26   Marriage and Divorce.
27   The Criminal Law, except the Constitution of Courts of Criminal Jurisdiction, but including the Procedure in Criminal Matters.
28   The Establishment, Maintenance, and Management of Penitentiaries.
29   Such Classes of Subjects as are expressly excepted in the Enumeration of the Classes of Subjects by this Act assigned exclusively to the Legislatures of the Provinces.

And any Matter coming within any of the Classes of Subjects enumerated in this Section shall not be deemed to come within the Class of Matters of a local or private Nature comprised in the Enumeration of the Classes of Subjects by this Act assigned exclusively to the Legislatures of the Provinces.

Exclusive Powers of Provincial Legislatures

92   In each Province the Legislature may exclusively make Laws in relation to Matters coming within the Classes of Subject next herein-after enumerated; that is to say,
   1   The Amendment from Time to Time, notwithstanding anything in this Act, of the Constitution of the Province, except as regards the Office of Lieutenant Governor.
   2   Direct Taxation within the Province in order to the raising of a Revenue for Provincial Purposes.
   3   The borrowing of Money on the sole Credit of the Province.
   4   The Establishment and Tenure of Provincial Offices and the Appointment and Payment of Provincial Officers.
   5   The Management and Sale of the Public Lands belonging to the Province and of the Timber and Wood thereon.
   6   The Establishment, Maintenance, and Management of Public and Reformatory Prisons in and for the Province.
   7   The Establishment, Maintenance, and Management of Hospitals, Asylums, Charities, and Eleemosynary Institutions in and for the Province, other than Marine Hospitals.

8 Municipal Institutions in the Province.
9 Shop, Saloon, Tavern, Auctioneer, and other Licences in order to the raising of a Revenue for Provincial, Local, or Municipal Purposes.
10 Local Works and Undertakings other than such as are of the following Classes:
   a Lines of Steam or other Ships, Railways, Canals, Telegraphs, and other Works and Undertakings connecting the Province with any other or others of the Provinces, or extending beyond the Limits of the Province;
   b Lines of Steam Ships between the Province and any British or Foreign Country;
   c Such Works as, although wholly situate within the Province, are before or after their Execution declared by the Parliament of Canada to be for the general Advantage of Canada or for the Advantage of Two or more of the Provinces.
11 The Incorporation of Companies with Provincial Objects.
12 The Solemnization of Marriage in the Province.
13 Property and Civil Rights in the Province.
14 The Administration of Justice in the Province, including the Constitution, Maintenance, and Organization of Provincial Courts, both of Civil and of Criminal Jurisdiction, and including Procedure in Civil Matters in those Courts.
15 The Imposition of Punishment by Fine, Penalty, or Imprisonment for enforcing any Law of the Province made in relation to any Matter coming within any of the Classes of Subjects enumerated in this Section.
16 Generally all Matters of a merely local or private Nature in the Province.

VII JUDICATURE

5 The Governor General shall appoint the Judges of the Superior, District, and County Courts in each Province, except those of the Courts of Probate in Nova Scotia and New Brunswick.

7 Until the laws relative to Property and Civil Rights in Ontario, Nova Scotia, and New Brunswick, and the Procedure of the Courts in those Provinces, are made uniform, the Judges of the Courts of those Provinces appointed by the Governor General shall be selected from the respective Bars of those Provinces.

8 The Judges of the Courts of Quebec shall be selected from the Bar of that Province.

9 1 Subject to subsection two of this section, the Judges of the Superior Courts shall hold office during good behaviour, but shall be removable by the Governor General on Address of the Senate and House of Commons.

2 A Judge of a Superior Court, whether appointed before or after the coming into force of this section, shall cease to hold office upon attaining the age of seventy-five years, or upon the coming into force of this section if at that time he has already attained that age.

100 The Salaries, Allowances, and Pensions of the Judges of the Superior, District, and County Courts (except the Courts of Probate in Nova Scotia and New Brunswick), and of the Admiralty Courts in Cases where the Judges thereof are for the Time being paid by Salary, shall be fixed and provided by the Parliament of Canada.

101 The Parliament of Canada may, notwithstanding anything in this Act, from Time to Time provide for the Constitution, Maintenance, and Organization of a General Court of Appeal for Canada, and for the Establishment of any additional Courts for the better Administration of the Laws of Canada.

VIII REVENUES; DEBTS; ASSETS; TAXATION

102 All Duties and Revenues over which the respective Legislatures of Canada, Nova Scotia, and New Brunswick before and at the Union had and have Power of Appropriation, except such Portions thereof as are by this Act reserved to the respective Legislatures of the Provinces, or are raised by them in accordance with the special Powers conferred on them by this Act, shall form One Consolidated Revenue Fund, to be appropriated for the Public Service of Canada in the Manner and subject to the Charges in this Act provided.

103 The Consolidated Revenue Fund of Canada shall be permanently charged with the Costs, Charges, and Expenses incident to the Collection, Management, and Receipt thereof, and the same shall form the First Charge thereon, subject to be reviewed and audited in such Manner as shall be ordered by the Governor General in Council until the Parliament otherwise provides.

104 The annual Interest of the Public Debts of the several Provinces of Canada, Nova Scotia, and New Brunswick at the Union shall form the Second Charge on the Consolidated Revenue Fund of Canada.

105 Unless altered by the Parliament of Canada, the Salary of the Governor General shall be Ten thousand Pounds Sterling Money of the United Kingdom of Great Britain and Ireland, payable out of the Consolidated Revenue Fund of Canada, and the same shall form the Third Charge thereon.

106 Subject to the several Payments by this Act charged on the Consolidated Revenue

Fund of Canada, the same shall be appropriated by the Parliament of Canada for the Public Service.

7 All Stocks, Cash, Banker's Balances, and Securities for Money belonging to each Province at the Time of the Union, except as in this Act mentioned, shall be the Property of Canada, and shall be taken in Reduction of the Amount of the respective Debts of the Provinces at the Union.

8 The Public Works and Property of each Province, enumerated in the Third Schedule to this Act, shall be the Property of Canada.

9 All Lands, Mines, Minerals, and Royalties belonging to the several Provinces of Canada, Nova Scotia, and New Brunswick at the Union, and all Sums then due or payable for such Lands, Mines, Minerals, or Royalties, shall belong to the several Provinces of Ontario, Quebec, Nova Scotia, and New Brunswick in which the same are situate or arise, subject to any Trusts existing in respect thereof, and to any Interest other than that of the Province in the same.

0 All Assets connected with such Portions of the Public Debt of each Province as are assumed by that Province shall belong to that Province.

1 Canada shall be liable for the Debts and Liabilities of each Province existing at the Union.

2 Ontario and Quebec conjointly shall be liable to Canada for the Amount (if any) by which the Debt of the Province of Canada exceeds at the Union Sixty-two million five hundred thousand Dollars, and shall be charged with Interest at the Rate of Five per Centum per Annum thereon.

3 The Assets enumerated in the Fourth Schedule to this Act belonging at the Union to the Province of Canada shall be the Property of Ontario and Quebec conjointly.

4 Nova Scotia shall be liable to Canada for the Amount (if any) by which its Public Debt exceeds at the Union Eight million Dollars, and shall be charged with Interest at the Rate of Five per Centum per Annum thereon.

5 New Brunswick shall be liable to Canada for the Amount (if any) by which its Public Debt exceeds at the Union Seven million Dollars, and shall be charged with Interest at the Rate of Five per Centum per Annum thereon.

5 In case the Public Debts of Nova Scotia and New Brunswick do not at the Union amount to Eight million and Seven million Dollars respectively, they shall respectively receive by half-yearly Payments in advance from the Government of Canada Interest at Five per Centum per Annum on the Difference between the actual Amounts of their respective Debts and such stipulated Amounts.

117 The several Provinces shall retain all their respective Public Property not otherwise disposed of in this Act, subject to the Right of Canada to assume any Lands or Public Property required for Fortifications or for the Defence of the Country.

118 Repealed.

119 New Brunswick shall receive by half-yearly Payments in advance from Canada for the Period of Ten Years from the Union an additional Allowance of Sixty-three thousand Dollars per Annum; but as long as the Public Debt of that Province remains under Seven million Dollars, a Deduction equal to the Interest at Five per Centum per Annum on such Deficiency shall be made from that Allowance of Sixty-three thousand Dollars.

120 All Payments to be made under this Act, or in discharge of Liabilities created under any Act of the Provinces of Canada, Nova Scotia, and New Brunswick respectively, and assumed by Canada, shall, until the Parliament of Canada otherwise directs, be made in such Form and Manner as may from Time to Time be ordered by the Governor General in Council.

121 All Articles of the Growth, Produce, or Manufacture of any one of the Provinces shall, from and after the Union, be admitted free into each of the other Provinces.

122 The Customs and Excise Laws of each Province shall, subject to the Provisions of this Act, continue in force until altered by the Parliament of Canada.

123 Where Customs Duties are, at the Union, leviable on any Goods, Wares, or Merchandises in any Two Provinces, those Goods, Wares, and Merchandises may, from and after the Union, be imported from one of those Provinces into the other of them on Proof of Payment of the Customs Duty leviable thereon in the Province of Exportation, and on Payment of such further Amount (if any) of Customs Duty as is leviable thereon in the Province of Importation.

124 Nothing in this Act shall affect the Right of New Brunswick to levy the Lumber Dues provided in Chapter Fifteen of Title Three of the Revised Statutes of New Brunswick, or in any Act amending that Act before or after the Union and not increasing the Amount of such Dues; but the Lumber of any of the Provinces other than New Brunswick shall not be subject to such Dues.

125 No Lands or Property belonging to Canada or any Province shall be liable to Taxation.

126 Such Portions of the Duties and Revenues over which the respective Legislatures of Canada, Nova Scotia, and New Brunswick had before the Union Power of Appropriation as are by this Act reserved to the respective Governments or Legislatures of the Provinces, and all Duties and Revenues raised by them in accordance

with the special Powers conferred upon them by this Act, shall in each Province form One Consolidated Revenue Fund to be appropriated for the Public Service of the Province.

9 Except as otherwise provided by this Act, all Laws in force in Canada, Nova Scotia, or New Brunswick at the Union, and all Courts of Civil and Criminal Jurisdiction, and all legal Commissions, Powers, and Authorities, and all Officers, Judicial, Administrative, and Ministerial, existing therein at the Union, shall continue in Ontario, Quebec, Nova Scotia, and New Brunswick respectively, as if the Union had not been made; subject nevertheless (except with respect to such as are enacted by or exist under Acts of the Parliament of Great Britain or of the Parliament of the United Kingdom of Great Britain and Ireland,) to be repealed, abolished, or altered by the Parliament of Canada, or by the Legislature of the respective Province, according to the Authority of the Parliament or of that Legislature under this Act.

THE THIRD SCHEDULE

Provincial Public Works and Property to be the Property of Canada

1 Canals, with Lands and Water Power connected therewith.
2 Public Harbours.
3 Lighthouses and Piers, and Sable Island.
4 Steamboats, Dredges, and public Vessels.
5 Rivers and Lake Improvements.
6 Railways and Railway Stocks, Mortgages, and other Debts due by Railway Companies.
7 Military Roads.
8 Custom Houses, Post Offices, and all other Public Buildings, except such as the Government of Canada appropriate for the Use of the Provincial Legislature and Governments.
9 Property transferred by the Imperial Government, and known as Ordnance Property.
10 Armouries, Drill Sheds, Military Clothing, and Munitions of War, and Lands set apart for general Public Purposes.

Table of Cases

Index

TEXAS A&M UNIVERSITY-TEXARKANA